SLOUCHING TOWARD ADUL[T]

SALLY KOSLOW is a journalist, a novelist, and the former editor in chief of both *McCall's* and *Lifetime*. She has written for *O, The Oprah Magazine; More; Real Simple; Ladies' Home Journal; Good Housekeeping; Reader's Digest;* and the *Huffington Post*. She lives in New York City with her husband; their kids have finally moved out.

Praise for *Slouching Toward Adulthood*

"Excellent . . . At last, a serious, well-researched book about raising children, which also includes that crucial characteristic every parent needs—a sense of humor."   —*USA Today*, "Top Summer Nonfiction Pick"

"'Our offspring have simply leveraged our braggadocio, good intentions, and overinvestment,' Koslow writes in her new book, *Slouching Toward Adulthood*. They inhabit 'a broad savannah of entitlement that we've watered, landscaped, and hired gardeners to maintain.' She recommends letting the grasslands revert to forest: 'The best way for a lot of us to show our love would be to learn to un-mother and un-father.'"   —Elizabeth Kolbert, *The New Yorker*

"An eye-opener . . . Koslow writes wittily about the infantilization of American youth as increasing numbers treat getting a job and moving out as just an option."   —*People*

"This book is hilarious! I burst out laughing on page one, and it just got funnier and funnier. But *Slouching Toward Adulthood* is also hard-hitting and painfully insightful—I found myself wincing with recognition. Backed by the latest research, Sally Koslow's thought-provoking new book should be required reading for today's parents and young adults."
—Amy Chua, author of *Battle Hymn of the Tiger Mother*

"A witty, provocative study that examines why so many millennials can't seem to launch into adulthood and now find themselves 'wandering—if not literally, then psychically.' . . . Observant and bracingly candid."
—*Kirkus Reviews*

D1160893

"There's a Koslow in all of us who wants to strangle Hannah, the character played by Lena Dunham in the popular HBO show *Girls*, when we learn that her parents had been subsidizing her life in New York City while she worked at an unpaid internship and pursued a writing career. . . . Koslow criticizes clueless parents as much as their narcissistic offspring. She argues that babying adult children tends to yield entitled progeny who can't launch their way into the conventional phases of adulthood. Koslow offers excellent advice, which makes this book worth reading to the end." —*Fortune*

"Smart, with plenty of insights and a lively prose style that should keep readers, especially the book's target audience of parents, wondering why their grown-up kids are back living in their basements, engaged." —*Booklist*

"Sally Koslow has written a funny, shrewd, and true account of a problem the boomer generation didn't know it had created: the consequences of helicopter parenting. We've pampered our kids so much they don't want to grow up. Who can blame them? *Slouching Toward Adulthood* is the book that explains why 'the guest bedroom' is a thing of the past."
  —James Atlas, author of *My Life in the Middle Ages*

"Koslow casts a keen eye on the 'not-so-empty-nest' phenomenon that besets today's baby boomer parents . . . and provides plenty of food for thought for parents and adultescents who want to understand each other and perhaps change things for the better." —*Publishers Weekly*

"Full of research, insight, and hilarious examples of what life is like for the long-suffering parents of 'adultescents,' *Slouching Toward Adulthood* is one of those invaluable books that identifies and illuminates a new phenomenon in our culture." —Gretchen Rubin, author of *The Happiness Project*

"Sally Koslow has really hit on something with her incisive *Slouching Toward Adulthood*. Memorable books that struck a chord about the path of life or the dissonance between parent and child—Gail Sheehy's *Passages*, Nancy Friday's *My Mother/My Self*—all had a kind of kitchen-table humanity and an ability to limn the unnamed conflicts of a particular moment. Beneath its jaunty two-drinks-with-your-coolest-friend ebullience, this book, as of its moment as those books were of theirs, has that resonance, too."
  —Sheila Weller, author of *Girls Like Us*

Slouching TOWARD ADULTHOOD

How to Let Go So Your Kids
Can Grow Up

Sally Koslow

A PLUME BOOK

PLUME
Published by the Penguin Group
Penguin Group (USA) Inc., 375 Hudson Street
New York, New York 10014, USA

USA | Canada | UK | Ireland | Australia | New Zealand | India | South Africa | China
Penguin Books Ltd, Registered Offices: 80 Strand, London WC2R 0RL, England
For more information about the Penguin Group visit penguin.com

First published in the United States of America by Viking,
a member of Penguin Group (USA) Inc., 2012
First Plume Printing 2013

THE LIBRARY OF CONGRESS HAS CATALOGUED THE VIKING EDITION AS FOLLOWS:
Koslow, Sally.
Slouching toward adulthood / Sally Koslow.
p.   cm.
ISBN 978-0-670-02362-2 (hc.)
ISBN 978-0-14-219682-3 (pbk.)
1. Young adults—United States—History—21st century.   2. Adult children—United
States—History—21st century.   3. Aging parents—United States—History—21st
century.   I. Title.
HQ799.7.K67 2012
305.235—dc23   2011043894

Printed in the United States of America
10 9 8 7 6 5 4 3 2 1

Set in Diverda Serif Com with Avenir Sid
Original hardcover design by Daniel Lagin

To Jed and Rory, who always make me proud,
and Rob, a wise partner in parenthood

A Note from the Author

Interviews for *Slouching Toward Adulthood* were conducted during 2010 and 2011. Since then, some people have moved, quit jobs, started jobs or graduate school or businesses, married, had babies, given up yoga, and so on. Also, in a few cases an interviewee has requested that the author not reveal his or her real name, surname, or identifying details, and the author has honored those requests. An asterisk (*) indicates a changed name.

Contents

Introduction

Two years ago, I began to dissect the minutiae of how many young Americans are enjoying adulthood's perks without its responsibilities. In looking at these lives, I also checked out parents' baffled views of their offspring—mothers and fathers who frequently see kids as self-absorbed and insecure. On both counts, I underestimated to what degree *Slouching Toward Adulthood* would hit a nerve. Since the hardcover edition was published, not only does everyone I meet seem to know or be a person who could have catapulted from the book's pages, but our entire country appears to be asking the question put to music in the inimitable 1960s musical *Bye Bye Birdie*: "What's the matter with kids today?" The answer, as it turns out, has as much to do with how Boomers have raised their children—with equal portions of indulgence and love—as it does with economic disappointments or evolving attitudes among younger generations.

As I'd hoped, the book found readers among my peers and their children in their twenties and thirties. On Amazon.com, a nursery school teacher, for example, urged "GenY, their parents, and educators to read this thought-provoking book. . . . Koslow acknowledges that for the most part Boomers were motivated by the best intentions while unintentionally not preparing their children for the realities of life. . . . My mother used an expression I hated yet have come to appreciate: 'Life is not a one-way street.' Koslow . . . makes the reader wonder if Boomers gave too much and asked for too little."

To be able to add my voice to a national dialogue has been gratifying. So, too—if you'll indulge me—the book's formal notices. A *BookPage* reviewer remarked that "Koslow's 'adultescents' are a new phenomenon, different from both F. Scott Fitzgerald's or even David Foster Wallace's slouchers, unprecedented in both scope and spiritual danger because of our new century's perfect storm of economic hardship and over-qualification." Former deputy book reviewer of the *Los Angeles Times*, Nick Owchar, recommended that last fall's presidential candidates read STA to get up to speed on issues affecting Boomer parents and their kids. In "Spoiled Rotten: Why Do Kids Rule the Roost?," an essay that reviewed my book along with several others, Elizabeth Kolbert of the *New Yorker* picked up on the term "adultescent," which, as far as I know, was coined by my son Jed in a family bake-off to identify the not-quite-adults in Mom's book. Around the time STA was published, HBO premiered *Girls*, the darkly comic sitcom hit fictionalizing the lives of four Brooklyn females. This caused *Fortune*'s Nin-Hai Tseng to offer my absolute favorite comment: "There's a Koslow in all of us who wants to strangle Hannah, the character played by [the show's creator] Lena Dunham . . . when we learn that her parents have been subsidizing her life . . . while she worked as an unpaid intern and pursued a writing career."

STA's publication brought numerous opportunities for me to

broadcast my message on television, radio, and blogs. For this, I am grateful, especially for the chance to rant on CNN.com, where the post went viral. Many of the 2,000+ comments were enraged: "The so-called 'lost generation' includes some of the . . . most qualified workers on the planet and we have the tuition bills to prove it. . . . Our elders waltzed into careers with qualifications that include two-finger typing, draft-dodging, and 'white person.' . . . Now they spend their days still not being able to get into their e-mail and stealing interns' ideas, yet they have the nerve to call young people 'self-entitled' because they actually don't want to spend their most attractive years grinding their bones into dust in humiliating jobs." Others acknowledged truth in my message: "Our generation does have an entitlement problem," one commenter admitted. "Many of us were told to expect the best if we studied hard and went to college, and consequently many people won't accept jobs they deem 'beneath' them, . . . and don't understand the concept of starting on the bottom rung and working your way up, and that having a degree doesn't mean you get to bypass all that."

It's good fun to join the media circus, but for an author, nothing beats comments from readers of the genuine article: the book. This I got, in spades. "STA gives voice to all the changes in the last generation—social, economic, technological, cultural," an Amazon .com reader observed. "We who eagerly flew from the nest . . . are micro-engaged in our young adult children's lives. Good or bad? That is Koslow's underlying question. She shows how new behaviors have become norms. Renting a U-Haul to help move your kid, say, once a year . . . Vacationing in very nice places with your adult children, on your dime. Welcoming boyfriends and girlfriends into your family, even including them in the aforementioned vacation. . . . Watching your daughter travel around the world working at yoga retreats after finishing an Ivy League degree? Waiting hand and foot on your son, who is living at home? So are a lot of other moms! This book . . . really explains . . . what the hell is going on in our country!"

Paul Rosa, sixty, who referred to himself as an "adultescent before it was cool," shared that during his twenties he drifted . . . to Colorado, California, West Virginia—"partying, girls!"—and went into show business with enough success to lose ten key years. Eventually he returned to his hometown, Pittsburgh, "far short of what I might have been," he says, adding, "My boys are not getting the 'you're so special' treatment. . . . This is a serious cultural crisis brewing, and really quite tragic, especially the breakdown in marriage and the lack of children."

"I read STA with equal parts amusement, amazement, and consternation," noted New Jersey resident Jay Steinberg, forty-six. "The cover story in an issue of *Money* recently grabbed my attention. 'What to Do with $1,000 Now (Plus: What to Do with $10,000 or $50,000).' What indeed? The article included a 'Take Care of the Kids' section. Got $1,000 lying around? Put it in the Vanguard Retirement 2060 Fund for Junior. Never mind funding your own retirement, assuming it ever occurs. . . . A suggestion in the $10,000 category: Buy your kid a safe used car. *Money* thinks a 2005 Prius would do, or a 2007 Hyundai Elantra. Seriously? I drive a '99 Corolla. This makes me angry! Why is *Money* advising us to spoil our kids? I was not raised with any sense of entitlement. . . . I cannot even begin to imagine accepting this kind of assistance from my own parents. I would be embarrassed. . . . Such an interesting moment we are living in."

I especially loved reactions from adultescents. "I have been one of those Facebooking Americorps Fantasy-Life Idealists," confessed Ethan Richardson on *Mockingbird*, a Web site geared to progressive Christians. "[Koslow's] observations hit the nail on the head. . . . She sees underlying motivations as well as generational plagues . . . and points the gun of responsibility back at the Boomers. . . . One of those amazing insights . . . is her perspective on our generation's bondage to choice. Koslow discerns . . . how choice, something anyone would say they like to have, ends up paralyzing those who make it their objective."

I would not call *Slouching Toward Adulthood* a sweet book. So I was curious—okay, anxious—to receive feedback from people profiled within its pages. It was with deep relief that I got an e-mail from Arlene Siegel of Grand Rapids, Michigan. "I read the pages about my daughter Naomi to many different friends and helped them understand . . . why Naomi is the way she is and how important it is to let our children live their lives."

When I interviewed Naomi Siegel she was juggling several jobs in Washington. Now she has relocated to California to become a doula and massage therapist. She isn't the only STA adultescent who's moved on. Some of the wiftiest drifters in the book have snapped into place like Legos. Colorado ski bum/leadership tour guide Ben White is now almost finished with a master's degree in social work from Smith College. Expat Julia Cuthberston has returned from Spain to earn a master's in public health at Columbia University, as did "Nicholas," who had been a male nanny waiting for approval from the New York Department of Education to become a licensed substitute teacher. Georgia Aarons, profiled in the "Oops, I Forgot to Get Married" chapter, not only tied the knot, she did it in Vera Wang at the estate of the 11th Earl of Sandwich. The wedding was splashed all over the *New York Times Style* vows section.

These are happy tales, all—especially if I omit details about the young man in STA who was recently arrested by the FBI on three white-collar felony counts. But for every twenty- or thirtysomething who finally gets his act together, I'm seeing another adultescent fresh out of college joining their ranks. National facts remain grim. More Americans age thirty-four or younger are sleeping in their childhood bedrooms now than at any other time in the past thirty years. Recent Pew Research Center reports show that almost 22 percent of young adults were living at home in 2010, up from 16 percent in 2000 and rising—the most since the recession that began in 2007. Here, however, is where perhaps something is changing: young people appear to have become sanguine—or flattened into passivity, Stockholm syndrome–style—about this back-to-the-nest stampede, simply because it's all they know. Seventy-eight percent admit that they're satisfied with—or at least resigned to accepting—their living arrangements, according to Pew. "If there's supposed to be a stigma attached to living with Mom and Dad through one's late twenties or early thirties, today's boomerang generation didn't get that memo," Kim Parker, lead researcher on the Pew study, says. How do parents feel about their twenty- and thirtysomething adultescents being home again? Let me guess: sometimes happy to be given a second chance at experiencing their children as they were ten years earlier, but stressed, frustrated, and worried.

The default rate on student loans is also currently so colossal—a trillion dollars, according to the Federal Reserve—that many economists predict a financial crisis like the 2007 housing market collapse. A higher percentage of tuition loans are in default than for mortgages or credit cards, and these loans aren't forgiven if you go through bankruptcy. They stay with you to the grave. At an NYU protest last year, students who anticipate a helluva time getting jobs after college called attention to their debt by wearing T-shirts with the amount they each owe emblazoned on the front: $20,000! $75,000! $90,000!

There's no mystery to the arithmetic: tuition at state schools, for example, once considered a prudent financial choice, has risen 72 percent since 2000, according to a U.S. Department of Education study. Adultescents and their parents simply don't have the dough to repay loans. According to the U.S. Census, the median net worth of people under thirty-five fell 37 percent between 2005 and 2010, and while it may also have been big news last fall when the national unemployment rate for Americans fell below 8 percent, for those aged eighteen to twenty-nine, unemployment remains, by some estimates, 50 percent above the national average. Joblessness has given rise to the moniker Generation Screwed, partly because Boomers, whose stock portfolios and home values have sharply declined in the past five years, are often unable to retire, which squeezes younger workers out of jobs. Another product of this reality show is that adultescents aren't buying homes. According to Harvard University's Joint Center for Housing Studies, between 2006 and 2011, home ownership declined by 12 percent among adults younger than thirty-five. Ditto for purchasing cars.

And what of parenting? The axiom—little children, little problems; big children, big problems—still holds. Parents continue to watch adultescents return to the nest with shiny diplomas and wonder if they will ever leave, yet can't bear the idea of letting go. Or they watch, white-knuckled, as their adultescents flit off to find themselves on other continents or get hearts broken by disappointments in work—or love. A new study conducted by researchers at Columbia University and Tel Aviv University accused overbearing parents of breeding commitment-phobic kids. Oy. I believe, however, that parents may be starting to realize that the help they offered ten years earlier no longer works. Perhaps the best thing they can do now, they realize, is to consider antidepressants or Zen Buddhism, take up a new hobby, and stop trying to solve kids' problems.

I invite you to dig into STA, and discuss it with friends or your book club. At the very least, I can assure you that if your family sounds suspiciously like those whose stories follow in these pages, take heart: you are not alone.

Sally Koslow, April 2013

Chapter 1

A PUBLIC DISPLAY
OF REFLECTION

Everyone is kneaded out of the same dough but not baked
in the same oven.

—**Yiddish proverb**

The clock struck noon. It was a weekday, bright and shiny. I gently
knocked. "It's late—sweetie, shouldn't you be getting up?"

A few minutes later, Sweetie staggered out of his childhood
bedroom in boxers, stubble, and a Beastie Boys T-shirt cherished since
tenth grade. Five months before, Jed had moved back home after a two-
year postcollege spin working at a San Francisco record label. A few
months earlier the plans for my son to open an East Coast branch of the
company had fizzled—not that this development appeared to have
cramped his style. A weekly unemployment check was financing
more late-night eating and drinking than my husband and I had done
in the last two decades.

"How's the job hunt?" I asked as he leisurely munched his bagel and paged through a magazine.

Mumble, mumble.

"No, really, how's it going?"

"Fine."

"What does that mean?"

This time I got the same look I received years before when I'd heard our son had his first girlfriend. "Who is she?" I'd asked, stoked with motherly glee.

"I release that information on a need-to-know basis," Jed answered, "and you have no need to know."

As Sweetie sat across from me at the breakfast table, I realized that *You Can't Go Home Again* wasn't on my son's English major syllabus.

All around us, sometimes in our own homes, we see young, well-educated Americans postponing full maturity and its attendant responsibilities. The beloved offspring to which I refer is most likely well over a decade into deodorant, partnered sex, and, depending on gender, tampons or even Rogaine. He or she is way past having earned the legal right to vote, defend our country, drive, maintain private medical records, enter into a contract, marry, smoke, go to jail, and—if he or she has hit twenty-five—rent a car or be elected to Congress. If a parent of such a person tweaks the hair and clothes, when her loving eyes gaze upon this child she may see some version of herself or her partner at the same age. This 2.0 reflection may look down on the reader, literally, from a greater height or have boobs that are a cup or two bigger—or perhaps it just seems that way, with her décolletage so often on display. There might be tattoos and tongue studs, but given Brazilians, landing strips, and manscaping, there's possibly not much pubic hair, although the parent prefers not to think about that.

Who are these people sandwiching a chunky stage between adolescence and adulthood, these individuals who resemble adults but aren't, exactly? The Margaret Mead who lurks within every parent can't help but notice curious discrepancies between the boy or girl under consideration and the grown-up we swear we were at the same age. We've come to think of "adults" as people who "settle down." Adults are financially independent and fiscally solvent, albeit usually with debt and a mortgage, usually tethered to a steady job or its reasonable facsimile. Trust fund kids never have seemed very adult, even—like Brooke Astor's greedy old baby—when they're eighty.

An adult isn't in a state of constant improvisation. An adult isn't shackled to his or her mother or father by cell phone or purse strings or both in a three-legged race toward an undecided destination. An adult doesn't crave constant stroking from Mom and Dad.

In the eyes of most real grown-ups, a random five- or ten-year slice of adulthood does not include going to school, taking a break, going to school again—possibly again and again—starting a job, starting another job, moving in with Mom and Dad, traveling here and traveling there, taking out loans, borrowing from the parents, and imbibing their grandparents' cocktails while accumulating credit card debt and purchasing cunning yet quickly replaced electronics.

Adults tend not to post their romantic status online, pulling back the curtains on their private life and publicizing intimate secrets. They don't fall in and out of love so many times they need Excel to track the relationships before they start to serially cohabitate, postponing marriage, kids, and getting fully established at jobs, much less careers. Adults may have sucked up the fizzy best seller *Eat, Pray, Love*, but they don't see Elizabeth Gilbert, its author, as their north star as they wing off for extended stays in Italy, India, and Indonesia. These young adventurers may also be unaware that Gilbert followed *Eat, Pray, Love* with *Committed*, where the author defends matrimony in pointillist detail. Adults feel that usually by the mid-thirties, they need to stop—and here I use the technical term—farting around.

WHERE WANDERING BEGINS

The road separating today's adult from yesterday's starts to diverge when parents drop off Jenny or Josh at college. For most of today's parents this is uncharted territory and not only because of Adderall replacing LSD, the unisex dorms and bathrooms, and the comfortably out same-sex relationships and transgender students. After visiting well over a dozen campuses during high school—Hogwarts, if the parents could afford it—taking thousands of dollars' worth of Sisyphean test prep courses, and perhaps enjoying a jolly gap year in a faraway land, most American kids from solidly middle-class and upper-middle-class families enroll in an institution of higher learning. Every September, you can hear a transcontinental sigh as moms and dads among the privileged, anxious classes articulate immense relief, glad to be exorcised of their itchy need to deliver a droning loop about safety schools and *U.S. News & World Report* rankings, boring even themselves.

Mom and Dad accompany their newly minted first-years ("freshman" is 1969 pre-feminist Neanderthal argot and even "frosh" has landed in the linguistic compost heap) to a campus. There, they unload many, many boxes, perhaps ordered with the help of Bed, Bath & Beyond's "Shop for College" service, where millions of college students quiz themselves to determine their decorating style and scrutinize a list of "recommended" products so they can mesh purchases with their roommates. Eventually families depart, perhaps after attending a misty ceremony designed to encourage Mom and Dad to bid their chickadee good-bye. Parents may delude themselves into thinking they are leaving kids to learn to fight their own battles—college is a growth experience!—and bushwhack through administrative obfuscation in order to land a coveted spot in Kick-Ass Poets 101. With that, Mom and Dad take their first deep, cleansing breath in eighteen years, and generally celebrate by having sex.

Some students major in something solid, graduate, and hop onto the hamster wheel to high-powered jobs, destination weddings, early parenthood, and homes furnished from Design Within Reach, West Elm, and CB2. That's the sunny side of today's America.

The underbelly of family life is that in what seems like seven minutes, for many other students—perhaps the brother or sister of the oft-extolled young person pictured above—floats a concept. College may not be the promised land, no matter that the particular school he is attending was his first-choice "reach," salivated over for three years while the school's Web site home page served as his computer wallpaper. No biggie. He'll transfer or meander along on the five- or six-year plan, possibly with a junior year in Zimbabwe.

Most boomer parents graduated after four years. If they hadn't, their parents—adults feared as much as respected—would have followed through on threats that scared the nonexistent sunscreen right off them. But it currently takes the average college student 4.5 years to get a bachelor's degree, and six-year stays have become routine—on top of red-shirting boys to start kindergarten a year late to allow them time to earn their chops on the T-ball diamond and grab an edge. This adds two or more full years—and sometimes staggering expense—for boomer parents to have dependent kids. That is, if students graduate. The United States now has the highest college dropout rate in the industrialized world, reports the Organization for Economic Cooperation and Development.

Tuition and fees at private, nonprofit colleges and universities have increased more than 4 percent per year for the last several years:

at press time, Bates College in Lewiston, Maine—to throw a dart and see where we land—charges parents more than $50,000 a year in tuition. Less expensive state schools add up, too: Penn State in State College, Pennsylvania, costs approximately $15,000 a year for in-state students. If parents aren't footing the bills, accumulated tuition becomes the adultescents' albatross: for the class of 2011, the student loan burden is close to $27,000. Adjusted for inflation, according to the National Center for Education Statistics, the cost of a public four-year degree nearly doubled between 1964 and 2009.

Longer stays in college grow partly from students wandering from major to major. Who wants to go to dental school when there are movies to write and direct? Snookums, how do you *become* a writer of screenplays or director of films, asks the sheepish parent. Snookums proceeds to accuse Mom and Dad of being bourgeois enough to suggest that college is about preparing for a job, not learning for learning's sake and/or finding himself. At this point many parents retreat, chastened, just as some students announce that they will go beyond reversing direction to dropping out of the college they walked on water to enter. A conservatory or culinary school! Playing professional poker! Becoming an organic farmer! Keeping bees! Why not? They don't require organic chemistry suffered through in a baccalaureate year, necessary to qualify for veterinary, dental, or medical school.

As parents watch the seeds of academic and social arrhythmia being sown, they start to wonder if in some way they enabled their kid's difficulty in finding himself and settling on a plan. Yes, I'm talking to you. Okay, me, too. Let's all be accountable; the fact that the term "enabled" hadn't joined everyday speech when baby boomer parents were the age our children are now is no excuse. And don't tell me you didn't realize WTF you were doing. Hey, you text. OMG, you were not born yesterday but probably in that buoyant post–WWII era.

But enough about you, or for that matter, them—our kids. Let's talk about the way things used to be. Let's talk about me, yet another poster girl for baby boomers.

ME, ME, TYPICAL BOOMER ME

I'm old enough to remember lusting after Sweet Baby James, who before God took his hair, had it hanging down to his shoulders. I'm young enough to be glad I dodged the napalm of heavy-duty sexual harassment and my mother's bullet bras, though I'm sorry I missed Elvis on Ed Sullivan. My deepest desire is that a mysterious benefactor will endow me with a gift certificate for whatever cosmetic surgery my heart desires and face requires. I still lace up my sneakers and "run." This makes me feel sprightly and virtuous until I hear, "On your left, ma'am" as every other person on the track passes me.

Sobering, all this, until I remind myself that I, too, lived with my significant other before we married, just as both my sons live with girlfriends. I actually married my guy, though our wedding didn't require a planner, nor did I have a bachelorette party in Cabo San Lucas that my girlfriends had to spend $2,000 to attend. In the seventies, life was simpler. Someone did throw me a shower. I received an electric knife I mistakenly tossed in the trash, a Salton hot tray I still use, and a fondue pot that I regret I sold at a yard sale for three bucks now that they cost $370 at Williams-Sonoma. For my wedding, all our college friends chipped in and bought us sleeping bags from Abercrombie & Fitch before the store rebranded and became, in the words of musician-writer David Byrne, "a kind of homoerotic, fascist chic outpost," where young Europeans queue up in the rain outside its darkened windows to load up on $48 flip-flops.

I digress. People my age do that. Drives our kids crazy, although it sometimes seems as if their entire postcollege lives are a digression. They don't want to hear about how it used to be at twenty-two or thirty-four. I tell them anyway.

After receiving a bachelor's degree from a Big Ten university, I visited a faraway city and was lucky enough to quickly find a job. Then again, I'd prepared for that position—it was at a magazine—by reporting for and editing newspapers during junior high, high school, college, and summer jobs. I could write an obituary of a hog farmer named Olaf in my sleep. After I received a postcollege job offer, I returned to my parents' home in Fargo, North Dakota—a place I never lived in again—to pack up my wardrobe, which fit into one wheel-less suitcase, then flew back east and started work the following Monday. I didn't own any electronics, just a manual typewriter that had been my high school graduation present and a hair dryer twice the size of my butt. A handful of college classmates were still living off their dads' credit cards—no one had their own yet—and getting their rents subsidized, but I supported myself, as did most young adults (which is how we thought of ourselves) with shy pride on my own dainty salary. Not that I had a choice. This is what my parents budgeted for and expected. I never questioned this fact of life.

I wasn't mature. What I was: eager to be grown up and I faked it till I felt it. A year later, I married my college boyfriend, who'd replaced my roommate, who moved in with her boyfriend. Not that I had any business getting married. Robert and I hadn't thought through marriage at all. We were harebrained and clueless and, above all, young, although I was older at marriage than many of my high school friends or my younger sister, who two years later married during college. When I got pregnant in my mid-twenties, it was not considered young.

Are the almost-adult people wandering now because their parents were children when they had them? Just a thought. Have we grown up yet? We can chew on that one till the flavor is all gone.

The twenty-three-year-old hubby and I are still married. Imagine. By yesterday's standards, this stability is normal; by today's, boring and batty. Recently, when a new friend of one of my sons realized that Rob and I were *both* the original, still-married parents of our child, he looked so gobsmacked I felt as if I'd stumbled out of a diorama at the Museum of Natural History.

I'm working in the same occupation, more or less, that I picked in fourth grade. Such a protracted attention span devoted to one professional pursuit makes the eyes glaze over in many people in their twenties and thirties, who find the concept of a lifetime commitment to a career field as stultifying as they do inconceivable. Not that there's much of a chance they'll do the same. Whatever the major—history, political science, or gender and sexuality studies with a minor in West African dance—a great many of the undergraduates I know barely looked for a job after they got bachelor's degrees. Instead, they flew off to a foreign country to teach English and eventually logged two or more years in victory laps at law school, business school, or garden-variety grad school, ensuring that they or their parents are on the hook for five figures' worth of student loans. With advanced degrees in hand, they may not be all that enthralled being a lawyer, a business-man, or a master—assuming that in this jobless-recovery economy they can find paid work. It continues to seem as if a whole generation is chasing a handful of opportunities. But no matter. They'll deal with that . . . later.

I hear you protesting. Some boomers we know and love—maybe you—have behaved in exactly the way I've described back in the day of be-ins and elephant bell bottoms. They dabbled with this or that and enjoyed the glitter of possibility before they fully engaged in a field about which they felt passionate, committed, or at least stuck with. We often call them creative, even eccentric, those charming exceptions with their libertarian jitterbug. But while I mean no offense to the freer spirits of the world—older baby boomers did get their summer of love—their collective squawks have ultimately never been vociferous enough to register on the Richter scale as a youthquake that changed society's norms. It's only now that what used to be considered less than conventional—postponing financial independence, jobs, marriage, a hovel of one's own—has become the norm for a great many Americans aged twenty-two to thirty-five.

When boomers were twenty-two to thirty-five and chose to go rogue, they joined the Peace Corps or, as my older brother did, Volunteers for Service to America (VISTA), a precursor to AmeriCorps started by the government in the 1960s to help fight poverty. Less idealistic young people may have mooched off of friends, squatting in grubby apartments. Rarely did these escapades, earnest or otherwise, last for more than a year or two. Rarely were they financed by parents. In 1960, about 70 percent of thirty-year-olds had become financially independent, moved away from home, gotten married, and started a family. By 2000, that number had dwindled to less than 40 percent. Now, every other kid you meet—a hefty slice of the pie chart—seems to fall into a loosey-goosey pattern, earnestly yet erratically finding his or her way, stuck at home in his old bedroom with the Star Wars posters or simply resistant to responsibility. In a significant shift in the zeitgeist, many, many people in their twenties or early thirties are wandering—if not literally, then psychically.

TWENTY-EIGHT IS THE NEW NINETEEN

A few years ago op-ed columnist David Brooks of the *New York Times*, with typical eloquence, observed, "There used to be four common life phases: childhood, adolescence, adulthood and old age. Now, there are at least six: childhood, adolescence, odyssey, adulthood, active retirement and old age. Of the new ones, the least understood is odyssey, the decade of wandering that frequently occurs between adolescence and adulthood. . . . There is every reason to think this phase will grow more pronounced in the coming years."

Something new and big is afoot and it's making parents edgy. We get that today's world is complicated. Twenty-eight is the new nineteen, quips psychologist Dr. Darryl Cross, citing British research that found that adolescence starts earlier than we thought—at eight—and lasts until at least twenty-eight. "Parents have not caught up to the fact that these changes are occurring and how to deal with them."

Months after I started my own research on this book, the *New York Times Magazine* published a lengthy feature, "What Is It About 20-Somethings?" For weeks it animated e-mail in-boxes. Parents sent it to kids and one another, and kids did the same. Bloggers of all ages feasted on the article. "Now safely eight months out of my twenties, I can look back at the past decade during which I lived in rural Arizona, rural Pennsylvania, three towns in the Berkshires, four neighborhoods of Boston, and New York City; worked as a holistic health counselor, Hebrew teacher, journalist, mountain bike leader, yoga instructor, backpacking leader, health food store cashier, farmer, editor, staff writer and writing instructor, and enjoyed a handful of committed relationships and many more handfuls of non-committed ones—with grateful distance," Gila Lyons posted. "I couldn't drive through a trailer park without being overcome with the need to live alone in a double-wide, and I couldn't pass through the suburbs without envisioning myself in an apron happily baking brownies for a backyard full of kids."

The *Times*' piece built on the considerable research of Jeffrey Jensen Arnett, a psychology professor at Clark University who has coined the term "emerging adulthood." Arnett maintains that today's patterns are analogous to what happened in the last century, when social and economic upheaval created a stage that became known as adolescence, which most people today assume was always part of our vernacular. The *Times*' reporting explored developmental psychology and how the brain matures (s-l-o-w-l-y), which brings to mind the thought that with their gray matter a work in progress, perhaps young people can't be expected to act like adults.

The piece raised many questions. "With life spans stretching into the ninth decade, is it better for young people to experiment in their 20s before making choices they'll have to live with for more than half a century?" Robin Marantz Henig, the author, wondered. "Or is adulthood now so malleable, with marriage and unemployment options constantly being reassessed, that young people would be better off just getting started on something, or else they'll never catch up, consigned to remain always a few steps behind the early bloomers? Is emerging adulthood a rich and varied period for self-discovery, as Arnett says it is? Or is it just another term for self-indulgence?"

Undoubtedly one of the most profound factors affecting what's happening now in our country is the economy, to which the *Times* gave only a nod. There are so many changes, so much misery and flux. Home prices may be tumbling, but the status of the real estate bubble is irrelevant if you don't have a job and/or money squirreled away for a down payment and mortgage. Twenty-two percent of young people between the ages of eighteen and thirty-four said they've been turned down for a mortgage, loan, or credit card in the past year, according to a survey from FindLaw.com, a legal marketing and information site. That's double the percentage of any other age group in the survey. As a result, many young people are now moving home to save on rent. The Census Bureau tells us that more and more adult children are moving back home. Between 2005 and 2011, the percentage of men aged twenty-five to thirty-four living with Mom and Dad rose from 14 percent to 19 percent—nearly one in five—while the number of female children living at home went from 8 percent to 10 percent over the same time period.

"This is not just a rotten moment to be young," writes Noreen Malone, twenty-seven, in an October 2011 *New York* magazine cover story, "The Kids Are Actually Sort of Alright." "It's a putrid, stinking, several-months-old-stringy-goat-meat moment to be young.... [W]e find ourselves living among the scattered ashes and spilled red wine and broken glass from a party we watched in our pajamas, peering down the stairs at the grown-ups."

Is it generous—or foolhardy—of parents to open their arms for returning offspring at a point when the older generation might also be supporting elderly parents or be well advised to start thinking of their own future financial needs? Add that to the list of questions. Meanwhile, the kids are back or may never have left. Maybe they can't leave because of heavy student loans, which soon will exceed a trillion dollars.

Parents may be fine with children being buffered by a certain level of emotional insulation between graduation and adult life, and many are not necessarily displeased by their kids' choices. I disagree with Dave Eggers, author of the best seller *A Heartbreaking Work of Staggering Genius*, who wrote that "the lives of people in their early twenties . . . are very difficult to make interesting, even when they seemed interesting to those living with them at the time." There is much to admire about our kids and their friends—their kindness, compassion, brains, humor, cocktails, far superior way of dancing, and technological facility along with much of their music, blogosphere, and comedic movies. I could watch *The Hangover* twenty times straight in one weekend.

If they and we are lucky, the generation to which we've given birth may live longer than we will: according to the Centers for Disease Control, the average life expectancy of someone born in 1950 is 68.2, whereas for a child born in 1980 the prediction is 73.7, and many families boast notably long-lived exceptions. My father lived to ninety-two. My mother-in-law is going strong at eighty-seven, throwing parties and taking herself on her first trip to Paris. Life expectancy at birth increased to 78.2 years in 2009, up from 78 years in 2008. Given more years on earth, maybe it's fine for younger people to raise a glass of barrel-aged bourbon and set cruise control for ten m.p.h.

Perhaps the drifting we see is also a sensible response to contingencies our children can't control. The big, bad real world we've helped to create for them in which to live as adults is a mess. The only thing a kid can be certain of is uncertainty and catastrophic federal debt. While boomers have raised their children with the best intentions, their carbon footprint has bloated and blood pressure risen as we've acquired stress, McMansions, gas-guzzling cars, basal cell melanomas, and a glut of possessions we don't need for which we've had to work longer hours than we'd like. What part does guilt play in our postcollege parenting? Even though our children have always been closest to our hearts, we have felt guilty as working mothers, or guilty as business-trip warriors, or guilty as observers of the fact that all our protests, donations, and marches to make the world a better place seem to have ended in a society with bigger class divisions, a disappearing ozone, and economic meltdowns. It's hard to turn to our child and say, as a responsible citizen, and with a final handshake as he walks out the parental door with his new BA, "Look at the paradise we've created for you."

We try to demonstrate support—dammit, that's the kind of parents we've prided ourselves on being! But while we're evidencing supersensitivity we're also coming unglued, because in many of our children we aren't seeing clear direction, only delay. We always expected that it might take our children a bit longer than it took us to get "there." But now, along with the ghost of Gertrude Stein, we wonder, is there any *there* there and where is *there*, anyway? Near the Maldives? Micronesia? Anyone?

Boomers are a fairly goal-oriented generation. We grew our hair and smoked our dope. Then we got jobs, families, bunions, mortgages, cataracts, and migraines. We raised children and educated them, often at schools we never could have gotten into ourselves. And let's admit it: whether we could afford to or not, we've spoiled kids to an unprecedented degree in human history.

Part of the indulgence has come in the form of stuff—clothes and shoes, sports and music equipment, electronics and computers. Some has been in experiences—lavish and frequent family vacations, big-ticket summer camps, and tours to visit colleges here, there, and everywhere. But much has been psychic, stroking our kids' egos with so much puffery that recent research points to young people becoming praise addicts who'd rather hear an accolade than have sex or eat their favorite food. Social scientists' data has shown that more young people see themselves as important or likeable than years ago. Grade-point averages have improved as the numbers of hours spent studying have declined, and teachers, perhaps influenced by parents, have done their share of stroking. High school students are getting more credits for taking advanced placement courses but are not scoring higher on standardized tests. The author of the book *Generation Me*, Jean Twenge, has found that a growing percentage of incoming college students have rated themselves "above average" in social and intellectual self-confidence compared with students in the 1960s, causing academics to wonder if we've bred a souped-up, antibiotic-resistant virus of over-confidence, not confidence. Intellectual confidence may be an illusion bolstered by grade inflation. According to Twenge and other academics who published a worldwide study in 2011 on this subject in the British journal *Self and Identity*, in 1966 only 19 percent of college students who were surveyed earned an A or A- average in high school, compared with 48 percent in 2009. Today's students enter college on a cloud of narcissism.

With the wisdom of hindsight, we saw our kids start to wander—and even encouraged it. With a soft heart, we tried to insulate them from hardship or at least everyday discomfort, failure, and struggle. We patiently talked through every choice and sorrow while we curated files on worthwhile, recherché programs because we were convinced that we'd spawned the next Mother Teresa, not just a daughter who rents Bollywood movies.

But who anticipated that kids' wanderings would last for years? Who anticipated that it might never end?

When my nephew graduated from Brown University and started a job the following Monday, his sister—who is a few years younger—rolled her eyes and said, "Zach can't wait to be an adult." It was not a compliment. One of the hottest comic strips today is *Dustin*, starring an unmarried, unemployed twenty-three-year-old who lives at home with his parents.

Mothers and fathers are confounded. Many of us were influenced by *The Hurried Child: Growing Up Too Fast Too Soon*, Dr. David Elkind's landmark book arguing for the preservation of childhood. Let kids be kids! "We do our children harm when we hurry them through childhood" is the essence of Elkind's theory. "Hurried children are forced to take on the physical, psychological and social trappings of adulthood before they are prepared to deal with them. . . . Growth into personhood in our contemporary society takes time and cannot be hurried. When children are pressured to grow up fast, important achievements are skipped or bypassed, which can give rise to serious problems later."

I respected this book many years ago and the twenty-fifth-anniversary edition published in 2006 is still selling briskly. "The contemporary parent dwells in a pressure-cooker of competing demands, transition, role changes, personal or professional uncertainties over which he or she exerts slight direction," Dr. Elkind observed. "By hurrying children to grow up, treating them as adults, we hope to remove a portion of our worry . . . (and) harm our children in doing so."

Perhaps it's turned out that all we've done is postpone our worry. I'm wondering if a generation of parents wasn't a little too zealous in drinking Elkind's brand of well-intentioned Kool-Aid and, as long as we're doing revisionist parenting, if a dose of Tiger Mother hurrying and harassing wouldn't have been in order—and isn't in order even now. We have the backs of this group of exceptionally cool people we love, but we want to figure them out. Is this a crisis—as our own parents said, "Little kids, little problems; big kids, big problems"?

WHO ARE THE WANDERERS?

Since the designation of "adult" doesn't yet fit the wanderers, what shall we call the postadolescent, off-the-old-grid kid traveling through today's wander years? Just as the word "teenager" didn't join our patois until the 1940s, I say it's time to introduce a name that the wander years' crowd can own.

Since this gang admires mixologists and logs a lot of time in cocktail lounges, I considered "adultini." "Adult-adjacent" was also on my short hit list, as was the spot-on British "kidult." I also considered the "Y-the-Fuck-Not-Generation," in honor of the Y Generation born between approximately 1975 and 1990. Dr. Arnett's term, "emerging adult," has garnered a following, but plenty of these young people are thoroughly stuck, not showing the most remote signs of emerging,

I'm picking "adultescent." Not to go all wonk on you, but by my definition an adultescent includes Americans twenty-two to thirty-five caught between adolescence and adulthood in an exploration that seems to go on forever, not unlike the Rolling Stones. Dr. Arnett speaks of the "thirty-year deadline." *If only.* After my research, that endpoint strikes me as overly optimistic.

I arbitrarily put the cutoff of adultescence at thirty-five, not because of any magical or critical thinking, but because I find it simply too dreary to think that someone past thirty-five is anything but an adult. Thirty-five—and definitely forty—is also the beginning of middle age, when you buy a pair of reading glasses and shift your focus more toward your limitations than your potential. And according to census data the median age of the United States is now 37.2—there are as many people over that age as under it. Our country is approaching middle age.

I'm not a sociologist, a psychologist, or, God help me, a self-help-book Barbie who with lapidary precision and a wagging finger tells others how to live. In this book, I promised myself not to even think about using the word "cohort," since I am not a formal social critic of any sort but merely a mother, contaminated by curiosity, who believes that if you see something, you say something.

For the last year, in a humble way, I have talked to other parents—fellow baby boomers, usually—as well as numerous American adultescents across the country and abroad with the hope of understanding what's going on. I have observed young people taking paths far different from the ones trod by their parents—and certainly not at all like mine. I've met people both delighted with their status quo as well as those who have, on occasion, been gnawed and spit out by the Jaws of Life. I've also met more than a few solid young people who, when they heard about the wander years as a concept, went apeshit with envy, because they thought it sounded like a lot more fun to live for the foreseeable future in Thailand than be an actuary in Arkansas.

As I've taken my own journalistic wander year, I have tried hard not to be judgmental. With me as your sherpa, I invite you along as I offer up my à la carte observations on how adultescents, overwhelmed by choice, seek and find adventure, here and abroad; move back home because they have no way to make rent; crave attention and often cash from parents, whom they frequently ask to help them move from place to place; create a mess; rack up debt; develop attitudes about money; imbibe *Mad Men* cocktails and the occasional prescription drug; get jobs only to quit them to start businesses or do good; postpone marriage and childbirth; have babies without partners—and more.

As Jane Eyre said, "This . . . will be thought cool language by persons who entertain solemn doctrines about the angelic nature of children . . . but I am not writing to flatter parental egotism, to echo cant, or prop up humbug; I am merely telling the truth."

"And your point is?" you ask. My goal is to capture a moment and to reflect our time. Make of it what you will. If you are a wandering adultescent, you already know you're not alone. If you are a parent of such an adultescent, you may not realize how much company you have.

Chapter 2

CHOOSE YOUR OWN ADVENTURE

My dad used to say that we'd all wind up working for "C" students. Joke's on you, Dad. I'm never getting a job!

—Anonymous

The first mega semi-independent decision that lays the ground for adultescence is "picking" a college. Until then, angst-y parents have engineered most of the big loop-de-loop choices for their budding scholar: red-shirting their child so that by holding him back from starting kindergarten, he'd get ahead; moving to the suburb with the highest SAT scores; gerrymandering within local school districts to wriggle into the primo public school or, at the very least, finagling for a better teacher, all with the hope of breeding and grooming their own thoroughbred. Come high school, the same parents dedicate countless dollars and endless travel miles to campus visits. Next, why *not* file as many as twenty college applications at $50 to $75 a pop? The fantasy, after all, is to try to make the "perfect" choice without too many family members winding up under the care of a psychopharmacologist.

The kid gets in. Somewhere. You'd think this is the end, that everyone can exhale, but for the wander years, it's really the beginning, because this is when choice explodes into a thousand splinters.

Once in college, a student's decision making picks up steam and intensity. Sorority/fraternity or not? This roommate or that? Dorm or apartment? By junior year, a major must be declared: Bachelor of Arts in Peace and Conflict, anyone? Sociology of Fashion, Magic, Historical Clothing? These are legit alternatives at fine institutions, and if you can't find a ready-made major, almost one thousand four-year colleges and universities allow a student to blend his or her own bespoke smoothie: Collective Cognition Studies, let's say, an academic mix tape of computer science, philosophy, psychology, and biology. That is, if Molecular Biology and Art Practice isn't more "you." For many adultescents, life has become a high-calorie pupu platter of possibilities so beyond the ken of Mom and Dad that parents can't even resent that they never got to try most of the options.

Once you get into college, it's a place where if you don't want to study hard, you usually don't have to. Type "college essay" or "term paper" into a search engine, and you can buy a paper—on "emerging adulthood," for example. *Emerging adults have reached a step up from childhood but are not yet ready to fully take on adult responsibilities. This part of life is open to many new experiences which can be very good for the morality of this upcoming generation of adults.* I give this paper a C–.

"For all my sons"—there are three, now in their mid-twenties— "college was mostly one long party," says Andrea Brockman, DDS, a Philadelphia dentist in practice with her husband. "My youngest,

Peter, is twenty-four, and still is in the party. His dream is to be a rock star. Meanwhile, he works at Starbucks. I think he should have a better-paying job or go back to school and find a career path. In a year I'll say, 'It's time. Make a decision.' Meanwhile we're still paying all his bills, because he can't afford health insurance or a cell phone and school loans."

Peter's brothers have drifted but landed, Andrea announces with fingers crossed. After college Seth wanted to start a business, then the economy went south and he couldn't get loans, so he returned to school. Now he's teaching science in an inner-city school, "struggling, but he's stopped the party." Jamey got downsized out of a corporate job. He's studying accounting.

In college, neither Seth nor Jamey, both liberal arts majors, took education or accounting courses. "My husband and I wanted our kids to get a well-rounded education, which would have included learning about business—basic marketing and accounting. But we discovered that unless you major in these things, you can't get into the courses," complains Andrea. "Then you graduate and all of a sudden find there are no jobs. This turns into disillusionment, which turns into partying with your friends in the same situation." Which turns into not much.

While Andrea vents about inflexible college curriculums, she also points out that her sons felt no incentive to excel at school because they lacked a plan that required them to earn good grades. "My husband and I knew we were going to professional school so we had to work hard, but our kids didn't feel that pressure. When I was twenty-four, I was engaged and had an advanced degree and a profession." While gnashing her teeth, Andrea blames herself. "I didn't press my kids to pick a path with a job at the end of it. These days I give them advice all the time . . . and see the curtain come down. Any discoveries they're making, they're making on their own."

FORGET PLAN B. THERE ISN'T PLAN A.

Who are we, if not the sum of our decisions? Yet as an authority on weighing the pros and cons of decision making, I realize I, boomer lady, do not possess what Henry James in *The Portrait of a Lady* referred to as "a roving disposition." Depending on your point of view, I have been dully unimaginative or laser-focused regarding job direction, remaining monogamous to an idea I hatched in fourth grade, to model my work life on the most intriguing woman with a paycheck I stumbled upon in the Upper Midwest tundra, Sheena of the *Daily Planet*, Lois Lane.

Following this dogged reporter's lead, I wrote for school newspapers. This led to summers at the *Forum*, my Fargo, North Dakota, newspaper. At college, between the teargas, the ironing of my hair, and the moonlighting at the *Wisconsin State Journal*, I covertly mailed résumés to national news and fashion magazines. During spring break of junior year, I skulked off to New York City, where most magazines get born, to job hunt. *Harper's Bazaar* offered me a copywriter's position. This would have been a get-out-of-jail-free card that allowed me to bypass a standard entry-level job as a dedicated slave to a 1970s Miranda Priestly, but I stewed about not getting a college diploma, declined the offer, and returned to my university to finish up a degree, although I didn't attend my graduation. No one I knew did. We collectively donated the cap-and-gown fee to a student defense fund for antiwar protestors who'd been jailed. For men at that time, the draft had been a volatile factor. The outcome of a lottery in 1969 left guys I knew who'd scored low numbers frantically asking hometown doctors to write letters citing medical problems that would yield a deferment. You never heard about more asthma and life-threatening cat allergies in your life. But within a few years, the Vietnam War started to wind down, and the moment of frenzy passed. Every man I knew got some sort of regular job or started graduate school, often after a trip, usually to Europe.

Following graduation I, too, took a summer swing through Europe, par for most boomers. My own trip, which I financed through money I'd saved from jobs the four previous summers, ended in New York City, where I interviewed at a few publishing companies. A magazine offered me a job. The salary was $90 a week, and no, I was not a scrivener in Colonial Williamsburg but an editorial assistant at the literary and imminently soignée *Mademoiselle*. My parents ponied up $100 to tide me over until my first raise, and with little thought, I moved to Manhattan, a relocation that was easy because once there, I didn't need a car. My parents certainly weren't going to buy one for me.

After I got a $10-a-week increase two months later, I never again asked Mom and Dad for financial aid because back in the day, my petite paycheck actually financed mass transportation, Chock full o'Nuts date nut bread and whipped cream cheese sandwiches for workday lunches and P.J. Clarke's weekend splurges, the occasional taxi or Broadway show, movies, clothes, vacations, rent, bottles of Mateus, and a summer visit to North Dakota, which my parents didn't subsidize. My live-in boyfriend drove a taxi and regularly delivered cookies for a bakery, so at any given time we had a freezer full of jaw-breaking, freebie rugelach for when we entertained, which was often.

I've never strayed far from my writing/editing/reporting comfort zone. I've been on staffs, freelance, sometimes both, and I've always convinced myself that whatever I was writing and editing was do-or-die important, that the earth would stop spinning if I didn't craft the best possible cover line, let's say, about how not to be fat after forty. I've also never regretted the professional choices I've made, just as I've stayed happy in the zip code where I moved at twenty-two.

An extreme case, my life story, and certainly a barely beige one?

No argument. But the CVs of most boomers I know differ only in the details. In every respect but fiscal I was fortunate enough to start with a pretty fine job, but plenty of my friends began with something dreary, knowing it was up to them to make it better. Most of us picked a path before we got too deep into our twenties and didn't stray further than moving from city to suburb or job to job within one or two industries.

Sounds like a snooze, you say, the equivalent of one endless loop of Golf Channel reruns? Most boomers I know don't think of their lives as dull. Hey, just look at our divorce rate! Our orthopedic injuries! Our suspenseful memory lapses! The shambles we've made of the environment and our country's infrastructure! The Sturm und Drang our kids create!

Any-hoo, choices. I've noticed that having too many options leads to snow blindness. It's not just Aunt Sally's wisdom: studies support the brain-draining oppression that multiple choices bring. Seemingly limitless possibility paralyzes us, a dilemma that social psychologist Sheena Iyengar, Ph.D., from Columbia University's School of Business, refers to as the paradox of choice in *The Art of Choosing*. In one experiment, Dr. Iyengar showed how shoppers who chose from more options were less happy with their purchases than those with more limited opportunities. "When faced with two dozen varieties of jam in a grocery store, for example, or lots of investment options for their pension plan, people often chose arbitrarily to walk away without making any choice at all, rather than labor to make a reasoned choice," reports Gretchen Rubin in her best-selling book, *The Happiness Project*.

A jam is the state in which many adultescents find themselves at graduation, feeling their lives are lousy with choices after they've been handed their bachelor's degrees. They hear the echo of their parents' trope wishing them Godspeed. *Find your passion! The money will follow! You can be anything you want to be!* Of course it helps that they've heard these mantras all their lives. By the time the diploma ink dries, many recent graduates begin to embrace the idea of life being one infinite Friendly's menu.

Assuredly, some graduates take their bachelor's degree and head straight to med school or Wall Street or public service. Applications for AmeriCorps positions, for example, nearly tripled to 258,829 in 2010 from 91,399 in 2008, the *New York Times* reports. Yet with bravado that astonishes most of their parents, many adultescents don't do the obvious and become instead stars in their own reality dramas. They pick a direction, reverse it, spin the dial, turn thirty-three degrees, win an all-expenses-paid free ticket to Bangladesh, start a novel, stay in a village with no paved roads, plumbing, or electricity but stellar cell service, crowd-source their next move on Facebook, get an MBA, jet to Equatorial Guinea, regroup in Kalamazoo, study an Eastern spiritual practice whose name their parents can't remember or pronounce, start a job, quit, ditch the novel and begin a screenplay, take a break to play more reindeer games, find a shaman, burn the half-finished screenplay, go to law school, where tuition has jacked up four times faster than the soaring costs of college, accrue vast loans, drop out, become a shaman, sell their car and fill a self-storage unit with their worldly possessions. Only then do they fly two stars to the right, straight on till morning.

"We live better than kings," Ari Siegel, a recent graduate of the University of Michigan, exclaims. That is, assuming you have some modest baksheesh at your disposal. "You book a flight anywhere in the world online and can be there the next day. You can function as an anthropologist, seeing things from a lot of different angles, living out *The Sun Also Rises.* Travel is an escape ... although," he adds, when he catches his breath, "the overwhelming amount of choice can create a person who doesn't have much of his own identity."

BUILDING A PERSONAL PORTFOLIO

> Those friends I had from college . . . a kibbutz here, a New
> Zealand sheep farm there. They've collected all these life ex-
> periences and now they're experience junkies—professional
> excursionists. That's what my real life is doing—it's out here
> collecting experiences, international ones. Harvesting grapes
> in Sicily, so to speak.
>
> —*Perfect Reader* by Maggie Pouncey

The way it often goes, with their parents' benediction (and a varnish of envy), adultescents unready to enter a career or move on to the next degree put their energy into crafting a tarmac of travel, unpaid internships, and exploratory jobs. Advanced planning is for sissies. Quicker than you can say "Meet me in Mumbai," *wanderjahrs* begin to turn into wander-lives.

"You'll always remember the wandering, not the office job," philosophizes Claire Leavitt, twenty-eight, a willowy Brooklyn-bred grad student living in Paris. "It's all about accumulating experiences. You want to build up your personal portfolio, to have dinner party conversation and be able to say what you've learned.

"My parents never pressured me to do something practical," Claire notes. "They believed college was for developing your intellect. Any pushback I got about my choices was from friends who were in, say, engineering, questioning why I wasn't trying to study something that prepared me for a job." She spent her first semester of her senior year in Hanoi, a popular choice. After graduation from a Big Ten university, Claire backpacked in Europe for a few months, and then got a job in Washington, D.C., covering congressional hearings. Soon she moved to

New Zealand, another short-listed hot spot. "I figured if I didn't do it then, when? I had a horrible case of wanderlust.

"Again, my parents were a lot more supportive than friends," Claire says. She returned to Washington and got another job on Capitol Hill. "I hated every minute of it, and at the same time fell in love with a guy who broke my heart. I was a cliché times twelve." This prompted the decision to enroll at the American University in Paris in an English-language master's program for international relations and public policy.

Claire hopes to go on to earn a Ph.D. in international relations and work at a think tank, making her living reading and writing. "The best part of my life now is academic. But a lot of my friends in Paris—they're mostly Americans—are less motivated, really lost. They see grad school as the icing on the cake instead of the cake that will help them get where they want to go."

She is aware of her advantages, not least of which is French health care. "The government even covers designer prescription sunglasses!" That and an American boyfriend with whom she's traveled to Greece, the Netherlands, Switzerland, and Africa—"really cool things I couldn't afford to do on my own." While her beau is twenty-two years older than Claire, she considers him the real kid in the relationship. "He acts thirty. I want to say, 'You've already lived most of your life.' But he thinks he has all the time in the world," a phrase she repeats minutes later to describe herself. "I feel perpetually twenty-two, though I don't want to end up at forty-one in a Lori Gottlieb situation," citing the author's book, *Marry Him: The Case for Settling for Mr. Good Enough*, which has struck terror in the hearts of many adultescent women. "I definitely don't want kids until I'm thirty-five."

"I've suggested to Claire that she might want to adjust down that age, especially because her boyfriend is fifty," her mother, Lorraine

Glennon, says. "But I don't sense that Claire's generation wants any mentorship—or needs it. This is where their entitlement comes in."

Behind many a wandering adultescent is a parent or two who wouldn't mind doing a *Freaky Friday*, playing a mother or father who swaps bodies with their child. And why not, when our kids have, compared to us, glossier degrees; better clothes, cars, vacations, and electronics; more significant financial support; and a more vociferous parental pep squad? "I always say my children live in a different class than I did," Lorraine jokes. Sort of.

"I was from an Illinois farming town of sixteen hundred people, not a bad place to be from when I grew up, though now it seems like meth city." Her husband, Roy, had a hardscrabble background in the Seattle area: his mother married four times and Roy ended up enlisting in the military. Roy and Lorraine went through undergraduate and graduate school on scholarships, using meager savings to swing a seventies beta version of wandering, crisscrossing the United States, taking odd jobs to support themselves.

"I worked in a lot of offices because touch typing is the one thing I do best on earth," she says. "In the middle of the trip, Roy and I married, partly to get some money to continue. We ended in New York. I taught a little, went to Europe for the first time at thirty, and had two kids when I was in my early thirties. I had no job trajectory or ambition." At thirty-seven she accepted a job at *Art & Antiques*. "Now I'm in women's magazines—but not *of* them," she says, careful to draw a distinction, "though I feel very fortunate to be able to make a living at all with my antiquated skill set. I love mucking around with long text. On many magazines, that's no longer in much demand."

Lorraine has been a booster for her daughter, Claire, and son, Tom, who's off to Uganda, encouraging them to make choices unavailable to her and her husband. "I've never been one of those parents who said,

'You've got to get home and get a job and settle down.' I was handicapped by my small-town mentality. Claire is so cosmopolitan. Her work ethic is incredible, but the externals of her life are very pleasant. She goes all over the place, even just for the weekend. This is what I want for my kids. It's worth it for them to have these experiences." Both kids have cobbled together scholarships and grants to finance their adventures. Claire predicts that she'll be about $50,000 in debt when she returns to the United States—"or maybe England"—to work on her Ph.D.

"My siblings and I were always hiding our real thoughts and feelings from our parents, where I think the kids of boomers are much more likely to confide in their parents," Lorraine says. "Today the lines of power just aren't as clearly drawn. . . . I've tended to elevate my kids, even when they were much younger, to peer status. Claire and I are extremely close. We talk constantly and I'm always giving my take on things, but I haven't offered macro advice like 'Have a five-year plan.' She does that on her own.

"These kids who win trophies for everything . . . have been mugged by reality, yet they still seem pretty optimistic," Lorraine concludes. "I guess that's because of the curriculum of self-esteem they've all had—this on top of their own sense of heightened entitlement."

"We come from people who brought us up to believe that life is a struggle, and if you should feel really happy, be patient: this will pass." That's Garrison Keillor speaking, the most articulate ambassador that the region of my childhood, the upper Midwest, will most likely ever export. Raising children in North Dakota during the 1950s and 1960s, my parents adhered to the philosophy above and apparently never got the memo about self-esteem. I didn't receive many compliments, for fear I might develop a swelled head.

But that was then. Now, even if you live in Fargo, it's hard to avoid noticing that creating self-esteem is what parents of adultescents seem to feel is their mission. Every decision they make on their kids' behalf becomes a tiny Lego block whose ultimate destination is creating a monument of self-esteem with a big brain, sports mastery, and superb social skills. The destiny of each child, parents have grown to believe, is to realize and maximize their own brand of distinction. Oprah may have started preaching to her viewers to "live your best life" in the 1980s. Perhaps she got the inspiration from boomer parents, who started being vainglorious about their children as soon as they had them.

Out of love—let's not lose sight of that—parents started helping kids with homework. "*We* have a lot of homework tonight," I'd often hear parents say. (I learned my lesson on that one. The one time I helped my older son write an important paper was during his junior year in high school. "We" only got a B, because his English teacher said his paragraphs were too short. They were short—about three sentences per paragraph, exactly the length of paragraphs in every magazine article I'd written or edited for the previous twenty years.) If kids didn't do well, we hired tutors. If they wanted to learn to play the saxophone, we bought one. I have the sax in the closet to prove this. If they got bullied, we called the school and intervened. No wonder child psychologist Daniel Kindlon, Ph.D., a Harvard adjunct lecturer in the Department of Society, Human Development, and Health, warns against what he calls our "discomfort with discomfort." "By the time they're teenagers, (kids) have no experience with hardship," he told *The Atlantic* magazine. "Civilization is about adapting to less-than-perfect situations, yet parents often have this instantaneous reaction to unpleasantness, which is 'I can fix this.'"

More students than ever are taking challenging courses in high school, but they are not scoring higher on standardized tests, and yet their grades in college are higher, thanks to grade inflation designed to make students—and parents—feel good about their efforts. Some colleges have had to hire full-time administrators to handle complaints from disgruntled parents about Jason's C+ paper or Katy's spooky roommate. These parents know from past experience, "I can fix this." Some parents even admit to editing their children's law school papers. Mark S. Schneider of the American Institutes for Research who headed the Education Department's research wing under President George W. Bush told the *New York Times* that a disturbing disconnect became apparent a decade ago, which is when many of today's wandering adultescents were in high school. "Students were taking more rigorous-sounding courses, but there was no evidence they had mastered the content." Yet the typical grade-point average in college rose to about 3.11 by the middle of the last decade, from 2.52 in the 1950s, according to a recent study by Stuart Rorjstaczer, professor emeritus at Duke, and Christopher Healy of Furman University. College students also spend fewer hours studying each week than did their counterparts in 1961, Philip S. Babcock of the University of California, Santa Barbara, and Mindy Marks of the University of California, Riverside, recently reported. It all suggests a scam—and some great, national coddling. No surprise that Pew Research Center found that three out of four Americans consider today's adultescents less industrious and virtuous than their elders, or that in a recent benchmark test, the Program for International Student Assessment, American students landed "in the middle of the pack; that's not where we want to be," said Stuart Kerachsky, deputy commissioner at the National Center for Education Statistics, an arm of the Department of Education.

The finding strikes me as mean and excessive. I know my kids weren't alone in each having a part-time job while at college. But the following is also true. "If you're my age or younger and privileged and American . . . we were told how very special we were," writes Claire

Dederer, born in 1970, in *My Life in Twenty-Three Yoga Poses*, one of the rash of memoirs by authors in or about their twenties and thirties. "We expressed ourselves, our special selves. It was more than a pedagogy, this idea of the specialness of every child. It was a belief system: 'wonderful you,' it might have been called."

If you're special, it's all about your idiomatic singularity. When you break free of teenage structure—tutoring, coaching, honing college application line items—you can make a fetish of your choices, every one, as the echo of commencement speech invective pushes you to march to your own drummer and to find and follow your dream, the cover songs for our culture. Does self-esteem take you the distance after college? Probably not as much as the satisfaction derived from accomplishments you've earned. Perseverance, resiliency, and reality testing are the qualities that predict success in life, author Jean Twenge's research says. Twenge also points out that "we treat our kids like adults when they're children, and we infantilize them when they're eighteen."

TAKE A HIKE, CORPORATE AMERICA

Ask Normandie Wilson where she lives and she'll tell you San Diego—for now. She's flying through her twenties free as the proverbial bird in the Henry Van Dyke quote that ends her e-mail signature: "Use what talent you possess. The woods would be very silent if no birds sang except those that sang best."

On graduation day from Oberlin College, Nicole Travota—Normandie's birth name—doubled over with a panic attack, blown out of the water by the question everyone my age is grateful not to have to answer again: *What am I going to do with the rest of my life?* Nicole had majored in religion and dance, and as she packed up her car to return to Hurricane, West Virginia, she "wished one of my professors had sat me down and said that if you want to be a dance major, you have to be either really talented"—which she didn't feel described her—"or exceedingly rich." Although her grandparents financed her college education, she arrived at Oberlin and did a reality check after she met students who got a handy $3,000 deposited in their checking accounts every month. "I was one of the few people I knew who worked during college," she says. "If I hadn't worked, I'd never be able to have a job now, because nothing at Oberlin prepared me to earn a salary.

"After graduation I had the brilliant idea that I would go to Key West and teach dance. I knew no one down there but by using My-Space contacted a teacher and drove to Florida with all my stuff." The job she thought was solid wasn't. She turned north and landed in New York City, where for almost two years she worked for a podiatrist, performing tasks for which she was unlicensed, like taking X-rays. After the doctor got busted for writing bogus prescriptions, Normandie Wilson—the name she gave herself—worked at a Sephora until she decided she belonged in Los Angeles. "I thought I wanted to act, but I ended up playing the marimba in an indie-pop band and working for a production company in Santa Monica, where my boss was a sexist pig."

Following a nasty boyfriend breakup, Normandie quit her job, stored her stuff, and spent eight weeks touring with her band. "We were eleven people in a van, no pay, sleeping on floors, spending at least eight hours on the road. It was one of the most trying yet best experiences I've ever had, because I tapped into an awesome network of friends." When Normandie returned to L.A., she took a "boring, depressing, stable" job as a bookkeeper in a guitar shop and reunited with her musician ex. With a taste for the road, the couple sold their belongings, hoping to perform in Europe. "We arrived in London with no plan, breaking up and getting back together a million times. I came back to Los Angeles penniless, sold my iPhone for five hundred and fifty dollars, bought a car, and moved to San Diego. Now I work part-time in a coffee shop, even though I have a degree from one of the country's most elite colleges," a ranking confirmed by *U.S. News & World Report*.

Not that Normandie lacks ambition. "At some point I want to have a good savings account and make a decent living, say fifty thousand dollars a year, by playing music, but those are my only material goals. I really believe if I continue to focus my energy, I'll be able to make an impact in the music scene."

Many mothers and fathers in America might gnash their teeth along with Normandie's parents, "driven crazy that I don't want to have a stupid blood-and-brain-sucking corporate 'steady' job." But does the world really need another manager? she asks. "I don't understand the trade-off of giving up the best years of your life inside a stuffy office kissing someone's ass for ten hours a day, unless you really want the fancy house and fancy car.... The recession has made me even happier, honestly, knowing that I've lived my life on the edge so far, since many of my friends who had jobs have lost them. Everyone I meet . . . is utterly envious of my freedom."

Contempt for corporations. Loathing The Man. Rebelling against the whalebone of structure. This echo from the 1960s is a familiar wander years' riff. "There's a very low tolerance for corporate bullshit," says Maxine Davidowitz, whose son Ben White has elected to stay in Colorado, where he went to college, rather than return to the East Coast of his childhood and adolescence. Ben lived first in Colorado Springs, then Crested Butte, now Aspen for three years—managing a ski rental shop and until recently doing a gig as an outdoor leadership tour guide.

"Ben knows he doesn't want to be a ski bum all his life, or even an Outward Bound guide," Maxine says. "He's looking for a more intellectual challenge. But administration and corporate politics drain my son. He had a job as a naturalist with the Aspen Center for Environmental Studies. It sounded wonderful to his dad and me, but Ben hated the time behind a desk. Recently, his alma mater, Colorado College, hired him as an interim program director. My husband and I got excited, thinking that as soon as the school saw how great Ben is they'd offer a full-time job and he'd be set. But weeks into the job Ben was already complaining. Ben has very high standards for how corporations and academic institutions should be run," a bar those corporations and schools fail to reach.

"This generation has a whole other set of values than the ones with which I was raised—get married, get a job," Maxine continues. "Around my son I find I have to really defend my choices, despite the fact that I've always found my work"—she is an art director—"to be so much fun there have been times I've almost felt I'd do it for free.

"My husband, Danny, is an executive coach who loves his work as much as I do. Ben's told both of us that he's found our dedication to jobs to be intimidating and stifling. I realize I can't take the template for my generation and try to press it on my son's. The mold doesn't fit.

"Ben is deeply philosophical and psychologically aware, astute about human nature. He's looking for a life where nature is central. He has most of the pieces in place—friends, spending time outdoors—everything except the big hole in the middle, what you do for a living. He's in an existential dilemma now, trying to decide if he should go to grad school in psychology, given that he's still not sure what his career goal is."

As a result, Maxine assumes the default position of an adultescent's parent: worrying. "If I take a long view, I'm reassured, because my son is very smart. But I care so much about his happiness that if I ask questions, it creates a terrible dynamic. When my husband and

I sense that Ben isn't happy, he feels our disappointment as surely as if he's put his hand in a fire."

"I come from a privileged perspective," Ben readily acknowledges. "My parents were able to pay for my college education, where a lot of my friends had to get jobs right away to pay off loans. But I also know people who don't have to bust their butts for sixty hours a week—and don't . . . friends with an urge to pick up and leave every few months because they've been afforded the opportunity to not choose one path."

Ben's approach to wandering has been more deliberate. "I was intent on making my life in Colorado. I wanted the intellectual and cultural stimulation of a New York lifestyle in a place that would allow me to walk out my back door and hike. I had the fantasy of living in a small town but still having an engaging, challenging professional life."

Ah, dreams. "As much as I love it here, I've gone through several different scenarios to make that life I wanted and there's always something missing," Ben admits. "Aspen is a place that people go [to] in order to never grow up. A lot of the people here have emotional issues and a drinking problem, and pot smoking is really prevalent within the field of outdoor education.

"The level of academic commitment is also very much absent," Ben continues. "There have been a limited number of people here who I really wanted to be with." For the moment, he is caught between bailing for graduate school and staying in his job. "I'd like to leave Colorado and return with a degree that lets me start a private counseling practice someday, but I don't know how feasible that is. A friend of mine who's a psychologist tells me he's never worked in a place less conducive to having a practice—people don't want to do anything about their problems and can't pay for therapy. And I don't want to live a life of poverty.

"There's so much thinking in my generation of 'Why commit to something if the world is still full of possibilities?'" Ben says. "I have many friends chasing AmeriCorps fellowships or teaching English in a foreign country, searching for something. It makes people hard to nail down." This affects forming bonds with other people and, certainly, romance. "I've had a few failed relationships with women who ran off to someplace like Thailand to do humanitarian work. I think some of these people will find themselves in their mid- to late thirties still uncertain and running away from confronting something within themselves."

Consider the annual "Modern Love" essay contest the *New York Times* runs especially for young people. "In 2010 the entire focus shifted to technology-enabled intimacy—relationships that grow and deepen almost exclusively via laptops, webcams, online chats and text messages . . . love so safe that what's most feared is not a sexually transmitted disease but a computer virus, or perhaps meeting the object of your affection in person," reports Daniel Jones, the column's editor.

One of the latest contest winners was Caitlin Dewey, who reflected on meeting a guy named Will at a Web journalism conference. ("If you have ever attended an Internet conference, you understand how pale skin, thick glasses and scruffy hair can be attractive," she writes. "Otherwise, I can't explain it to you.") Will and Caitlin returned to their respective cities and began a "safe, sanitized" relationship via Skype and webcam. "The Internet brings people together with hash tags and message boards, but it never satisfies them," she explains. Yet "no matter how much you love someone's blog or Twitter feed, it isn't their posts you actually want." So eventually, Caitlin traveled 540 miles to meet Will for a weekend. He took her to dinner—and spent the meal reading his e-mail. Later, back in his apartment, his focus wandered to his Web site's traffic, not the young woman at his side. For Caitlin Dewey, IRL—*in real life* in online parlance—was no success.

"HE'S ONE OF THOSE SMART, DRIFTY YOUNG PEOPLE . . .

who, after certain deliberations, decides he wants to do Something in the Arts but won't, possibly can't, think in terms of an actual job; who seems to imagine that youth and brains and willingness will simply summon an occupation, the precise and perfect nature of which will reveal itself in its own time.

This passage from Michael Cunningham's novel *By Nightfall* might have been inspired by any of the adultescents I've met, young adults endowed so generously with talent, intellect, and options they're like fireflies with perpetual batteries, gracing one sky and then another and another, calling to mind the aphorism "too smart for their own good."

"It's been hard to be out of phase with the image of what I was 'supposed' to be doing," says Jonathan,* twenty-eight. "Take an Ivy Leaguer, Phi Beta Kappa overachiever and put him in a world that says if you don't climb the ladder by thirty-five, you'll never get there, and it's tough. I've often gone through big phases of trying to 'get back on track,' telling myself that my years of adventure were over."

Jonathan is a high school salutatorian who went on to earn high honors at Yale while exploring nonstop. First there was debate, speech club and math club, the constitution team, chorus, and jazz band. That was high school. "At Yale I filled in the gaps with the outdoors club, climbing, the carillon society, pit bands, Tai Chi, and a juggling group called the Anti-Gravity Society, which put on a Halloween show with fire breathing and torch throwing." Occupied with all these interests and obligations, Jonathan did not immediately choose a major. "I debated between math and music. My father argued that if I wanted to have more doors open to me, music might not be the most strategic choice. I ultimately picked math because it required fewer courses.

"I've had lots of achievement, but not so much attention given to where I want to go with it. I wrestled with that in college and I'm still figuring out what I'm passionate about." Not that Jonathan feels compelled to comply with a time line imposed by society. After Yale he biked and hitchhiked in New Zealand, then did an about-face and became a consultant for a company in Washington, D.C., supporting the Environmental Protection Agency. "After two years I started feeling that I didn't have the time or space to reflect," he says, so he spent a year in Belgium on a fellowship to study the carillon. "This was a cocooning period, not the eight-to-ten I'd had in Washington with a rich social life." In Belgium Jonathan arrived at the realization that he loses steam on the introspective side if he doesn't have a community. "I discovered that the people I need in my life are a rare thing and I can't just walk into a bar and meet them."

Meanwhile, he entered the "biggest and most prestigious contest for carillon and almost won," after which he'd planned to come back to the United States to get a job. "But while I was procrastinating, I got an offer to perform at Renaissance festivals, which are full of people who move five times a year and live out of a tent. I had the chance to not get on with my life"—and be an intellectual carnie. "With the Renaissance festivals you get the whole stratification of society, well-educated and not, a neo-hippie society with a lot of music and potluck. I got housing through the festivals or stayed with friends. Does that mean I mooch? How do I make sure I'm giving more than I'm taking? That was one piece of the puzzle."

Now Jonathan is on less of an antihero path, with an apartment leased in Boston and a job working for his brother doing cancer research. Choice can be delightful. It can also be overstimulating, confusing, and panic-inducing, creating a juggernaut of doubt and indecision.

"I'm trying to take the structured and traditional model I had in D.C.—formal job, formal housing, all my friends buying nice things—and balance it with adventure, connection, learning, and growth . . . to find the middle ground that sustains me. I have the sense that I've broken through a lot of the *shoulds* and the *musts* and am looking for a life that fits the living, breathing me, rather than my imagined sense of self. I think you can live a whole life that way, and live it well, provided you're not deferring happiness for that day when you find the 'one right thing.' I'm not sure that it's so different from those who start out with a firm and sensible plan—after all, things change for them, too.

"I suppose it's possible that I'll never 'amount to much,' and that thought still doesn't really appeal to me," Jonathan admits. "But it doesn't feel that likely, either. I have some nascent projects going on that are pretty exciting. Generally I feel like I'm in a good place. I've come a long way."

Chapter 3
SEEK AND YOU MAY FIND

With choice, entitlement, and specialness topping off the lexicon of a generation, wanderers frequently seem to seek seeking. The search may span continents—or penetrate inward—with sincere, even reverential, attempts to feel whole or fill a void.

One thing's certain: here's the church, here's the steeple, open the church, and, excuse me, you'll see not many adultescents. A joke circulates among theologians that people in their twenties and thirties view God as a divine butler and cosmic therapist, on call 24/7, helping them feel better about themselves but demanding little in return. You hear a lot about being "spiritual" without being "religious," with adultescents admiring belief systems untainted by intolerant theological judgments. Many people twenty-two to thirty-five years old, along with their parents, find New Age beliefs attractive simply because they don't see their Sunday School dogma at work. Practitioners don't necessarily visit an ashram, but many seek out Eastern prayer or study techniques of soothing New Age treatments, an appealing alternate to attending the religious institution of their childhood, the one they consider irrelevant now that it's boisterously rejecting gay marriage or evolution.

Some young people are rejecting Christianity partly because of their parents' hypocrisy, claims Dave Wager, who runs Silver Birch Ranch, a Christian camp and conference center in White Lake, Wisconsin. "Parents have talked about the sin of gluttony while being gluttonous. They have talked about not being greedy while they bought summer homes, sports cars, and go on expensive vacations. They speak of the importance of sexual purity while . . . allowing Internet porn to escalate to unbelievable levels."

And while maybe it's too woo-woo for cynical you (and me), the shift toward New Age spiritualism might be explained by Neptune being in Sagittarius, says Los Angeles psychic Ally Mead. "For people in this age group, the challenge is to find meaning. Neptune defines how a generation will present itself and Sagittarius is the sign of the seeker, so they're bound to become a very spiritual generation that breaks down walls and incorporates foreign people, customs, and languages into their world. Travel, learning, and metaphysics will all be part of this transition for them, as they learn to put aside materialistic concerns in favor of personal meaning."

Does a regular yoga class, for instance, not offer amounts of "community" equal to a church or synagogue social? adultescents often say. That group "ommm" can bring a chill to your spine and balm to your soul and it's been twenty years since yoga was New Age. Now it's in every American gym, church, and synagogue basement, and for many adultescents is more than exercise. Meet Abraham Heisler, who has trained at the headquarters of Ananda Marga, a global yoga and meditation organization founded in 1955 by Shrii Shrii Anandamurti, living for a year at the group's headquarters in Missouri, studying vegetarian diet and yoga. "I got deeper and deeper into it, very close to taking vows to become a monk," Abe, thirty, says. He pulled away before the final commitment, fearing that the choice would separate him from family.

Abe started college at Syracuse University, majoring in film, and transferred to the State University of New York at Binghamton, where he switched to history. He recognizes a pattern. "I go away from something and return to it later." After Ananda Marga, he went back to his home of New York City to live with his grandmother, teaching yoga and waiting tables, then decided to enroll at the New York Film Academy, "film being one of those things I'd started studying at fourteen." He was able to finance the $30,000 tuition costs through an inheritance.

"To be honest, I just wanted to get film skills," Abe acknowledges. "I never planned to be a big-time filmmaker. But my teachers were applauding my work—they still show my thesis film to incoming students. Doors started opening and I went through them."

After film school, Abe felt a pull toward Vermont, where he taught break dancing until he came back to New York to sell beads, teach film to high school students, and write a screenplay. "Producer friends urged me to get investor backing. And my ego went through the roof. I spent two years trying to raise money while working as a cameraman for a news channel and director of photography for low-budget features. But in this economy no one was willing to invest in a no-name director on an independent film. When that came crashing down, I had nothing."

Not quite. Abe made his way to Melbourne to live with his Australian girlfriend, Satya, and perform hip-hop music. That's when Ananda Marga approached him to make films. This led Abe to "a whole lot of flying here and there—Taiwan, Indonesia, Singapore, and Haiti—working with an organization I love, but it put a spoke in the wheel of my relationship with Satya. We broke up, I went to India to meditate on what I wanted to do with my life, and when I saw her again we decided to get married."

Next, thanks to a friend from Tasmania, Abe moved to Los Angeles to intern with one of the producers of *My Cousin Vinnie*. But although Abe says he's "made contacts, and film is something I love and people think I'm good at, it's not my end goal." That would be teaching meditation, "to help people express their potentiality. I feel I'm ready to go back to studying, to give me more career options, like counseling, the life coach thing, some therapy . . . and I'm looking to do a master's degree in east-west psychology at an institute in San Francisco." Meanwhile, he remains in L.A., supporting himself through editing, while his wife, an aeronautical engineer with the Australian Air Force, has been traveling in South America, because "she'd like to transition to something more socially conscious, perhaps with an NGO.

"I look at life from a yogic perspective," Abe explains. "People have potential experiences that we need to go through in order to feel fulfilled. These experiences come in any shape or fashion. We all go through ups and down, one flowing motion, never a stagnant pool. Everybody is a walking story," some more like hasty blog posts than polished literature.

"It's a wonderful thing for a young person to be able to explore, either literally or the world of ideas, to be somewhat playful after years with your nose to the grindstone," says Dina Heisler, an educational consultant and Abe's mother. "Every generation has had people who took off and went to sea or followed the call of Bob Dylan's long and dusty road." In the tradition of many wander years parents, Dina herself spent six months hitchhiking in Europe. "You change skies, have novelties."

Yet if you're a baby boomer, chances are that you left all that behind years ago and got a job, a spouse—at least for a while—some kids, a mortgage, or maybe all of the above. "Hopefully, there's a point at which you hit a more mature stage, finally determine and commit to your passions," Dina says. "Abe's stepped over that threshold by getting married, but he's still in limbo. Typically, when you say 'I am an adult,' there are lots of markers that point to this—things that connote stability. Those markers are less available to him. He's somewhat adrift, a Peter Pan."

Trust in her son bolsters Dina. "Abe cares about himself enough to make healthy choices and has found ways to support himself. He's used my credit card very sparingly and has always paid me back. For a luftmensch"—lovingly invoking a Yiddish word that roughly translates to "an impractical contemplative person having no definite business or income"—"he's got a very practical, responsible side. If Abe says he's going to do something, he does it. I think he is trying to figure out next steps, but it's hard. The freelance lifestyle has great lows, because he's thrown on his resources all the time.

"I've never felt it was particularly helpful to tell someone else what to do," Dina continues. "I can't kiss the boo-boo and make it all better. I don't offer advice unless I'm specifically asked. It's a tricky balancing act, being a parent—you have a lot of influence, especially to make kids do the opposite of what you say. We aren't objective and some of us want to be involved simply so we can feel we're still needed. Sometimes you have to examine your own motives. It can be most helpful, often, to disengage.

"Abe is clear about his priorities—he's an artist, an idealist, a dreamer, very much a visionary who sees possibilities. He's also clear about his spirituality and the role it plays in his life. I've been surprised by yoga being such an essential force, but it had a salutary effect on him—after he started practicing yoga and meditation I saw the Abe

I remembered before he was a teenager. I liked who he was becoming and have become more reconciled to the idea, but the spirituality thing is very upsetting to my ex."

The ex doesn't disagree. Dina and let's call him Sam* split up when Abe was eleven. "Dina is more of a booster for Abe's choices, very enamored with Ananda Marga, and I'm not quite there," Abe's father says. "I've been skeptical, more on his case about 'settling down' than his mother."

It took Abe's dad nine years to get his college degree, which he received in 1972, and he didn't have a conventional job until he was twenty-five, but that hasn't stopped Abe's wandering from being a source of friction for him. "In those years many of us were making a revolution and didn't have time to settle down," Sam explains. "That period was also more forgiving economically. I'm worried for Abe, who is without a steady income. I try not to be overbearing or judgmental. Mostly I listen and ask questions, but I've hounded him about health insurance, which he doesn't have. This is where I think he is really at risk.

"Abe's immediate circle has a lot of 'seekers.' People who graduated from college in the 1990s were more career-focused and scared to strike out on their own. Josh, our son who is six years older than Abe, has followed a much more predictable path to a teaching career and is open and accepting of my point of view.

"I have all the anxieties you'd expect from a parent concerned about a child's welfare, but I also see where my son is following values established in our home," Sam says. "We never focused on material pursuits for either of our boys. The old radical in me wants to applaud and support, while the weathered realist bites his nails and hopes for the best.... I wonder how parents with more traditional backgrounds and personal choices handle children who pursue unconventional paths?"

GIFTS FROM THE UNIVERSE

> "Chipped mugs," she calls them. They roam in packs. The
> beaches of Sinai . . . ashrams in India, music festivals with
> drugs and free love in France, Spain and the Negev.
>
> *—The End of the Land* by David Grossman

Again and again, beneath their humor and shrugs about the flux and
fluidity infusing adultescents' lives, what you hear from parents is love,
pride, and frustration. "My friends and I all live vicariously through my
daughter Naomi," says Grand Rapids, Michigan, resident Arlene Siegel.
Like Dina Heisler, Arlene logged six months hitchhiking abroad more
than thirty years ago. This experience established the baseline for her
parenting philosophy: "not to clip my children's wings and to go where
they are." When Naomi was a junior, she took a semester in Copenhagen; Arlene visited her there, as she did when her son taught English in
Taiwan. "How can I not support their choices?" she asks.

Naomi Siegel is a poignant source of comfort for her mother. "I
have MS," Arlene explains, "and on days when I'm doing very lousy,
she talks me through Reiki," a Japanese technique for stress reduction
and relaxation that promotes healing. "Within minutes I feel better.
I'm constantly in awe of Naomi. I'm probably my daughter's number
one fan, although I don't know if I've ever told her that."

What some people might call making your own luck, Naomi,
twenty-six, sees as gifts from the universe—which on her behalf has
had deep pockets since she graduated from the University of Wisconsin. "A week before graduation, I didn't even know what I would be
doing that summer so I decided to stick around Madison," where she
worked at an after-school program, studied Reiki, and immersed

herself in the spiritual community outside the university. "Then my family chipped in air miles and got me a ticket to Taiwan, where my brother was." Since then she's been on the move.

Like Abe Heisler, Naomi's spirited wanderlust has been fueled—depending on your level of skepticism—by old-fashioned ingenuity or a New Age sensibility. While living in Asheville, North Carolina, working as a job coach for people with disabilities, she wrangled a full scholarship to a program in Israel and India, a development Naomi attributes to, quite simply, magic, which she allows is so abundant in her life that she's had to turn a blind eye to much of the logic she'd studied as a philosophy major: "I was going through a lot of transformation, opening up to the abundance in the universe. I felt a spiritual tug to go to Israel a few months earlier when I'd been at a music festival in Minnesota and my friends and I started experimenting with a phenomenon of manifestation," her version of "ask and you shall receive." "Free things started coming our way—tickets to the festival, meals, and more. I was feeling really empowered. My friend said, 'Why don't you manifest a ticket to Israel?' I started planting seeds, e-mailing programs and organizations that were looking for staff. A week later I was offered a scholarship and a living stipend."

In Israel, Naomi spent five months offering Reiki at a trauma support center. In India, she created teacher training and an environmental art curriculum while living in Hyderabad, a city in the south-central part of the country. On the weekends she visited remote villages, finding places to stay and people to hang with through the lulu of a resource CouchSurfing.org. Need to crash in Kazakhstan? Log on to the site and see if one of the, say, six hundred posts for futons, sofa beds, and air mattresses may be available for you. Every year, more than two million couch surfers, most of them in their twenties and thirties, avail themselves of this remarkable service in almost eight thousand cities in 241 countries.

After nine months of travel, Naomi was ready to return to the States. She visited her family in Michigan, earned some money, and drove a car received as a high school graduation present to north of Reno, Nevada. Here she attended the Burning Man arts festival, a Woodstockian extravaganza featuring three-story sculptures in the desert and adultescents camping in tents, yurts, and RVs. Next, she and her circle of "nomads, hippies, and free spirits" trekked to Berkeley and California's Humboldt County, where Naomi worked on a farm.

Hawaii, where Naomi turned twenty-six, followed. Since then, she's been nesting in Bellingham, Washington, where she landed with only $200. She posted an ad at the local food co-op offering to trade work for housing and two days later found a place to live. After several changes of address, home is the basement of a six-bedroom house shared with friends. Naomi juggles several admirable part-time jobs— caring for a woman with autism, nannying a baby and toddler, helping to run a healing center, and creating programming for a cancer support center.

"I wake up every day and ask, 'How can I be of service?' and often find myself swooped up and taken to fill different roles. I don't make long-term plans, but allow things to unfold and hold faith that I'm always provided for. Again and again, this has proven to be true beyond measure. My life feels very full and I see myself living this way for the foreseeable future. Saving money? No. I have faith that money will always be there." Health insurance, too, thanks to her parents' generosity.

"I feel mine is a bolder generation than my parents' because we've been given a sense of safety and security that has allowed us to be more courageous. Wherever I go I know I will find someone with a similar worldview and be taken care of." Her parents, she says, have been proud of the contributions she has made to various communities.

"I've never asked for much and they probably knew I wouldn't listen if they'd given me advice."

Arlene Siegel considers her daughter exceptionally self-sufficient. Nonetheless, she's concerned about what she sees as a proclivity on Naomi's part to belittle people her own age who lead plain vanilla lives—high school friends, for example, who've hunkered down in Grand Rapids, married, had children, and have already worked in the same job for years. "I have to remind Naomi that everyone gets to make their own choices," Arlene says. A graver concern: her daughter's safety. "When she first started doing this couch surfing business, she's so trustworthy I was afraid she'd get into jeopardy, though knock on wood, that hasn't happened.

"I hope at some point she'll have a more settled life," Arlene confesses, then shakes off fantasy. "I don't think she's that kind of person. Naomi goes where she feels a calling, and often people follow her. She has an electric personality and friends all over the world. It's interesting how these gypsies find one another."

PASSIONARIES CALLED BY GOD

Old-time religion might be good enough for plenty of folks, but most adultescents aren't in the hallelujah chorus. This is not to say they aren't spiritual: according to a recent Pew study about religion among Millennials, the number of young adults who claim that they pray every day rivals the slice of young adults who said the same in prior decades, but they attend fewer services and are half as likely to affiliate with traditional religious institutions as boomers were as young adults. A large majority of Millennials—72 percent—describe themselves as "more spiritual than religious," according to a survey by LifeWay Christian Resource, and about one in five have left their childhood denomination; a quarter are completely unaffiliated. Adultescents express their godliness and devotion differently from older generations and are decidedly more liberal than their parents, more likely to accept homosexuality and to see evolution as the best explanation of how human beings got here. They are eager to put their energy where their mouth is, making social action a priority.

For the last two years, Stephen Prothero, Ph.D., chair of Boston University's Department of Religion and author of *God Is Not One*, has asked students to concoct their own religions. "What strikes me most about my students' religions is . . . how similar they are," Dr. Prothero recently wrote in an essay, "Is Religion Losing the Millennial Generation?" "They want to be tolerant and non-judgmental. Most . . . were fully compatible with other religions. Their founders stress that you can join their religion without leaving Catholicism or Judaism or Islam behind." Also he notes that his students long for "happiness now. . . . Priests, rabbis, imams and ministers would do well to engage in interfaith dialogue . . . with this 'spiritual but not religious' generation . . . slouching not toward Bethlehem or even atheism, but toward new ways of being religious."

"When I grew up people thought of a generation as twenty-five years," observes Riess Potterveld, president of Pacific School of Religion, which prides itself on "being as far left as you get positioned within American religion." PSR has a student body that embraces Roman Catholics and Unitarians as well as mainstream Protestants and is located near Berkeley, California, centers for Buddhism and Judaism, where its students may take classes. "Now things change so rapidly, a generation is closer to eight years, maybe six, and each generation clusters around different values.

"This generation tends to delay every stage—they marry later and have closer-knit communities of friends than people my age," says

Riess, the form of address he prefers. "And where our students all used to want to be pulpit leaders, now only about half go in that direction. Many aren't part of organized religion at all, but in their journeys have developed what they consider to be a spiritual call to God and bring a broad view to our school, which was started in 1866. The end trajectory for these 'passionaries' might be nonprofits or even law, business, or biotechnology, but they have a sense that they'll use their vocation in some sort of spiritual dimension transforming the world.

"Some corporations have found their younger workers really don't just want to earn a living as much as belong to an organization having a deeper impact on our global society, reaching the poor, trying to create some justice. This is a register against hopelessness and despair when we have social problems on which we never seem to make much progress. It's a very positive trend I started seeing about ten years ago and it's increased, this idea that people can have a passion not necessarily tied to a specific vocation."

Riess Potterveld has four sons between the ages of thirty-four and forty and says he monitors the world through their experience. "They're environmentalist and feminist, grew up with a complete openness and lack of prejudice about gender orientation, and are committed to all those things they think will empower people to live out life more holistically.

"They travel more than I did, have more of a global sense, and are comfortable with diversity, which they seek—they find it abhorrent to be a monoculture environment. When we get together with our boys and ask them where they'd like to have dinner, for example, they never say 'generic American'—they want Thai or Japanese or Indian, and my oldest son and his 'wife,' who've been together for years, refuse to marry until all their friends, gay or straight, have the same opportunity."

Ben Cherland, twenty-eight, could be a younger Potterveld son. Since attending Concordia College, a small Lutheran school in Moorhead,

Minnesota (across the river from my hometown and popular with many of my closest and brightest high school friends), Ben has been seeking answers to spiritual questions. "I spent the year after college at a Lutheran retreat center, where I found the directors to be incredibly intolerant and intentionally hostile to the queer community—people who are transgender, gay, and lesbian. I was frustrated and angry with what I perceived as a lack of understanding about larger issues that perpetuated people's suffering. So I went to Union Theological Seminary in New York City to learn how to put these people in their place and show them the ignorance of their ways.

"I had no career goal in mind." This was fine with Ben's parents in Regina, Saskatchewan, both of whom have doctorates and are "big believers in higher education," he says. "I went to Union not to become a minister—that was the furthest thing from my mind—but to learn how to argue with folks on the Christian right." Nondenominational and progressive, "Union flipped me on my head. When I entered I was hostile to the idea of becoming a pastor, but after that it seemed feasible." In 2009 he earned a master's of divinity, concentrating on Christian ethics. Now he's studying at Luther Seminary in St. Paul.

"Not that I'm settled," Ben stresses. "This year will be about discerning whether or not becoming ordained would be a good thing for me and for the church. I hope I can find some peace with where I'm at while I uncoil the concept of being religiously engaged among my generation." Top of mind: the impact that becoming a minister will have on his social life. "I'm a single twenty-eight-year-old and my prospects of finding any kind of life partner"—a woman, in his case—"aren't feeling great at the moment. I'm attracted to women outside of the religious traditions I'm trying to participate in, yet I'm looking for someone I can share my morbid fascination of religion with. I feel like I'm asking for a lot."

Mike Pacchione, thirty-three, is also trying to figure things out. September 11, 2001, was the day Mike was, he reports, "'saved,' as we Christians say." Mike's father was an unaffiliated Protestant, his mother Jewish, and he was raised without religious tradition. "For my entire life I'd been wrestling with issues of faith and Jesus. On September 10, 2001, I'd stayed up into the wee hours outlining my thoughts and figured out that Jesus made logical sense. The next day I'd planned, as my first Christian act, to buy McDonald's hamburgers for everyone at the office, but I woke up to reports of planes flying into the World Trade Center. At the time I lived in Philadelphia doing ticket sales for the Phillies, and thought, things could be ending here soon. I got down on my knees and said, 'Lord, I get it.' Suddenly Christianity made emotional sense, too.

"It wasn't until a move to Portland in 2005—which is ironic, because it's über-liberal, one of the least-churched cities in the United States—that I grew my faith, which I've learned is about a relationship with Jesus, not telling people what they can and can't do." He leads a small "community group," a hybrid of Bible study and community service affiliated with a nondenominational church that attracts people in their twenties and thirties.

Mike moved to Portland because he got a good deal for grad school in communications study. "I always thought I wanted to get a Ph.D., do research, and ride that out for the rest of my life, but when I went back to school I realized being a research-based professor was too isolated and theoretical for me. Teaching public speaking is . . . it has a practical application." Mike is now an adjunct professor at Portland State, teaching public speaking, and therein lies the rub. "I try not to make loud, obnoxious anti-secular noises . . . but I hear students say bad things all the time *in speeches* about Christians without thinking twice. They would be far too PC to make similar remarks about someone's nationality or race, but somewhere in their education and upbringing they basically received the green light to assume everyone is anti-Christian. The mental filter doesn't weed that out."

Back on the East Coast, Portia Carter* has been similarly alarmed by remarks she's heard from people her own age, many of whom she considered to be her friends. "I saw racism for the first time when Somalians moved to our town and kids I grew up with complained about them taking 'our' jobs. I grew up very privileged, with a stay-at-home mother, a sports-car-driving doctor father, two homes, and three other cars. I played flute, studied ballet, and did other privileged white-girl activities, but I also had huge crushes on Bono and Sting and their activism sparked something in me. But at my nice Catholic high school I learned that people can be greedy and selfish. How can you call yourself Catholic if you spend two million dollars to fund an anti-abortion campaign but not send a check to Haiti? Jesus didn't say just take care of the white middle class—he wants us to take care of everyone. I began to struggle with a guilt complex and wish that my family understood me better. I wanted to do activist things and meet the Somalians, and had no one to talk to about this. My school had no social justice component."

Portia's parents encouraged her to apply to college wherever she wanted, without regard to cost. "I wanted diversity," she says, and chose Trinity College in Hartford, Connecticut, where she majored in international studies, concentrating in African studies, with a minor in both French and human rights. During junior year she spent four months visiting Senegal. "I had no idea what I wanted to do after graduation. I considered going directly on to get a Ph.D. in African studies, but after I handed in my thesis, a friend from Guinea said he'd raised money for a project in his country. I wound up spending two months there, helping to build a well in a village and fix a school building."

When Portia returned, her parents announced that they were divorcing. "I did not see it coming. We were together as a family for a week on vacation, my sister went back to college, my brothers returned to our house with my mother, and she insisted that I stay in our ocean house with my father. My mom was grieving. I look and act a lot like my dad, and she and I had a difficult time during my adolescence because of what I wanted to do with regard to social justice. She didn't want to be around me.

"After two months I was desperate to get away from the family stuff. I returned to Hartford to be a part-time community organizer and got another volunteer job in exchange for rent in an apartment I shared with some AmeriCorps volunteers in a druggy neighborhood. It was a lot of upheaval in one year, but my parents' split was a blessing in disguise, giving me the freedom to separate from them. I needed that. I was accepted into the Jesuit Volunteer Corps and moved to Texas to do pro bono work with a refugee resettlement organization, helping people seeking asylum, especially torture victims."

The Jesuit Volunteer Corps is a faith-based program that allows people twenty-one to thirty-three to dedicate a year or two of their lives to serve others in the United States and around the world through community service. The program is based on the Jesuit principle that we should all strive to see God's presence in everyone and everything. Portia is one of 350 volunteers, all of whom receive modest stipends for food, housing, transportation, health insurance, travel to and from retreats, and sundry costs. It's not the norm for volunteers to sign on for a second year, but Portia has—at the job she wanted most, to work with Jesuit Refugee Services, an international organization that works in refugee camps abroad. Her one-year position is in the Washington, D.C., national office. After that, her path is unclear.

"I'm under a lot of pressure from my family to 'grow up' and go to grad school," she says. "They think I'm wasting my intellect because I graduated with the top of my class. But a lot of my peers went to grad school and now regret it. They can't get a job. They're heavily in debt. Throughout my whole journey I've struggled because I've been able to take greater risks because of my privilege. So while I hesitate because of this, I also realize that a master's is the new bachelor's degree. There's no way around that. I might take the GRE and get another degree, possibly in public policy.

"Most people in their twenties right now are in a transcendental funk because of the economy," she says. "We're waking up and finding out that none of the opportunities we were promised are there. People don't talk about this because they want everyone to think they have it all.

"The twenties? It's not at all like being on *Friends*."

Chapter 4

"HONEY, I'M HOME"

Was the whole empty nest thing . . . so bad? Was it so bad
no longer to have a daughter's frustrated artistic tempera-
ment bleeding daily on the carpet . . . ?

—*Birds of America* by Lorrie Moore

After the kids left, I felt the rounded satisfaction you undergo
at reaching the end of a challenging but rewarding experience. We'd adjusted to having no kids at home and—full
disclosure—it hadn't been hard.

Sure, Rob and I missed the homey ritual of nightly dinners, rushed
because the boys had five hours of homework ahead. We fondly re-
called folding misshapen, dryer-warmed T-shirts commemorating
rock concerts of days past. We remembered with a tear the monosyl-
labic grunts to "How was your day?" as well as the daily sight of our
sons' sweet faces covered with stubble when they stumbled out of bed

at noon after a hard night of drinking. But if we were being honest, we liked that it was once again simply Rob, Sally, and the dog.

It was pretty damn roomy, that nest—until it wasn't empty anymore. When we learned that our son Jed, at twenty-five, would be returning from San Francisco to live with my husband and me in our New York City apartment, I imagined it as a grown-up stroll down Sesame Street. Our two sons are five years apart and when Jed came back, his brother, Rory, five years younger, was halfway through college. It had been years since Rob and I had enjoyed the pleasure of Jed's solo company and we were looking forward to his stay, which we expected to last a month or two—three, tops. We'd heard that Jed had become a skilled cook and we could almost taste lip-smacking meals in our future augmented by bonding conversations with our witty young adultescent. Since he was past the legal drinking age, we would even serve wine with dinner. Party on, family.

When our DJ-ing, concert-promoting, English major son had hatched a plan to move to the West Coast after graduation to become a paid intern at a small record label, he presented it as a fait accompli. Rob and I recognized that Jed's fatwa was historically consistent with his approach in the previous decade, when he'd imposed his own personal HIPAA law. He'd never sought our opinions in selecting courses or a major ("Why would I ask *you two* when there are so many more qualified people to help me make this decision?"), nor did he want us to know what his grades were. "They're not yours, they're *mine*," he pointed out. Parents could go broke paying tuition, but grades were the student's and only the student's business, Jed announced. And the college agreed.

In the Bay Area, Jed found apartments through Uncle Craigslist, made friends, and scrounged for furniture. He didn't own a car or ask us to buy him one, but navigated the city via mass transportation, thank you very much. The internship turned into full-time work where he discovered talent and created contracts for bands. He managed on his wages, which increased with his responsibilities. Never once did our kid demand a parental money transfusion. Rob and I grew proud. Some mature, capable guy we've raised, we'd say with a high five.

After two years he was ready to return east. San Francisco's attractions were dimming, he explained. The record label where he worked decided to take Jed up on his suggestion that they start a New York City branch with him in charge. As the summer of 2001 ended, Jed and his thirty-four deadweight boxes of vinyl records decamped to his former bedroom in the family apartment while he began to plot how to jump-start his company's eastern outpost.

Seven days later, two airplanes flew into the World Trade Center's towers. That morning, mother and son, like the rest of America, stared incredulously as the reports unfolded, each more gravely inconceivable than the one before. Hours later, to our colossal relief, Rob straggled in and our other loved ones were accounted for. By the evening, one of Jed's college friends and his older sister, whose lower Manhattan apartment was now uninhabitable, had landed at our home, where they slept on couches for a few weeks. The following month Jed's employer, like so many others, ditched the idea of the Manhattan branch. Jed was let go with no severance. It was a start-up, after all.

Our son took this setback in stride. In New York City post-9/11 we all felt as if we were on some new psychotropic drug to which we hadn't adjusted. Everyone seemed to be sleepwalking through a horror show. A twenty-five-year-old's job loss, especially when he had parents to live with and a weekly unemployment check, was far from tragic. We sensed that Jed was also relieved to be unburdened of the pressure to figure out how to start a new branch of the record label, though he had never been a slacker. He had worked every summer between college years, had a part-time job during each academic year, and, unlike most of the students at his small New England liberal arts college, hadn't taken a gap year or a semester abroad, choosing during his junior year to be a dorm resident adviser. He was in no way feckless, just a kid relishing a break. Completely reasonable, his dad and I thought.

After a few weeks, however, our parent-child relationship began to echo the colicky tone of junior year in high school, few families' finest hour. My husband and I found ourselves unable to staple our mouths. Have you updated your résumé? Looked online? Scheduled informational interviews? Called X and Y? How about Z—and A, B, and C, especially C? Networked, networked, networked? Priced health care, which we insisted that he find. (This was before the days when parents could cover a child Jed's age on their policy, a national acknowledgment that someone well into his twenties isn't an adult.) While you're at it, could you please make your bed? Do your laundry? Not clog the kitchen drain? At least walk the dog?

As weeks morphed into months, our nagging escalated in direct proportion to our evaporating sense of humor. Yet aside from squabbles that had become the downbeat of our days, Jed's life seemed—to us—as he would say, sweet. Every night, he met buddies for dinner, movies, or drinking, staying out long past our bedtime. This put him on a cycle of sleeping far later than his early-rising parents, which guaranteed that we'd start each day pissed. We have a close extended family, and when they began to ask, "What's up with Jed?" my husband and I became embarrassed and defensive.

In early summer Jed casually mentioned that he'd been offered a position. He was thinking of declining. Sales weren't his thing, wouldn't be lucrative, the job sounded dull, and what was the rush to work again? Within his crowd, joblessness seemed to present no stigma, and given that he didn't have to pay rent or take care of many financial responsibilities beyond medical insurance, transportation, and social life, he was managing on his unemployment check.

That's when Rob and I started a conversation one shout short of an intervention. "Do you have any other options? Are you nuts not to take this job?" we screeched, though less politely.

"If you've never been hated by your child, then you haven't been a parent," Bette Davis said. Allow me to cut to the chase. With a significant shove, Jed accepted the job offer. A few paychecks later, he moved to Fort Greene, Brooklyn, to share a basement apartment with members of a band fittingly called Oddjobs. Thus ended one of the shabbier after-school specials in our family history.

The number of adultescents now living in their parents' homes looks like nothing less than a stampede. As the ageless singer-songwriter Tom Rush recently said in a concert, "Kids used to rebel and leave home. Now they rebel and stay home."

Everywhere, chicks are coming home to roost, victims in a flat-lined economy where, according to recent census figures, the tally on overall unemployment is fourteen million, approximately the population of Illinois and Rhode Island combined. For those eighteen to twenty-nine, the unemployment rate is 14 percent, which rivals the levels that age group experienced in the Great Depression. Stymied in their hopes to land a job, being poorly paid if they actually get a job, laid off by Goldman Sachs and the local Dairy Queen alike, felled by divorce or academic failure, adultescents are often drowning in debt. Talk about raising the debt ceiling. At my alma mater, the University of Wisconsin, 60 percent of graduates wind up owing an average debt of $20,000 when they get their degrees—and the school is public, not private, and within the Big Ten, one of the good deals.

Adultescents are numb with indecision about what move to make next. The other day I noticed a cartoon by Christopher Weyant featuring a derelict relaxing on the steps of a mausoleum, captioned with "I thought I'd never have to move back in with my parents." But a lot of people do. Winding up in your old bedroom has become more of a movement than an indignity.

Here, a cheat sheet with statistics running from grim to grimmer:

- In the graduating class of 2011, it was estimated that 85 percent of graduates moved back home, according to a poll conducted by the consulting firm Twentysomething Inc.
- According to census estimates, by 2010 some 5.5 million people aged twenty-five to thirty-five were living at home, an increase of more than 25 percent since the recession. More than 40 percent of those 5.5 million people earned less than $11,116 a year, which put them on the cusp of poverty.
- A 2010 *New York Times*/CBS poll showed that 46 percent of Americans think the younger generations will be worse off than their parents.

It's a whole lotta upset, a whole lotta digits, especially as you estimate that for every stat representing an adultescent return, you can usually count two parents hyperventilating and gasping, "What now?" and "This wasn't what I signed up for." When boomers thought they'd ended child rearing and could begin to reboot—financially and personally—the kiddies are b-a-a-a-ck.

"The first thing I see when I wake up in the morning is my name in lights," Dylan Suher, a 2010 graduate of Washington University in St. Louis, writes in the *New York Times*. "Specifically, I see a giant sign that hangs over my bed. Smothered in glitter and festooned with stars and Christmas lights, it spells out my name in cardboard letters. It was commissioned for my bar mitzvah, and was later used to decorate my childhood bedroom—the bedroom in which I now sleep.... Moving back home was the rational choice ... under the circumstances. I had little work experience and few marketable skills when I graduated, and I knew I would have to take a series of unpaid internships.... But the fact that a choice is responsible doesn't make it pleasant.... I'd kill to put five miles between myself and (my parents') unsolicited job and dating advice. I don't think they know or remember what it's like to send off résumé after résumé, to finally get a job, and still not make it out of your parents' house. The feeling of failure."

"Just because I don't have a life doesn't mean I don't deserve to live," states The Onion, America's Finest News Source, with Ben Stiller, star of beloved man-child movies *Zoolander* and *Dodgeball*, gravely reporting on Shaken Man–child syndrome, "the second leading cause of death among men-children after choking on Buffalo wings.... If all else fails, you can leave your man-child on the steps of a local movie theater or a Chipotle restaurant in the hopes someone else takes care of him. Anything is better than hurting him." Hardy har har.

For adultescents to decamp to their parents' immediately after college is, of course, as classic as a white shirt, and although flabby, unshaven boy-children guzzling Bud, playing video games, leaving the refrigerator open, and cutting toenails in the living room are a collective national image, female adultescents wind up living at home, too.

"I don't want to share a two-inch spot with a roommate in the middle of nowhere or spend two thousand dollars a month for a studio apartment," says Zoe Jordan,* twenty-five, a young woman with uncompromising standards who's continued to live with Mom near Manhattan's Lincoln Center since she graduated from The New School in 2007. Zoe is not rushing to move out. Staying in this comfy, convenient nest has allowed her to be a serf in Mayor Michael Bloomberg's community affairs unit; with few household responsibilities, she has been able to launch a food blog. "The arrangement works because I have a very good relationship with my mother, who's not on top of my head, like most of my friends' moms are," Zoe says. "She welcomes my company"—partly, Zoe acknowledges, because Mom split up with Dad more than ten years ago.

"This is a more entitled generation than their parents' and grandparents'," says William J. Doherty, Ph.D., professor of family social science at the University of Minnesota. "They come home to live because there's nowhere else they could live better."

"Young adults today are willing to sacrifice independence in exchange for material comforts," Katherine S. Newman, Ph.D., dean of arts and science at Johns Hopkins University and author of *The Accordion Family*, told the *Minneapolis Star Tribune*. They'd also rather stay with parents than relocate to a place whose the only allure is a salary.

"Go West, young man," Horace Greeley editorialized in 1865 in his newspaper, the *New York Tribune*. Battalions of young men hitched their dreams to this command and transplanted themselves to build our country's midwestern and western regions. Within our country, the Midwest shows reasonably strong job growth, but I've yet to see a groundswell of enthusiasm for moving to fly-over country. In the face of dreary national unemployment figures, my home state of North Dakota has the lowest unemployment rate in the nation and is in the midst of an oil boom yielding high-paying jobs along with farms whose crops are paying record profits, yet it struggles to lure young workers.

Many parents—not wanting to be buzz-kills and nourishing dreams for their children, through whom they may be living vicariously—continue to encourage plans for striking out in glamour cities like San Francisco, Los Angeles, and New York. And in cases where parents are meekly suggesting that adultescents look at other options, young adults often tune them out.

"After college you've got to beat the odds *not* to move back home," Barnard College senior Alexandra Katz acknowledges as we chat over coffee at a café near the Columbia/Barnard campus. I'd reached out to her, impressed by a column she'd written for the *Columbia Spectator*:

> The cost of admission to adulthood is greater than it once was. It's not that we want to be in school until our late twenties. It's because jobs that were once attainable with a college degree now require additional education. It's not that we want to move back into our parents' homes. It's that we need to save money in order to afford ever-increasing housing costs. This isn't a question of whether or not we want to remain "children" for longer. Our generation isn't looking for a longer childhood—we are struggling to overcome the barriers to adulthood.

One of the scariest parts of life after college is figuring out housing, observes Alexandra, who has set her sights on New York City. You get the sense she'd rather eat spiders than try a different city or go home to live with her parents in West Roxbury, Massachusetts, an urban suburb primarily distinguished by Boston accents of the sort we hear in movies starring Ben Affleck and Matt Damon. This move would, she says, make her feel as if she'd failed. This is how Alexandra believes that a cousin, who also attended Barnard, must have felt after she recently graduated with a 3.9 grade-point average, sent out résumés by the heap, and got not one nibble. Her cousin scrapped her dreams to conquer New York City after graduation and returned home instead to the big small town of Boston.

Thinking about how to manage your finances after college

becomes torturous. "Even if I spend half my salary on my rent, it's going to be expensive," Alex says. "My friends and I who want to live in New York City have all accepted that we'll be six people crammed into a tiny apartment facing an airshaft in Harlem or one of the less gentrified parts of Brooklyn. I'm figuring I might earn thirty thousand dollars and rent would be about eight hundred and fifty dollars a month, and I'm really good at managing money. I've been on financial aid throughout college and have taken all sorts of internships, though they've been mostly unpaid."

A few friends have already lined up "ridiculously high-paying banking jobs," she adds, "so the rest of us are thinking, well, we can't live with *her*." Pursuing a financial industry job is not, however, an option this young woman says she would consider. Alex has majored in political science and, thinking like the ACLU lawyer she dreams of becoming, has ideas on how public policy should change with respect to housing for young people. Just as new health care legislation now allows parents to keep children on their insurance plans until age twenty-six, she feels the government should develop affordable housing for recent college graduates. But getting back to the here and now, she grimaces and admits that she doesn't see how she'll be able to live in New York plus save for law school, which now generally costs more than four years of college. "My parents would like to help, but they can't. They have another child in college," her sister, Samantha, a student at George Washington University.

I consider that in the less complex and more stable world of the 1970s, after I'd graduated from the University of Wisconsin in Madison, I was easily able to move from my Great Plains hometown to Manhattan. No Brooklyn or Queens for me. Rental apartments were plentiful and cheap—few had been converted to condos and co-ops at that time—and I paid in rent no more than the recommended one-quarter of my slave wage as a magazine editorial assistant. Granted, my sweet, clueless parents never realized how many junkies were roaming my block on West Eighty-third Street, right off Central Park. Neither did I. I suspect that had either of us understood that I'd chosen to live in a truly scary part of town, I would have immediately begged to move in with an aunt and uncle in Nowhere, Long Island. But by the time I was mugged in my vestibule just steps from Central Park, I felt too feisty and dug in.

"My parents have always said, 'Your twenties are for finding yourself,'" Alex Katz says. So I was eager to speak to Jill Stanzler-Katz, Alex's mother, a social worker with a practice near Boston, where she counsels young women and their parents.

"Girls have historically been taught to get their self-esteem by making other people happy," Jill says. "I'm interested in helping parents teach kids early to feel good about themselves." Her vision of cloud nine for her own daughter includes seeing her fulfill the dream of trying to live in New York. She and her husband, Alex's father, Jeff Katz, who runs a nonprofit focused on changing adoption laws, support their daughter's postgraduation goal with full parental passion, albeit without a financial stipend.

In Jill I recognize myself, a woman lucky enough to find work that she loves. "I see clients all day and get home at night and can hardly speak, but I like helping people function in a healthier way," she says, and with equal earnestness adds: "We spend so much time working, we owe it to ourselves. After you put in years and money getting educated, you should try to make good choices." For her daughter, this will depend on escaping "the Ivy League bubble."

The previous summer, Jill heard Alex complain that "people are so ahead of [her], already studying for the LSATs with track records more luminous than her own. In this bubble everyone's competitive and

Alex feels she has to keep up. I get that, but it's hard for her to step back and decide whether or not to buy into this thinking. She doesn't trust her own skills and talents enough yet. I want her to have the strength to find balance." All of this, Jill is certain, will develop in due time.

"I hope Alex will support herself for a few years, get to know herself better, then decide if she still does want to go to law school." The last thing Alex would want "is to return home to live with us," though if this scenario came to pass, Jill says she'd see it as a "necessary transition." Still, speaking as a therapist as much as a mother, she maintains that it's often unhealthy for kids to come home after they graduate from college. Too much shrinkage. Home is where young adults revert to what Jill calls whiny, please-Mommy-take-care-of-me "baby selves," distinguished not only by the desire to be coddled but by arguments and nitpicking.

BOOMER MOMS: TAKING PUSHY UP A NOTCH

The same two-act play has run in the home of Barbara Crowley of Dallas, though her adultescent daughters are solidly in their twenties. Within months, Evelyn, twenty-nine, and Jaime, twenty-six, each unexpectedly moved home. Jaime arrived first. She'd been a ski bum with a boyfriend in Jackson Hole, Wyoming, and had applied to graduate school to earn a Ph.D. in clinical psychology. After being accepted by programs throughout the country, Jaime decided to go sensible, picking a local university to take advantage of in-state tuition. She informed her parents that she'd live at home for the first year of her program to make life easier for her.

"My husband, Geoff, and I were okay with that," Barbara reports. They never expected Jaime's older sister, who'd lived for four years in New York, to show up, too. It's tough for Texas kids who move to the

Northeast, Barbara has noticed. "The experience often has a short shelf life. Unless they find someone to marry, something like seasonal affective disorder kicks in after two to four years." Barbara's daughter Evelyn had been working for a fashion magazine, being praised for her efforts, then suddenly started asking questions like whether she really wanted to spend her days writing about blindingly beautiful Yves Saint Laurent topaz Swarovski-crystal earrings, price upon request. "Kids this age become rudderless, looking for the next best thing. To my husband's and my dismay, Evelyn quit her job without another one lined up. When she arrived in Dallas and looked back, the magazine industry had collapsed. She saw Sodom and Gomorrah, with layoffs everywhere."

The Jaime-and-Evelyn show happened when the Crowleys had just sent off their youngest child, a son, to Northwestern University. Their empty nest, which they'd started to savor, refilled after months. "People who told me 'It's so nice—your daughters are back' had it wrong. For starters, the two don't get along. Having them here again in their twenties? Not fun. I found that I reverted to a housewife stereotype as servile as my grandma. If you raised your kids like I did— overly motherly—it's very hard to get out of that mind-set when adult children return. A remnant of you worries the same way you did when they were teenagers. It became high school revisited—the laundry, the cooking, the concern about the girls' driving in our urban sprawl, the getting home late and the making sure they got up on time. I fell back into complete mom-mode."

That is, the boomer generation's deviant twist on mom-mode, because, as Barbara points out, her own mother was entirely comfortable being far more hands-off. "Are we boomers making up for a loving, nurturing environment we didn't get?" she asks. "Do we feel as if we were neglected? I raise these questions all the time."

As do I, because few boomer mothers I know behave unlike Barbara Crowley. When adultescents return home, mothers tend to reinvest full throttle in their dormant parenting role as if they were choreographing a flash mob. We've all heard the Jonas Salk quote, "Good parents give their children roots and wings." But I wonder if every mom I know hasn't secretly installed a chip under her kids' skin to make sure they are returned to us like lost dogs, simply so we can bluster and blow in one more giant gust of motherhood.

"When you've been the coach, architect, and main cheerleader of your child's development for twenty years, it's difficult to back away, especially if kids are struggling," observes Dr. Sylvia Gearing, a Dallas psychologist. "Many women have to be encouraged to refrain from the bad habit of overidentifying with the child. This can be a Herculean feat."

Barbara's daughter Evelyn has now moved to Los Angeles to pursue a master's degree studying film. This means all three of Barbara's children depend once again on the family income for tuition and health insurance. "Geoff and I feel pretty bankrupt—no one is completely off our payroll," fueled primarily by a struggling family bakery business. "Try selling thirty-dollar fruitcakes in the shape of Texas in the recession. We're a good year and a half at least from seeing any of these kids 'launched.'"

In order to keep their son in the lifestyle he'd become accustomed to at college, Anita Carcich and her husband felt they had to upgrade their cable to premium service. "I'm also getting a lot less sleep now," says Anita, a legal assistant who gets up at 5:45 every weekday morning in order to commute from New Jersey to Manhattan. "I'm an Italian mother. When my son is out at night, I can't rest until I hear that key at the door, which happens anytime between midnight and four A.M."

Gary has been living at home for one year since his college

graduation. His major was journalism, and he hasn't been able to find a job. "The future is depressing, actually," Anita says. "I'm not seeing a lot of progress or Gary actively pursuing getting a job. But he's not sitting at home doing nothing—if he was, I'd kill him. He's delivering pizzas and cleaning grout. I think he should try to get an internship, even if it's unpaid, but my husband says that's ridiculous because it would wind up costing our son to commute into the city and he has loans to repay. At least it's not as bad for us as it is for a lot of our friends, whose kids are in the same boat but twenty-eight."

BRING ON THE FAMILY-SIZE HAMBURGER PACKS

When my oldest child became a teenager, I discovered I couldn't make the rules up fast enough. He'd hit new stages before I even recognized they'd arrived. But this is not how it works with returned adultescents. Rules? What rules?

"In my generation, we generally do far more for our children than what was done for us," says Marie Hartwell-Walker, EdD, a licensed psychologist and marriage and family therapist and the mother of four adult kids, two of whom are currently living with her and her husband in their rambling, seven-bedroom Amherst, Massachusetts, farmhouse. "When do you stop parenting? When does childhood end? These are big questions." Few boomer parents have figured out the answers.

The return of an adult child feels as jarring as an alarm clock going off during a sweet dream on a cold winter morning. Rationally, parents usually accept the arrival of their kids, yet their emotions are scrambled. After they vacuum off the welcome mat for an adultescent, how and where do they draw a line in giving help, be it portioned out in psychic duct tape or paid bills? Parents not only don't know how to renegotiate a new deal for themselves and their kids, they don't realize that they have the right to do so. Rarely do you hear anything as concrete as "You can stay here for a while, but we need a plan for your transition out and, by the way, no freebies."

"Having done our best to move out of our own parents' homes as soon as we could to get on with adult life, we never expected our own children to return," says Dr. Hartwell-Walker, author of *Tending the Family Heart*. "Yes, we love our children to death. Yes, we do want to help them out. But at this stage, we didn't think we'd still be buying milk by the gallon and family-size packs of hamburger. We thought that just maybe there'd be a little extra money to go out to dinner, indulge in a movie, or even take a trip or two. Then we become upset to find out that the only place where our kid can afford to live on what he makes is one room in a wet basement in an unsafe part of town. We may want to stop active parenting, but we also want our children to be safe and have an opportunity to get back on their feet. Parental feelings become a mix of being glad to help, weary of accommodating, resentful for feeling like they have to do so, and guilty for feeling resentful."

Can you say ambivalent? It's complicated? And how about judgmental, especially if parents say or at least think "I told you so," frustrated by pinheaded or entitled choices their kids have made—and that the parents cautioned them against? Dr. Hartwell-Walker harrumphs at adultescents who want to move back in with parents after they have found a job but just don't love it—and thus quit—or because living rent-free allows them luxuries: payments on late-model cars and iPhones to replace last year's BlackBerry.

"The parental safety net isn't always used for safety. Sometimes it's for lifestyle. We're in danger of infantilizing our adult children, who are failing to distinguish between *want* and *need*. When I speak to my peers, everyone has stories of old jalopies and apartments furnished in Late Attic," Dr. Hartwell-Walker says. "There was a pride from having come through that successfully. The shared remembering has helped make us strong. A lot of kids will miss that."

Hearing her speak makes me drift back to my own first apartment, shared with my boyfriend before we were married. (Did my parents know we were cohabitating? Without a doubt. Did we discuss it? Never. I believe this is when the don't-ask-don't-tell philosophy came about.) During a business trip months after I joined the staff of *Mademoiselle*, Robby surprised me by filling our tiny hovel with thrift shop and curb-side finds. I remember with fondness this $185-a-month, cockroach-friendly hole and its higgledy-piggledy decor. Not so fondly that I didn't want to upgrade by the next year to a bigger, safer place, but with a tint of distinct sepia nostalgia.

What Dr. Hartwell-Walker says next snaps me back to reality: she has no sympathy—nada—for kids who want too much. "When I see parents overdo it, as a therapist I try to find a gentle way to tell them they're not helping their children. The subliminal message that comes with all the giving and doing is, 'We don't think you can do it on your own—we need to do it for you.' "

Saying this apparently snaps Marie back to reality, too. "I want to be careful about how I generalize because I don't think all kids today are spoiled. A lot of them work hard." Not every kid who returns home suffers from bombastic dreams matched only by their lack of direction and flabby self-discipline. In *The Trophy Kids Grow Up: How the Millennial Generation Is Shaking Up the Workplace*, author Ron Alsop wrote, "If there is one overriding perception of the Millennial generation, it's that these young people have great—and sometimes outlandish—expectations." Dr. Hartwell-Walker takes issues with such a slur. "Yes, there are those who spend more time in the virtual than the actual world, making relationships with people they will never meet . . . kids who think they are entitled to get what they want just because they want it . . . students who debate their professors' evaluation of lacklus-ter work on the grounds that they 'tried hard' . . . with parents who want so much to do a better job than their own parents that they go overboard and extend adolescence sometimes into the thirties. These are parents who can't seem to find a way to tell their kids to grow up and get on with life.

"But there is only a *slice* that's spoiled," she stresses. In this cate-gory she excludes adultescents who've graduated from college and try mightily to get a job, only to bump into continuous rejection, just as she offers profound sympathy for those who lose jobs due to economic upheaval. Some of these adultescents take a severe hit to their self-esteem—in therapeutic patois, a "narcissist injury," a major rip in per-sonal worth. Returning home to loving parents can sometimes at least bandage that boo-boo, and it is unequivocally the smartest step, she maintains, that both parents and child can take. In the case of many adultescents today, the majority of empty-nest parents are simply say-ing, "Let's all get real; you, my child, have a problem and we have a house with an extra bedroom. Honey, come on home."

So goes the system that once existed in the United States. But peo-ple used to marry earlier and living with parents didn't last long. Also, today's adultescents who've returned home are less likely than those who've preceded them to stick to their parents' schedules and kick in for expenses. When my son Jed lived at home, for example, we rarely ate together.

"The big shift is this extended period where young adults have no major responsibility to work or family," says Dr. William Doherty. "They're tethered to the family in the sense that they live at home, but not as contributing members. That's really new and different from gen-erations where young adults lived in family life—and, for example, had dinner every night with their parents—until they married. Now the young people are responsible only for themselves and even then rely on parents."

Throughout the world most people do not launch at twenty-one. In many parts of the Middle East and southern Europe it's the norm for adults to stay at home until marriage. A study published by the London Centre for Economics reports that in Italy 85 percent of men aged eighteen to thirty-four still live with their parents. They're called *bamboccioni*: big babies, and recently an Italian judge said that a sixty-year-old father still had to pay an allowance to his thirty-two-year-old daughter living at home. Among twenty-five-year-old men, for instance, 61 percent of Italian men have never left home, while the numbers are lower for women: 39 percent. In Poland, 55 percent of men this age have never left, along with 35 percent of women. In Spain, 54 percent of men and 33 percent of women have not yet left home. In Hungary, 49 percent of men and 27 percent of women have not. In Portugal, it's 44 percent of men and 30 percent of women.

The Japanese have an expression for people in their twenties and thirties who are unemployed or underemployed: *freeters*, thought to be a shortening of the English word "freeloader." Many freeters wind up living with parents in quarters that are notoriously tight. If an American is depressed about the current job situation and wants to experience a moment of schadenfreude, take note: "Japan has the worst generational inequality in the world," Manabu Shimasawa, a professor of social policy at Akita University, told the *New York Times*. Even pre-earthquake, pre-tsunami, and pre–nuclear radiation crisis, the news was filled with grim accounts of how college graduates face an all-time low in employment.

In the United Kingdom, 28 percent of men and 13 percent of women have not yet left home by age twenty-five. (The gender differences are similar in the United States, since young American women tend to depart sooner than young men.) In England they're called "kippers"—kids in their parents' pockets—and more twenty- and thirtysomethings are living at home with their parents than at any time in the past twenty years, according to the Office for National Statistics. In the past, British adultescents have tended to leave home earlier than their European cousins, but the latest figures show that 25 percent of men aged twenty-five to twenty-nine now live with their parents, almost double the proportion of women in their late twenties (13 percent) who still live at home.

Canada illustrates the same trend: 43.5 percent of Canada's four million young adults aged twenty to twenty-nine were living with their parents in 2006, up from 41.1 percent five years earlier. "Your kids may be doing it and the kids down the street are also doing it, so it's not seen as a failure to launch," says Monica Boyd, a sociology professor and Canada Research Chair in Immigration, Inequality, and Public Policy at the University of Toronto. "Thirty or forty years ago it was kind of weird. We've had a sea change.... Living at home after college occurs at such levels in Canada, the United States, Europe, and Australia that it's clear this is what being a young adult is all about. What is almost happening—particularly for those in their early twenties—is that not to be living at home is what is unusual."

MAKING A MOLEHILL OUT OF A MOUNTAIN

"After five years in northern California trying to write a novel, my twenty-nine-year-old son, Jack,* came home last September," says Rebecca Levin* of Hudson, Ohio. "He has about ten friends who've also come home, so he doesn't feel out of it in the same way kids our age would have felt—there's tremendous social reinforcement. My son works in a restaurant. We don't have a regular arrangement for when we see him, but he knows if he puts his laundry in the basket, it will get washed. If he has a girl over, that's awkward, but probably worse for her than me."

Jack graduated from college after five years. Now he works in a pizza restaurant. "I've decided not to think about what my son is going to do in the future. I used to say, 'Oy, what did I do wrong?' But when I found out how common this is and it hit me how radically different this generation is from mine, I stopped blaming myself. While this happened, my niece, along with her lawyer husband and three-year-old child, moved into the home of my parents, who are ninety-three and eighty-seven. Four generations now live together because my sister and her husband (my niece's parents) visit on weekends.

"Parents like me are dealing with cultural change. My child isn't the only one coming home. It's a huge percentage . . . so I don't feel personally guilty anymore. I've started to look at the bigger issue. It's economic—and we don't know where that's going—and with so many other kids coming home, it's becoming acceptable. My friends are starting to joke about it, which makes it easier. I've learned to make a molehill out of a mountain.

"My husband and I are optimists. We think that if our son gets sick of living with us he'll have an incentive to get a better or second job and move out. I don't think this trend will last forever. Maybe all these kids will get together and start rehabbing foreclosed houses."

Marie Hartwell-Walker, the mom from Amherst, Massachusetts, most certainly does not consider it inappropriate or surprising that two of her own four adultescent children have recently settled back into the nest. She is equally unruffled by the fact that during forty-five years of marriage, she and her husband, Fred, have, after becoming parents, experienced a mere six-month child-free blip. Her older son quit college and began to care for autistic children, work he found rewarding but paid only $11 an hour. At that point he returned home, eventually reentering college to complete a degree. "I see him moving out when he graduates," Dr. Hartwell-Walker says. "We've talked about the end time."

When she speaks about her other son, she points to a portrait of an eighteenth-century Native American chief rendered in dark tones. Long dark hair hangs loose, strands of a beaded necklace surround the chief's neck, and a woven blanket covers his right shoulder. The portrait is so lifelike that it startled me when I walked into the living room. "I have an eighty-thousand-dollar painting to represent what's become of my other son's art school education," she says, gesturing toward the canvas. "He's well educated, but with a fine arts degree he couldn't find a job. For a while, he put up tents for weddings, but then he injured himself, so now he can't find a job in either art or physical labor because he can't swing a hammer, although he looks exactly like what everybody wants to look like when you go to the gym." This son is also back in school, to become certified as a fitness trainer. Dr. Hartwell-Walker expects him to move out soon. "The clarity of the arrangement is what makes these stays work out or not. When an adult child is living at home indefinitely, the whole family experiences a low-level 'why isn't this over?' anxiety. It puts everyone in a tangle."

WE'RE NOT IN KANSAS ANYMORE

The heartland has experienced much of what the coasts tasted first—layoffs, numerous adultescents out of work, as well as young moms whose hopes of staying home with babies have been dashed because their husbands are unemployed. "Often when parents experience boomerang kids, it makes the mother and father feel as if they haven't done their job correctly," says Gina Heyen, a licensed marriage and family therapist practicing in Wichita, Kansas. "It's especially painful for them to see their kids suffer."

Wichita is the country's aircraft capital, home to manufacturing plants for Boeing, Lear, and Cessna, among others. As airlines and other Fortune 500 corporations have stopped ordering new jets, jobs have been swept away. "It hasn't been this bad around here since the Depression," Heyen notes. "In the clinic where I work, we've seen a huge increase in depression and anxiety, with more people seeking medication than counseling. I'm not surprised by the latter—it's an expression of our society's desire for instant gratification.

"We're strong on family values here," Heyen says, which calls into question a parent's role when kids' lives go off the rails. She cites a solid, long-term marriage that threatened to shatter when a prodigal daughter in her thirties returned home with more than $60,000 of debt. Not long after, her sister, in her twenties with heavy student loans, showed up, too.

"The girls started to use the house mostly as a hotel. Only after the daughters had been home for a few years did the family come to me for counseling. By then, the father was feeling overwhelmed, dipping into his retirement savings because he felt as if he was still the provider who had to pay, pay, pay. The mother took a different approach. She had other ideas for how to use their money. 'We're done,' she'd decided. 'In fact, we've been done having kids at home for a very long time.'"

The nuts-and-bolts plan Heyen hammered out helped the family to steer the daughters toward networking, volunteering, and researching state programs for the Department of Housing and Urban Development (HUD), Medicaid, disability, student loans, and consumer counseling—resources this family never needed before and didn't know how to access. The father decided to research the programs with the daughters to see if utilizing them would create more financial independence for everyone. "The mother wanted them gone in thirty to sixty days, but the standard of living the girls would have faced under those conditions was a concern for the father. She had to compromise on a six-month time line."

In Sharon Gilchrest O'Neill's practice of more than twenty years in Westchester County, New York, she used to see virtually no cases of boomerang adultescents. Now she sees many: "I try to work with the parents first. They usually have to be reminded that the number one rule of parenting is that a mother and father need to work as a team to make sure that kids don't play you off one another. It's important to talk through boundaries. Will you let your adult child drink at home? Smoke pot? Does the child get his own room back? What bathroom does he use? Will a boyfriend or girlfriend sleep over? 'I don't want to see some guy walking around in his underwear,' one dad complained." Like a referee joined to a judge, O'Neill reminds parents that it's still their home, no matter how old the kids are.

"Often the parents feel that because the child is in the twenty-to-thirty age group, they can't set boundaries." Hooey, she says. A return home can get especially tricky for both parents and kids when, while they lived on their own, adultescents have grown up more than their parents realize or can accept. "I saw one sensible girl of twenty-five who came home though she didn't really want to," O'Neill reports. "She'd lost a good job in finance and, as a result, hadn't lived up to her own expectations, but she couldn't afford to have her own apartment anymore. While she'd been on her own, she'd gone to therapy and addressed having a mom who always wanted to know everything about her." Now the mother is in therapy with O'Neill, trying to reinvent her idea of what it means to be a loving parent. This starts with no longer cross-examining her daughter every day in hopes of creating closeness.

Certainly, there are ugly stories told by both parents and adultes-cents forced to return home. "I married and moved to North Carolina with my husband, where he was stationed for the navy," says a young mom who chooses to remain anonymous. "The next year I had my son and found out that my husband was cheating on me with a married nineteen-year-old neighbor whose husband was in Iraq. That summer my husband left me, saying he didn't want to be a husband or a father anymore. Soon after, he was deployed to Iraq. I stayed on in base hous-ing for another six months but became broke and lonely. My daughter and I moved back home to Pennsylvania. We didn't really have a choice, since the navy was going to take away our housing when my ex returned from Iraq."

She's landed in a fresh hell. "My mom spends no time with my daughter. My dad wishes we'd never moved back. My job doesn't pay enough for me to get ahead with savings to get out of here and I feel like I never will. Subsidized housing in our area has a long wait list. I'm depressed knowing we aren't wanted. I swear that the only reason why my parents haven't kicked us out is because my mom doesn't want to live alone with my dad and because I do the laundry and a lot around the house to keep things neat and clean. I'm a live-in housekeeper. Sometimes we just choose the wrong path and it takes us back to a place where we never want to be again."

BED AND CABLE: THE MIDDLE-CLASS TRUST FUND

"My parents let me rest like I was Jenny coming home to Forrest Gump," says Jonathan Harms, twenty-seven, of Rapid City, South Dakota.

"I took a shot at a dream, working in the music business for three years, and eventually became an executive. The choice to come home came swiftly. I was on a tour. The band I was managing was fighting, and my business partners back in Nashville seemed to be organizing their own alliance. I called my folks in Aberdeen, South Dakota, knowing they'd be cool with me coming home to gather myself for a few months before another adventure."

To Jon's surprise, being home felt so comfy he's never left the state. "South Dakota is in my blood," he's realized. "I want to be a part of it, maybe even start a family. I didn't see that happening in the rock-and-roll business—too many hours and not enough trust. I get along famously with my parents. We laugh and watch HGTV. They are very supportive and understand that I'm in a different stage in life than, say, a college student. I was close to getting married in Nashville, but it just didn't work out. My mother is a great friend who hasn't pushed me to find a girl. My dad, the well-rounded professional that he is, helped me to hone my vision for another shot at a future and career. He made sure I knew it was okay to be at yet another crossroads.

"We Digitals have invented new ways of interacting—Facebook and Twitter—but it's as rare to find a no-wind day in Fargo as it is to find a deep interaction," he adds. "We are very much in touch with our emotions, though, and perhaps the stock we put into them is the strength we use to pick up and go when we see a fun opportunity or run when we are uncomfortable. That, and the fact that our boomer parents have worked hard to . . . fund our gallivanting. There is much to see and experience, but I think wandering is out of my soul. I'm young and not so dumb anymore."

After living at home for several months, Jon moved five hours away to Rapid City, South Dakota, where he's working full-time at a publishing company while going to school to earn an MBA. His mother is tutoring him by phone in calculus and statistics. After living rent-free with his parents, he found a house that he plans to convert to a rental.

"To celebrate my adulthood I also bought a full-size Chevy Silverado," he says. "I've never been in debt except for my student loan, but in the last, oh . . . six months, I got my first credit card, a house, and a truck, huzzah! But I'll be honest. My parents still help me out with bunches of money. This last weekend they drove to see me and bought new trim for the inside of all my windows and curtains for them, too. I can't believe how expensive a set of curtains is!"

Not long ago, Tracey Benson* was a wife and Rolfing therapist—being Rolfed is to receive a deep-tissue massage some liken to masochism—dwelling in hipster Brooklyn. Her husband, Allan,* had gotten a job with compensation high enough to allow her to sell her practice and start a Web site–based business that sold high-end artisanal foods. Within the year, however, Allan lost his job, and Tracey's business, for which she took out a $50,000 FDA loan to start, became a sinkhole: there were few buyers for designer pickles in a frank-and-beans economy.

Financial worries widened the fault lines in an already shaky marriage. "I left my husband shortly before our son Chris's* first birthday," Tracey says, the same time that she was facing the repayment of the loan. A few months later she moved in with her family, who'd returned from living in London and Singapore and had settled in New Haven, Connecticut, equidistant between Tracey and her older brother in Boston. "I needed their support," she says, but when she first moved to New Haven, she was embarrassed to tell new friends that she was living with her parents. "I had to remind myself that some of my friends had set up businesses thanks to trust funds. Except for college tuition paid for by my parents, I've been supporting myself since I was fourteen. My mother and father couldn't give me a trust fund, but they can give me love and a roof over my head when I've needed it. It's been a healing experience for all of us—far better than declaring bankruptcy and living in a chicken coop in Brooklyn."

Tracey and Chris each have a bedroom in her parents' town house and he is in preschool across the street. With her parents helping to care for their grandson, Tracey has been able to reopen a Rolfing practice and start teaching an online marketing course for other practitioners. Both endeavors supply income. She splits the cost of groceries with her parents and does the marketing and cooking, but the Bensons don't ask their daughter to kick in for household costs they'd be covering were she and their grandson not living with them. "Support from my parents has allowed me to work because I don't have to panic about child care," Tracey says. "There was a brief period in Brooklyn when Chris was in day care. At the end of the day I was in a tremendous rush to pick him up, dump him in a stroller, get on the subway, get him home, and the next morning do it all over again. My move home has relieved me of that pressure."

Tracey and her parents continue to care for Chris, along with her ex-husband, who has relocated to New Haven and begun to manage a restaurant. "There's not a big negotiation about who's going to look after Chris at night. Honestly, my son is in heaven to have this much quality time with his grandparents. I was very close to my grandparents when I grew up. I'm thrilled that he has that connection, too. We all thrive from this situation." She looks forward to being solvent in about a year. At that point she'll leave her parents' home but expects to stay in New Haven. "Now it would be weird to up and move a thousand miles away. I have a Greek friend who says, 'You should live close enough to your parents so they can walk over but not in their bedroom slippers.'"

That sounds good to me. I have one son a continent away in southern California and another one a borough away in Brooklyn. I don't see nearly as much of either of them as I'd like. I look longingly at real estate ads and wonder what it would be like to have different apartments under the same roof in a Brooklyn brownstone or side-by-side Santa Monica bungalows.

Not that my kids share this dream. Not at all, and probably a good thing.

Chapter 5

THE U-HAUL AS UMBILICAL CORD

Life can only be understood backwards; but it must be lived forwards.

—Søren Kierkegaard

When my friend's daughter Jessica, MBA in hand, recently moved from Washington, D.C., to Boston, it involved a futon, a small library's worth of books, a set of Calphalon cookware from her grandparents, and the most important app of all, Mom. Having received a schlep-alert, Mama Julia loaded the SUV and drove it down from New Hampshire to pack, haul, unpack, hang photographs, joust with cable companies, wait for deliveries, assemble furniture—she is both Click and Clack, traveling with her Phillips head screwdriver *and* an Allen wrench set.

I asked Julia why she was doing all this. When she was thirty-two, the age daughter Jessica is now, Julia had a husband, two kids, an aging golden retriever, a business, and a four-bedroom home. I don't remember her mother driving up to New England to help her move, though I do recall Julia hanging wallpaper and refinishing floors when she was in her seventh month of pregnancy.

Jessica is her mother's daughter: smart, resourceful, and energetic. Yet Julia says, "I don't want Jessica to have to do this alone. I feel for her."

Considering the high-powered consulting position that Jessica was assuming, I wondered what her future bosses would have thought of this intervention. But who was I to judge? A month earlier my older son, Jed, also thirty-two, had decided that it was time to graduate from living with housemates. Although he was raised in what I considered to be a bastion of sensible values, Manhattan's Upper West Side—when my kids were young our zip code was so crunchy I felt obligated to wait until I traveled to the East Side to slip on stilettos—Brooklyn was now Jed's borough du jour. Along with every other local liberal arts major, he had apparently caucused in Prospect Park and decided that Manhattan was a gulag of dorkiness and greed. I found a certain delightful symmetry in my son's choice of Brooklyn, from which my own father had fled in 1936 to Fargo, leaving behind subways and egg creams, though taking with him his accent and Dodgers devotion.

As soon as I learned that Jed was moving, I, who consider decorating magazines porn—I know it when I see it— started salivating at the thought of fording the East River to accompany my son while we peeped into Romanesque Revival mansions and Victorian brownstones. I broke into a dreamy smile just thinking about the mother-son bonding and saw myself spouting axioms like "Buy less but buy better" following an afternoon of apartment surfing by hitting the Brooklyn Flea, where the grilled cheese sandwiches could make a pig of an anorexic.

But no. "I can manage on my own, Mom," Jed said at my attempt to bulldoze into that area of his cortex where decisions get made. With no help from me he found a home suitable for himself and innumerable boxes of vinyl records. Nonetheless, when it came time for his actual physical move, he quickly accepted an offer from my husband in the form of a rental truck.

What is it about boys and their trucks? I'll tell you. Trouble. Early on a hot summer Saturday, Rob and I, primed for adventure, picked up a U-Haul. Judging from the turkey sandwiches and homemade cupcakes I'd packed, you'd have thought we were going to Yellowstone Park, not transferring belongings from Boerum Hill to Carroll Gardens as well as driving hither and yon to fetch furniture bequeathed by various donors.

As tasks invariably do, our mission took more than twice as long as anticipated. It was nearly midnight when the last monster armoire needed to be delivered out of the truck's womb. My hubby, 1948 model, gave the mahogany galoot its crowning push. The next thing I heard was Rob moaning like a woman in her twenty-third hour of labor.

"Gee, Dad, maybe you better rest," Jed said as I ran to my manly man's side while he slunk off into the dark to ice his ego as well as his wound.

Like other former high school athletes of his vintage, Rob is no stranger to orthopedic attention. For the past decade, it has taken us an extra twenty minutes to clear airport security due to the sorry outcome of a football injury, a titanium shoulder, which requires a suspicious pat-down. You'd think Bionic Man would know when to call a physician, but since guys rarely do, it took days before he noticed that he no longer had a bicep, just a long appendage hanging from his shoulder like a salami.

"You popped a tendon!" Dr. Gristle-Bone declared. "Don't worry—we'll operate. If you'd waited any longer to see me, I'd have had to use a cadaver tendon," he added, sounding disappointed. I briefly considered what it would be like to sleep next to a partner who was an exclusive nutty blend of Jewish, titanium, and cadaver. That was not to be. After emergency surgery, three months with a brace that turned Rob into RoboCop, every minute of physical therapy our insurance plan would cough up—*poof*—my husband was repaired. And if Jed called tomorrow to say he was changing addresses again, faster than you could say OxyContin Rob would be behind the wheel of a truck.

When adultescents whistle, Mom and Dad—slaphappy indentured servants—run, though rarely do parents expect reciprocal service. During the last five years, Rob and I have exhibited a gypsy streak and moved four times, yet I didn't ask Jed or his brother, Rory, to pack as much as one carton: I wouldn't want to impose (and they didn't offer). Yet I don't consider it a burden when we haul ass on our sons' behalf. The two of us and many other parents see moving kids as love distilled into duct tape and brown corrugated boxes. With one-third of people in their twenties moving to a new residence every year, the U-Haul is a born-again umbilical cord. Parents like feeling needed. We want to satisfy that hunger as surely as we want to eat, sleep, or have sex.

The relationships boomers have with young adult kids are a tight weave of guilt and love. If both parents worked when the children were growing up, Mom and Dad likely bought into the quantity versus quality-time argument; now that the kids have left, parents invariably have more time on their hands and long to make up for what they missed. They may also sense that at some level their adultescent children are ill-equipped to handle quotidian problems, hold themselves responsible for the developmental delay, and jump in to help all too easily.

"My wife and I recently picked up a U-Haul, found ourselves

driving on the parkway—which was illegal—and then had the joy of loading and unloading all of my son's stuff—a five-hour task," says Howard Glattner, who lives in Bucks County, Pennsylvania, and recently drove to Washington, D.C., where their son, twenty-five, is a law student.

"Could your son have done this on his own?" I asked.

Howard hesitated before he said, "Probably."

"How many times have you done this?"

"Ten," he estimated, between his son and a daughter.

"Did anyone ever do this for you?"

"Of course not," Howard howled. "I'd never have asked for this kind of help, and also, I lived at home with my mother until I was twenty-seven, just as my wife lived with her parents, so we didn't need it. But we want to help our kids in any way we can. *It's all for the kids*."

When I was a young wife and already Jed's mommy, a young woman I knew—your basic brainiac, Chinese major who'd just graduated from Swarthmore College—was moving from Fargo to Manhattan. Her father, a busy physician and father of five, was driving her 1,450 miles to lend a hand. When I heard this, my jealousy was that of a four-year-old whose best friend got a Ginny Doll with a straw bonnet, lacy anklets, and a canopy bed when all *I* got was a used coloring book of state birds. I, too, had made this Fargo-to-Manhattan trek and had moved twice more since then within the city. The farthest my father had driven me was a mile to the airport on the first leg of the trip. Forget the fact that it never crossed my mind to expect any other kind of support, that I managed fine in Gotham without his looking over my shoulder, that my independence bolstered my self-worth, or that no one else I knew in the Midwest of the 1970s had parents who'd dream of being so pushy. Still, when I heard about this other dad's labor of love, I felt retroactively deprived.

I'm sure that memory was embedded in my brain when the opportunity arose to assist in Jed's move. It was an opportunity for Rob and me to be useful and close when there were so many ways in which our son, perhaps wisely, had shut us out of his life. Do adultescents accept help to make nice to parents or because they haven't developed the skills to cope on their own? Do parents offer their ministrations out of an inability to separate from children? Or are other dynamics in play, and if so, what the heck are they?

Talk to Dayna Schmidt, twenty-seven, and you find that the impulse to ask Mom and Dad to spring for the garbage can–size cylinders of bubble wrap and commandeer a move begins with sheer practicality. "I've relocated every year since I graduated from high school," explains this small-town Kansas native who longed to "go over the rainbow to somewhere far, far away." Her journey, thus far, has led her to various addresses in Des Moines and Chicago. Every time she's switched apartments, her parents have been at her side, just as they recently assisted her brother in moving cross-country.

"When it comes to a U-Haul, my mother and father have this insane ability to Tetris things into a very small space," she says with admiration, referencing the wildly popular video game where players fit falling blocks into a grid. Parental capability is, however, a single piece in the puzzle. More compelling: you can ask friends only so many times, but parents are always willing.

"Almost everyone I know moves a lot," Dayna says with the same nonchalance she might use to report that most people she knows get haircuts. "Every so often you meet someone with a smooth plan, but more people my age wander around in every way. I don't think many are really stationary. Right now, the economy has a lot to do with it, but that's not the sole reason. Growing up we were, to a point, coddled. Our boomer parents wanted us to have it all. We were raised hearing,

'You're great! You can do anything! You get a trophy just for finishing the race!' Few of us realized in real life you get the trophy only if you're first and, hey, there's hard work involved."

As far back as elementary school, Dayna imagined herself working in television. She received a degree in broadcast journalism from Drake University but left the field after an internship and an entry-level job because—good morning, reality—she "got depressed seeing all that bad news and sitting in a dark room editing film." She also had friends who wanted to become marine biologists, she recalls, "but only one person I know actually became a marine biologist." Could this be because many of these students, raised in landlocked Kansas, had never put a toe in an ocean? Perhaps, but what Dayna suggests is that "there's far more trial and error and decision making involved in life than my generation was told it would require, and no one ever helped us figure it out."

The disillusionment that's sent her peers wandering has served Ms. Schmidt well. After tossing aside her vision of cloning Christiane Amanpour and encountering turbulence in the form of anxiety about relationship and job loss, and facing "just your average I-don't-know-what-the-hell-I'm-doing-with-my-life blues," she recast herself as "a certified quarter-life coach for twentysomethings." A life coach helps you identify aspirations and reach goals, Dayna explains. Clients, whom she recruits through social networking and word of mouth, are required to sign on for at least six sessions. Business, Coach Schmidt says, is booming.

Another Chicagoan, clinical psychologist David Gursky, Ph.D., explains that adultescents, a demographic that constitutes much of his practice, happily erect an electric fence to stop Ma and Pa from invading their space. They turn to parents primarily for crisis management—and you can put moving at the top of that list. For this behavior, Dr. Gursky does not dump on the younger generation. He contends that while boomer parents are often skilled problem solvers, they tend to be dismal failures at the no-pyrotechnics task of mentoring because they were too stressed and busy to have taught their offspring fundamental life skills, like learning to pack for a move, arrange for utilities, or paint a room. He seconds Dayna Schmidt's belief that the parents of adultescents bought into "the self-esteem movement and were fearful of 'hurting' kids by placing limits." Allowing young adults to find their own way has resulted in their drifting right up and into inevitable roadblocks, at which point parents come to their rescue.

"The big complaint I hear from parents is that their young adult kids call only in a crisis—when, let's say, they lose their iPod, need to prepare for an interview, or move," says Natalie Caine of Los Angeles. She turned this parental Sturm und Drang into a cottage industry six years ago by establishing Empty Nest Support Services, which provides seminars, online classes, telephone consultations, and workshops. Adultescents want to "touch in with their parents," Caine says, using her term for the quick hit of a phone call or drop-in visit. "They want encounters to be as brief as possible, which makes parents feel used or betrayed. Mothers and fathers get included in the moment of drama, then children move on and parents never hear about the exciting resolution. *How's the apartment working out? Did you think you did well on the interview?* Well, parents aren't going to get that resolution. I always tell them to lower their expectations."

Parents may lick their wounds, but that doesn't stop them from renting, loading, driving, and unloading those trucks and dragging boxes up flights of stairs. They do it to experience a sense of purpose, which as a society we often lack, suggests Elizabeth Lombardo, Ph.D. Her practice includes boomers as well as a significant number of people in their twenties whose parents have sought out and are paying for their therapy, something she says she can't imagine previous generations doing.

"Our oldest daughter, Melanie, is twenty-seven," says Tracey Fieber of Esteban, Manitoba. Tracey has four children in their twenties and has helped each of them move multiple times. The last trek was a thirteen-hundred-mile round-trip from her daughter Melanie's home in Winnipeg, Manitoba, to a town outside Calgary, Alberta, requiring a team that included Tracey, her husband, their son-in-law's parents, and Melanie.

"We left our home eight miles from the U.S. border on a Thursday night, driving three hundred miles in snow to Winnipeg, where the next day we packed and loaded everything onto trailers. We started driving to Calgary, but a blizzard forced us to return to Melanie's home, where we had to sleep on the floor. In the morning, the roads were snow-packed with glare ice and trucks jackknifed in ditches and cars rolled over. We waited in line on the highway along with hundreds of other vehicles until it opened." The trip to Calgary took two days. When the worker bees arrived, they spent a day unpacking and hooking up appliances. Tracey arrived home on Tuesday. "Both sets of parents love helping our kids where possible, and making their life easier," Tracey says. "If asked again, we'd do it in a heartbeat!"

Fifteen and counting is how many times Erika Hoffman of Chapel Hill, North Carolina, has helped her four twentysomething children move since they graduated from college. "It's a gift of time as well as money and makes me feel as if I still have something to do with their lives," she says. "My husband and I have toted furniture in trucks, bought mattresses, stocked refrigerators, helped sign up for utilities and cable services, and taken roommates out to dine before we depart.

"It's like tucking tots into bed," Erika says. "Even after night lights, bedtime stories, and bath rituals were long over, I routinely stuck my head into each of my kids' rooms to say good night. Often, my teens were asleep or making sure they appeared that way, so loath were they to receive a peck on the cheek. Poor things got it anyway!

"My children didn't need the assurance of knowing Mom cared. They took that as a given. *I* needed to guarantee they were safe and sound before I could snooze. It's the same way with moving them to new abodes. Kids this age don't want our help as much as we want to give it. Afterward I pick out souvenir salt and pepper shakers for them when I travel, buy five-hundred-thread-count Egyptian cotton sheets, and fill their cupboards with paper towels and toilet paper to last a year. Maybe they will think of me, for a second, when they reach for the whisk broom that I bought."

"I don't see parents helping kids move as 'an issue' if it's fun for everybody and a parent simply wants to continue to play a nurturing, caretaking role," says Elizabeth Lombardo. "There's nothing wrong with wanting a connection. The trouble starts when parents focus mostly on giving and kids focus mostly on receiving . . . when children over-rely on parents or parents find their primary purpose in living through a kid. I'm thinking about moms, for example, decorating whole apartments and homes, especially for sons. 'When you come home from work, it'll be all done!' these mothers will say."

Uh-oh. Would this have been me had Jed not said, "No, thanks anyway, Mom." His *are-you-crazy?-over-my-dead-body* was strictly subliminal.

Adultescents are closer to their parents than those of the same age in previous generations, yet more distant in other ways. "I'm seeing a lot of financial reliance, young adults who expect parents to keep paying for them and bailing them out," Dr. Lombardo says, "yet greater emotional and social distance."

Dr. Gursky has noticed a change. "Earlier in my practice"—he is forty-eight—"when I observed an adult in his or her twenties who wasn't mature and capable, I was stunned. Now the mature young adult is the exception, especially among men." Here he blames (beware: the dark side of Tetris) video games.

"They've dumbed down a whole generation of young men, making them zoned out, lazy, and self-absorbed. Whenever I see a young man as a client, I invariably want to grow him up and encourage him to take on many of the traditional chivalrous values of an older generation. What young women really want is for their boyfriends and husbands to assume a healthy partnership role in the relationships. Young adult women are doing all the hard work in their marriages. They make life easy for young men, and all the guys do is sit on their butts."

Not every individual aged twenty-two to thirty-five is, of course, an adultescent. Randy Rutkin of Henderson, Nevada, the proud mother of "self-reliant and self-sufficient" Kate, does not feel her daughter fits this classification. The last time Randy helped Kate, twenty-five, move was when her daughter graduated from the University of Southern California and took a teaching job in San Francisco, where she's also completing her master's degree. Yet Rutkin, who is an adolescent therapist, is careful to add, "I think Kate's behavior is unusual for her age group. She's definitely in the minority."

As the years have passed, each generation seems to be taking a longer time to grow up. Boomers were allowed more leeway than their parents, and their children's attitudes are continuing the cycle in an ever-loosening spiral. What Rutkin is seeing in her practice—"far more than five or ten years ago"—are parents who've never set limits or boundaries, have abdicated their natural authority as parents, want their kids to like them as friends, and have given children a blatant sense of entitlement. "These are parents who are intimidated by their kids. I predict that the generation coming up"—today's teenagers—"may be even more wandering than people in their twenties and thirties are now."

Chapter 6
ADULTESCENTS
WITHOUT BORDERS

I thought maybe I'd understand my parents better if I'd spend
some time thinking about immortality in a really old place.
Read some good books. Get some thoughts down.

—*Super Sad True Love Story* by Gary Shteyngart

ifty years ago, *Europe on $5 a Day* changed travel. By the 1970s,
Arthur Frommer's bible, full of fetching pensiones to look up,
was already a classic. His smarty-pants publisher suggested that
readers rip their guidebooks apart to cut down on the weight they had
to carry once they'd finished traveling in one country; this prevented
the book from being passed on to a friend and vastly multiplied sales.
I was merely one more American reader who'd hopped a charter flight,
crosshatching Europe on overnight trains to save on lodging while
I highlighted Mr. Frommer's tips. With a budget of a thousand bucks,

I covered ten countries in as many weeks. My college class could have thrown a mixer at the Spanish Steps.

Americans may be sadly deficient in our ability to chat in languages other than English, at high decibel, wherever we travel. "It's embarrassing," President Barack Obama acknowledges (this from a Harvard man with an international background who admits he knows only one language). "When Europeans come over here they all speak English . . . then we go to Europe and all we can say is *merci beaucoup*." But being monolingual hasn't stopped Americans from exercising our passports. According to a survey by Continental Airlines, twenty-somethings will typically visit nine different countries before they are twenty-five, and most first traveled to a foreign destination when they were eight years old.

Until Prince William took one, boomers thought a gap year meant laying in a good supply of straight-leg jeans and pocket T-shirts. But a recent survey of three hundred thousand students entering college found that slightly more than 1 percent had waited a year to start college, according to the Higher Education Research Institute at the University of California, Los Angeles. A small number, perhaps, but in the 1960s and 1970s it was the atypical and extremely lucky student who spent a junior year abroad, and almost no one took a gap year. This changed when the boomer generation—and not just the über tier—began to identify themselves as global citizens. Since then, they've seen to it that their kids get around. At fifteen my boys traveled to Japan, Peru, and Chile on YMCA trips and many of their friends did the teen tour circuit. Half the Jewish kids I know under the age of twenty-six have taken advantage of a completely free, ten-day "Taglit-Birthright" trip to Israel, a social whirlwind that my sister refers to as BirthRate. The Internet, Skype, and better cell service than you'd find in, say, Los Angeles have also profoundly green-lit our broadened global perspective.

On American campuses we don't hear much outraged rhetoric about how only students from privileged countries and backgrounds have the freedom and resources to explore other cultures, doing volunteer work, tackling outdoor adventures, or traveling purely for pleasure. Nor do travelers appear to be daunted by tsunamis, earthquakes, or terrorist attacks. Four times the number of students study abroad compared with twenty years ago, according to the Institute of International Education. Africa, Asia, Latin America, and the Middle East are vying with the United Kingdom, France, Spain, and Italy as primo destinations.

After graduation many adultescents continue to say *hasta la vista*, buying one-way tickets to faraway lands. A critical difference between today's adultescent sojourns and Frommer-esquepades of the past is that yesteryear's trips tended to last a month or two or six months at the most, while today's travels last at least a year and sometimes stretch on indefinitely. A friend in Vermont tells me that at least six friends of her son, now twenty-eight, headed to Thailand after college and have never returned.

Some of these latter-day Gerald and Sara Murphys sally forth strictly for kicks, though for others, living abroad is an expression of idealism and a response to what they've started to regard as the United States' bad juju. The country of their birth may have given them the Big Mac, the Constitution, and the chicken dance; still, they'd like to explore an alternative to a nation that, they've concluded as they've reached the age of majority, falls short on health care, smart energy policy, maternity leave, public transportation, day care, and vacation days, and has started wars, compromised its environment, and allowed infrastructure, public education, and Social Security to deteriorate while political corruption, Wall Street bailouts, the Tea Party, obesity, genetically modified crops, foreclosures, NASCAR, creationism, salmonella, credit card debt, *The Biggest Loser*, and—perhaps most important to them—unemployment have flourished.

Growing numbers of U.S. citizens are looking for work in Australia, for example, where China's thirst for iron ore and energy is transforming the country into an economic powerhouse. Daniel Davila, a twenty-three-year-old timber floorer from Camarillo, California—a Los Angeles suburb buried in the Golden State's housing dust bowl—moved across the Pacific two years ago after he'd been forced to take a job stocking shelves at a grocery store for barely minimum wage. In Perth, a mining boomtown, he earns in one day what he was paid for a week's work in the United States. A former hedge fund banker in his early thirties, Garrett Mclaughlin, moved to Sydney to study for an MBA. As he entered his final semester he says he's already had several job offers.

The Overachievers: The Secret Lives of Driven Kids, published in 2007, kicked off with a profile of a high school senior named Julia Plevin. "On the surface, she seems to have it all, a straight-A student without exception since sixth grade," chapter 1 gushes. It continues with shout-outs for Julia's heavy-hitting advanced placement classes, dedication to yoga, distance running records, and more. But Julia isn't just "The Superstar," as the book anoints her. "My daughter is a trend spotter," says her mother, Amy Plevin. "We're speaking of the first second grader in Potomac, Maryland, to wear a key ring on her backpack. The next year, every backpack jingled. Whenever we shopped, Julia would want what you'd find in the stores the next season. Her mind works differently. She makes connections that I don't see until she points them out. In a sense Julia represents her generation—she always seems to know what's cool."

What's cool now is working abroad, exactly what Julia has been doing for several years. Her senior year at Dartmouth coincided with the tanking of the economy. "Almost desperate" about what to do next, Mom recounts, but ever the strategist, Julia applied for a position through Princeton in Asia, an organization that has been placing college grads in Asia since the 1890s. Julia's second language was Spanish, but what the heck? When she was offered a job at the International Union for Conservation of Nature, an environmental NGO, she landed in Ho-Ho-Ho Chi Minh Hanoi, a city that satisfied her top requirements: rich in cultural events, a no-gluten diet, and the chance for avid exercise.

Moving to Vietnam, Julia says, was the ballsiest and best thing she's ever done. "Hanoi is so alive, so raw, exactly what I need—chaos—which keeps me energized. In America people move from private box to private box all day long, from their house to their car to the mall to the office to Starbucks to the gym and to Walmart. In Vietnam there are no boxes. Life is lived on the streets. I love that."

Her first job? Not so much. She quit, started a Web site, blogged, wrote for a local English-language magazine, and—chop-chop—became its managing editor, all while tending a flowering social life. Initially she befriended fellow Western expats from Holland, Germany, Switzerland, Italy, France, and Canada, along with other Americans. As she picked up Vietnamese, she acquired native friends as well.

Reduced to a postcard, here is Julia's life: "A dreamy *Sex and the City* job, going to wine tastings, hotel and bar openings, and art events, learning how to manage a magazine, opportunities to travel the country and Thailand, Myanmar, Laos, Cambodia, and Malaysia. There are many other places I want to live—France! Italy! Argentina! Spain! Israel!"

Professional opportunities keep calling out to her as well. Business school? More writing? Design classes? She sees them all as options, although her dearest dream is to become a fashion editor of one of *Vogue*'s editions in, say, Japan (despite the fact that among young people, Japan's unemployment is astoundingly high, since the cultural preference is for older workers). "But I can't think about what I want to do next year or have a five-year plan because I'm so focused on daily life here," Julia says. "Not that it's easy. I drink a lot more than I did in college, find it hard to go for long runs, and sometimes the traffic and noise get to me." They definitely got to her parents—when they visited they were "overwhelmed that when I could live anywhere in the world I chose a polluted developing city. Go figure, eh?"

"Hanoi is growing so fast, there are cement mixers and gigantic bricks everywhere, with bikes, motorbikes, and honking trucks and cars all competing for the same bit of street" is how Amy Plevin, Julia's mother, describes the city. "I had to go back to my hotel just to take a breath." Yet the tumult fails to stop her from seeing the benefits of her daughter's choice. Julia was the kid who called Mom between every class at Dartmouth. Now she is fearless, because, as she says, in Vietnam if you're timid, you'll be outmaneuvered. Amy's bigger anxieties are long-term. First, there's the worry that Julia's transient international life will turn permanent. "I picture grandchildren I won't know and family holidays that Julia isn't part of." But assuming her daughter's expatriotism soon ends, a more immediate concern is how her daughter's foreign work experience will translate to the American job market. "My daughter has had three interns working for her in Hanoi, but she could come home and find herself an intern," Amy remarks drily.

IT'S NOT ABOUT THE JOB

Herein, the rub. For adultescents living abroad, life is less about the value added to a résumé than the lushness of the experience, where even tweedy toilet tissue may seem exotic simply because it didn't come from Target. Actual work adultescents do is, for the most part, beside the point.

Teaching English is the default job for our young expats. Over the last three years, Teach Away, one of several organizations placing English-speaking teachers in foreign countries, has seen applicants aged twenty-five to thirty-five increase 200 percent because teaching is a virtual synonym for sustained traveling. "The goal is not to get settled or to find a career job," David Frey, the organization's spokes-person acknowledges, "but to see the world." In 2010, the company received more than fifteen thousand applicants. Few of the teachers hired were experienced in that profession or graduates who aspire to continuing careers in education.

Consider Anna Nichols. After she got her bachelor's degree from a small Methodist college in Birmingham, Alabama, her parents ex-pected their daughter to be self-supporting. Sizing up the American job market and hungry for attractions beyond antebellum mansions and rib joints, Anna found a job in Székesfehérvár, Hungary, teaching high school English. The work turned out to be "difficult, unrewarding, and often thankless," but when the school year ended Anna wasn't ready for Alabama.

"I'm very interested in marrying someone foreign," she allows. "I love the idea of having bilingual children with a rich cultural back-ground. So when an au pair job fell into my lap, I gladly took it, excited to learn a third language and make new friends." Now Anna is living in Vienna, working for a German family who expects her to do laundry and cook as well as babysit for *drei Kinder*. "Being an au pair makes teaching in Hungary look like heaven."

"What Anna's learned," her mother, Laura Nichols, says, "is that she would definitely prefer *having* a maid to being one—and that she may not want to have a large family." To her mother's relief, Anna is planning to return to the United States for graduate school.

After graduating from Bowdoin College several years ago, Douglas Cuthbertson spent a year teaching English in Sendai, the largest city north of Tokyo (and sadly, now deeply affected by the 2011 earthquake, tsunami, and nuclear plant disaster). "It was much more difficult than I thought it would be," Douglas says. "The language barrier was daunting. No one spoke English and I was functionally illiterate, unable to use ATM machines, read street signs or labels at the grocery store, or ask basic questions. I started learning as much Japanese as possible. The teaching itself was so-so—the school did not know how to make effective use of me other than as a human tape recorder spitting out the proper way to pronounce English words for awful tests the students are required to take. But teaching wasn't the main reason I went to Japan. I came to view my days at school as . . . a fascinating sociological experience in learning about the culture.

"When most Americans go to a foreign country, they think something along the lines of 'It's amazing how similar all people across the world really are in so many ways!' But the longer I spent in Japan, the more I realized the Japanese are radically different from Westerners with thousands of invisible hierarchical, social rules. One of the best parts of the year was when my parents came to visit. I asked my mom at the end of the trip whether she was used to Japan. 'No,' she said. 'It's like being on Mars.'"

After Doug came back, he attended law school, joined a top-flight law firm, and twice on business has visited Japan, where his language

skills have proven valuable. Not every adultescent working abroad returns to the United States as quickly as Doug Cuthbertson, nor does the
work experience end as happily. More typical for expats is seeing one
year abroad melt into another, inertia nourished by the goodies and
glamour of Not-America. Only late in the game do some of these adultescents recognize how derailed you can become spending your twenties abroad.

A mother of a son in his mid-thirties puts it this way: "Jeff has
worked in Germany three times as well as in Argentina. He speaks
perfect German as well as Spanish and French and is good in almost
everything. The first time he went abroad, I was very admiring. But he's
never been able to leverage the experience at home, and it gets harder
to get on track as you get older. You don't want an entry-level job in
your thirties."

An expat adultescent is rarely thinking ten years down the road,
however, when the decision is made to go abroad, nor is it likely to be
a choice made in concert with parents. "Our children don't ask us
things first, they tell us," says Judy Cuthbertson of Hamden, Connecticut, Douglas Cuthbertson's mother. "My husband and I know people
whose kids really discuss things with them, or at least talk about options. Ours say, 'I'm going here. This is what I'm doing.' They don't want
us to talk them out of something.

"I could turn it around and say our kids don't value our opinion or
aren't as close to us as other children, but I don't really believe that.
They know who they are, and in some ways this makes it easier, because if they don't like the result of their decision, they don't blame us.
Also, I see kids—girls, especially—who call their parents to a ridiculous extent, a habit that starts in college and never stops, with mothers
checking in on kids on the hour, with kids calling at night to reassure
their parents that they've arrived home safely. 'Should I get a latte or

not get a latte?' I have friends who say, 'If my daughter phones one more time, I'll shoot her.'" And if it's not actual voice contact, it's a text.

Julia Cuthbertson, Doug's sister and Judy's daughter, wasn't that kind of girl. "When Bush was reelected I had absolutely no desire to stay in the States," chuffs this Middlebury graduate. She'd logged a few semesters in Spanish-speaking countries—Argentina, Ecuador, Peru, and Spain—so it wasn't a stretch to move to Madrid. For almost five years she has taught English while Spain has cast a spell. It's not all about sangria and sun, tapas and siestas. Over-the-counter birth control pills: only 17 euros a month. Zipping off to other European countries for a weekend: 30 euros. Hot days and cool nightlife: priceless.

Judy Cuthbertson didn't blink when Julia left for Spain, since Douglas had established a family expat tradition. Plus, her daughter had already flashed her adventurous soul by starting college a semester late so she could live in Argentina. Nor was Judy surprised when one year in Madrid turned into two and two into three. "It was four that got me."

"Each time I announce that I'm staying another year my mom gets annoyed," Julia says. "I remind her to stop nagging or I'll never come home, then assure her that I'll be back soon, which—finally!—is true. Although I wonder how I'll ever afford the thousand-dollar-a-month rent and the high cost of traveling and the eight-dollar glasses of wine." (Note to Julia: $8 a glass is now a bargain.)

What's motivating Julia's return is, ultimately, work-related: she's applying for a master's in public health. "I've had a hard time rationalizing staying abroad as my age creeps closer to thirty and I'm still teaching disrespectful teenagers. I'm getting frustrated enough that all the drinking wine on *terrazas* is not outweighing my long days. I want to begin a career in a field that I am passionate about. In my case, this is impossible to do in Madrid. Most people here have careers that fit into traditional slots—doctor, lawyer, engineer, teacher, and architect. No one knows what public health is. It's too interdisciplinary! There are really no other opportunities for Americans in Spain besides teaching English or working illegally at a bar or café."

Pining for family life is another draw for her return, Judy suggests. "Julia misses things she didn't miss a few years ago . . . like the idea of her clothes totally smelling like grease from frying potato latkes, sitting around the fireplace with her brothers, or laughing with me as we watch crummy TV." She's also grateful for the evolution of her daughter's assessment of both the United States and Europe. "When Julia got to Spain, I worried that she was so starstruck she saw everything as black and white. I understood her attitudes but felt a little as if she was rejecting us. As Julia's matured, she's developed a balanced view of the world. She doesn't see the United States as the land of milk and honey but recognizes that there are issues in Europe, too."

Julia says she has grown to see the United States as "too focused on work," but that there are positives she misses. Take customer service. "Spanish bureaucracy is slow and complicated, especially annoying when you have to constantly renew residency cards and have forms signed." Another is work ethic, albeit with a caveat: "I have always been bothered that many Americans pride themselves on taking so few days off. What kind of a life is that? Even my own parents have insinuated that the reason I've stayed in Spain is because I like all the time off and the partying." The last is American diversity: "I see a significant portion of the Spanish population as xenophobic and mildly racist, with an older generation that's had a hard time adjusting to the immigration boom that started about fifteen years ago."

Julia's evolution has also been Judy's. "The bottom line is that I now know my daughter will always have a much wider vision of the world than I will ever have. I have friends with kids who live right down the street, but that isn't who Julia is and part of me envies her."

LIVING ON THE MARGINS

"I am definitely one of those people who mythologize Europe," confesses Laura Warrell, a native of Kent, Ohio. In her twenties she married a Frenchman and lived in France for a year. The couple moved together to Boston and New York, where she did the drill of aspiring writers who wish to pay their bills—fact-checking and freelancing. "Then my husband and I divorced. I had that moment when I thought, 'If I'm going to do anything fabulous, this is the chance.'" That meant returning to Europe—"drinking in cafés, writing wonderful books, talking to artists and painters."

She moved to Spain and three years later, Berlin. Outsider status afforded freedom: "When you don't have your family, friends, and culture surrounding you, you're nakedly yourself. You define yourself, which is invigorating, but what I also determined was, yeah, Berlin is where it's at, progressive and exciting, and I'm not German. I wasn't going to be able to find my place there," because to be an expat can mean staying forever isolated. "I have friends who live in Europe, have married Europeans, and speak languages fluently but still don't feel Europe is theirs," Laura observes. "Local cultural references aren't yours, the references that mean something to you mean nothing to the locals, and this goes beyond *Jersey Shore*. There is a certain kind of person who can live abroad forever, someone who doesn't need to feel as connected as I do to a community."

Laura returned to this side of the Atlantic and more than a hole in her résumé found reverse, continuing culture shock. Friends had moved on with their lives and been difficult to replace. "The bigger thing is the feeling that life will never be as interesting as when I was living abroad, that the United States is comparatively boring," she says. "When I hear that people want to live abroad, I say, 'Do it, but don't think it will be easy to come back to normal life in the United States and get a house with a picket fence and a nine-to-five job.'"

"People who travel like I do are either running away from something or running to something," says Carl White. "I was running away. I was very successful but an asshole, a little arrogant. Now I feel I'm running toward something, which is my business. I have a goal."

Born in St. Petersburg, Florida, Carl graduated from Northeastern University and Stanford Law School. After he passed the bar, he practiced law for a large corporate firm in Boston, working on a community outreach project. "My superiors told me the project was going to help the community, but the way I looked at it, the project could hurt it just as much. Pretty quickly I needed a break and asked if I could go to Costa Rica for a few weeks to learn more Spanish." He left and never returned to the job. That was a decade ago, during which Carl has bartended in England, done private security work in New Zealand, taught English to executives and high-ranking government officials in France and Spain, and directed a school in Italy. He's not just learned more Spanish but become fluent in French, Italian, and German.

"When I was growing up, I had a scholarship to go to a private school that was ninety-nine percent white, so as an African American I was used to being on the outside looking in," Carl recalls. "Most Americans have a very difficult time doing what's been easy for me. It's been exciting to be paid to live this life that people do when they're retired or rich and famous. I can't tell you how many times I'd walk around and say, 'Wow.' But obviously, your perspective changes as you get older."

Carl recently turned thirty-five. Four years ago he settled in

Berlin, living in the gentrifying Kreuzberg district, trying to start a business he describes as an upscale Chuck E. Cheese's–styled children's educational center. "German people are intelligent and open-minded, but it's hard to make friends and the country is all about following the rules, organized but inefficient. Trying to start a business has been expensive and frustrating. As long as I'm moving forward, I'll stay. But if I feel I'm getting nowhere, I'll return to the States. I've given myself two years.

"I'm not an asylum seeker. Even though the States is going through a hard time—I hear a lot about people running way from student loans—I still think it's a great place to live." And yet he'd return with trepidation. "I worry that I'll have to go back to school, that my experience won't translate."

Chapter 7

DEAR GOD, THE MESS

Whosever room this is should be ashamed!

—Shel Silverstein

f I were to paint a mural of the wander years, each brushstroke would represent a mildewed towel, a ripe sock, a thong dropped by the side of a bed whose linens hadn't been laundered since . . . whenever. Like the person who dirtied them, yesterday's dishes would be lounging, crusted in hues ranging from the pink of penne with vodka sauce to a burnished marinara red. Wastebaskets? Full. Windex? Empty.

Many column inches have raged elsewhere about how when they cheered on baseball teams, boarded ships, or applauded at Broadway shows, adultescents' grandparents and great-grandparents wore their Sunday best (sweet archaic term). By 1995, when today's adultescents were tots, the tide had turned. *Newsweek* magazine famously ran a cover story, "Have We Become a Nation of Slobs?" Its scolding tone forever shamed many Americans into cleaning up their sartorial act. My husband, for one, started shaving on Saturday morning.

Fast-forward to now. Clothes and grooming aren't the issue. If a guy sports stubble, chances are it's intentional. (Jake Gyllenhaal and Bradley Cooper, I'm talkin' to you.) The first words of most young women I know were "How do I look?" If a thirty-three-year-old wants to wear pajamas to a meeting where she's pitching for VC funding, better her than someone my age.

Comfy casual is also the dress code for those who work in most start-ups, which are often crowded into small spaces that the public doesn't see. In these cases, there's no compelling reason to dress up, as there isn't when you work at home.

An unspoken rule among adultescents is that "if you dress up too much, you run the risk of not being taken seriously," Seattle-based Web-meister Erica Zidel told the *New York Times*. "In entrepreneur culture your look should be laid back. But while corporate dress has become more relaxed, hygiene has not. Dressing 'down' doesn't mean grooming oneself less; it means wearing clothing that expresses who you are. If anything, I think young professionals who 'dress down' wind up looking more put together than those who wear traditional business attire. Comfortable clothing allows people to be more confident."

It's interiors, not exteriors, that cry out for a comment and a squeegee. Offspring of the Tide generation are not only often untidy, they're seemingly unaware and unrepentant about their surround-sound squalor, whether it's in their own abodes or lending an aura of grunge wherever they tread. When adult kids bring their slatternly ways along on a family visit or to roost under boomerang living arrangements, the shit hits the walls, sometimes literally. Across the land, you hear parents wailing, "*How* did I raise such a slob?" as they assess the mess.

"My thirty-year-old son is a successful sculptor in San Francisco, yet so messy that as much as I love him, I'm relieved when he leaves after a visit," says Tricia Patton,* of Mendocino, California, who speaks for many. "I'm upset that I feel this way about my own child, whom I adore. Yet when he stays in our perfectly lovely guest room, he throws the pillows on the floor and never unpacks; brings weeks' worth of dirty clothes and fills the laundry room with piles; makes a complete hodgepodge of the kitchen, eating an entire jar of pâté or tub of hummus at a sitting, then leaving the empty container in the sink. He likes my steam shower, so I tell him, 'Use it, but I don't want to know you've been in there.' There will be wet towels all over the house. He likes to lie on the floor, petting our golden retriever until she sheds. I could go on and on. In his own loft—which I'm afraid to visit—I suspect he cleans when he can't stand it anymore, but whenever he's here it's like this huge wind has come roaring through. In every room you can see where he's been.

"I used to say, 'Please, at least make your bed,' and he'd answer, 'Why?' His work has been shown in major museums, but he still acts like a little kid. I taught him to clean the same way my parents taught me—I sent him to camp!" But while Tricia's homemaking skills may have been outsourced to Camp Make-a-Mess, where she was taught to fold a taut hospital bed corner by someone who actually knew how to make one, perhaps during his summer experience her son was whittling a hash pipe. Chances are today's camp counselors wouldn't know a hospital bed corner if they bumped into one in the woods; if they were asked to teach campers bed-making technique, they would ululate in mass protest.

Tricia is a psychotherapist, and following one of the commandments of her trade, she's learned that she can't change her son—only herself. "Through the years I've slowly stopped being controlling. When my patients complain about this problem, I tell them they should be happy their child wants to come to see them, period. A mess can always be cleaned up." A bad relationship? Sometimes unfixable.

A CONTAINER STORE OF EXPLANATIONS

It's no great mystery to deconstruct the shambles that adultescents turn their surroundings into when they return to the nest. At any age part of the luxury of coming home is clemency, which includes being able to savor cozy creature comforts and lapse into gemütlich habits. That parents may hope that their child has moved beyond these habits toward civility is beside the point.

"My daughter turned twenty-four last week, and so far she has been the prototypical conscientious perfectionist who does everything right—straight A's, runs ten miles a day, writes thank-you notes and mails them on time, is lovely to her parents, is beautiful, popular, and always has a boyfriend who adores her, volunteers at the soup kitchen, and tutors underprivileged children pro bono," says one Denver mother. "Her sole discernible flaw is that her room is a wreck. I think it's the only way in which she can imagine to rebel. I suck it up and try not to explode."

When kids move back home in the last stage of adolescence or beyond, they regress, says Carl Pickhardt, Ph.D., an Austin, Texas, psychologist and author of *Boomerang Kids*. "The first cause of sloppiness is anarchy: young adults feel they should be able to freely operate and don't want to be bound by external rules. The second cause is independence: they want to live on their own terms, and the last is the freedom to express their personal selves."

When adultescents return to the womb, mothers and fathers also regress, Dr. Pickhardt suggests. Sergeant Mom, reporting for duty. Then again, counselors ministering to the acrimony springing from boomerang arrangements stress the importance of the older generation laying down ground rules. Thus, parents are damned if they do and damned if they don't. People I know deal with their adultescents' pigpen ways by closing a door along with their eyes and mouths. They save their true shock and fury for when they see how young adults live on their own, particularly if it's in parent-subsidized housing.

"I helped Jake go through his apartment when he and his fiancée moved to a condo," says Paula Platt* of Kansas City. "The place hadn't been dusted since he moved in four years ago, so it was like a hazardous materials site. Anything I moved set off a cloud of something. At their new place it's a combination of way too much stuff for a small space and the fact that they never put anything away, so there are papers, coats, laundry, clothes, dirty dishes (they wash the ones in the sink, but there are always a lot of strays), books, magazines, plants, food boxes, empty bottles, a litter box that needs cleaning, and recyclables everywhere—and the last time my husband and I were there they announced that they'd cleaned before we arrived.

"My husband refuses to stay there. I can take it overnight. In their defense, my son and his fiancée both work full-time and cleaning comes after volunteering to help people with taxes, tennis, poker, the gym, singing in a choir, and belonging to a book club. I think keeping things in order is a really low priority, not something they object to," she says, trying to understand these curious adultescent folkways. "They seem to be chill about it, though, and have tons of guests and cook all the time, which is better than a sterile apartment with no social life, and they keep track of everything they need. I doubt a bigger space would make much difference. They are considering getting a cleaning service once a month, but there's not much outside help can do about the chaos. The problem goes way beyond clutter."

"There really is more mess today," concedes University of Texas psychology professor Sam Gosling, Ph.D., author of *Snoop: What Your Stuff Says About You.* "It's not just in the parents' imagination." Few adultescents travel lightly. Most are the owners of a prodigious amount of stuff—electronics, sports and cooking equipment, musical instruments, clothing, shoes, books, furniture, wine and spirits, automobiles, and for every third adultescent male, coffin-sized turntables for DJ gigs. I caught myself before I wrote "proud owners" because it would be pride in ownership that generally leads to the maintenance, respect, and order that may go lacking.

One reason there's stuff here, there, and everywhere is—I suspect—because much of it, item by item, costs less than a generation or two ago. This makes it easier to accumulate and, because it's not as expensive, less valued. I'm thinking, definitely, of clothes—as I often am. H&M, Zara, Uniqlo, Club Monaco, Joe Fresh, Topshop, and their assorted fast-fashion ilk cleverly market to young customers (and the boomer who forgets she's not young, which would be me and many of my friends). If these shops had been within easy reach when I was twenty-five, my wardrobe would have been five times as large; if IKEA and Target—the hipster Kmarts—had also been available, my apartment would have looked like the Collyer mansion, a reference lost on adultescents. Even if the pleasures of drive-by shopping don't seduce you, eBay, Craigslist, Freecycle, Groupon, Amazon, Etsy, and the like enable cyber-consumers to fill every nook and hook, no matter how modest a budget. The more stuff, obviously, the greater the grunge potential.

We can blame cheap stuff—and China, if we must—but parents of adultescents also need to take the rap for at least some of the mess they excoriate. Anyone American and twenty-two to thirty-five has grown up in a throwaway society. Parents and child alike have been trained to covet what's new and to toss what's broken instead of repairing it, to value time and convenience over saving money, all leading us to a buy, baby, buy mentality. To not own a smartphone is, for example, border-line embarrassing, an expression of being a Luddite rather than conservative consumerism. And while many boomer women were forced to suffer through home economics, most toss clothes that need to be mended rather than take out their sewing kit, if they own one.

In addition, middle-class parents have typically exempted their kids from—and here I will lip-synch my mom's litany—making their beds, loading and unloading the dishwasher, cutting the grass, taking out the garbage, setting the table, raking the leaves, shoveling the snow, and dusting and vacuuming the home. Families have been so manically focused on boldfaced college application line items and the lessons, tutoring, teams, and studying that lead to these accomplishments that basic chores fall into the crowded gutter. (Does this fuss stem from best-in-show parenting hoops that my parents never heard of or does it emanate from deep fears that said children could possibly slip into a lower class stratum? I wonder.) Extracurriculars and good grades have been perceived to be more valuable than facility with everyday homemaking and maintenance. Rushed as we always are, we've found it easier to take care of household tasks ourselves—if we take care of them at all—than to devote time to patiently explaining to kids how to separate lights from darks and wash a wood floor. That is, if we even know how to do these things. In affluent homes, which undoubtedly breed the most wandering adultescents, there is often a housekeeper, a gardener, and other outsourced employees to keep the mess in check. No big surprise that most young adults can conjugate Spanish better than they can unclog a sink or rake a lawn.

"There is a line between supporting your children and enabling them," says Christine Hassler, life coach and author of *20 Something Manifesto: Quarter-Lifers Speak Out About Who They Are, What They Want, and How to Get It.* "Intrusive and often controlling child rearing has caused many twentysomethings to be unequipped for life outside of the nest, which is why so many never leave or move back home after college. It's the children of such cockpit parents who most often fit the stereotypes of entitlement, with a consistent need for validation, failure to self-start, mediocre work ethic, and a general lack of soft skills—the repertoire you can't bullet-point on a résumé. Just like many in this generation who haven't been taught to listen or problem-solve—because these children have been managed for so much of their lives they've never had to develop these skills—they don't know how to clean a house or mow a lawn. No one can teach you how to solve a problem unless you have a problem to solve.

"I remember being taught to do laundry at eight," reminisces Christine, who is thirty-five. "That's pretty unusual now. One of my clients told me that when her car stalled on the freeway, she pulled over to the side, hysterical, called her father for help, and waited until Dad arrived, never realizing she could have phoned AAA, a service she didn't know she had."

The downward slope toward American grubbiness began decades ago, when boomer moms threw in their unwashed towels along with the toilet brushes in favor of Rolodexes and matchy-matchy power suits accessorized with ribbon ties. In the 1970s, I remember feverish feminist diatribes about distribution of housework, with rants pointing out that women had higher standards than men and therefore wound up in charge. But my sense is that women have dropped their standards, along with yesterday's undies—on the rug, not in the hamper—and men haven't picked up the slack. Not one American woman I personally know under the age of seventy has done spring-cleaning, ever. With women on the paid-job circuit, straightening and sanitizing haven't risen to the top of anyone's list, and the collective working women's kvetch continues to be that their husbands, those

witless chuckleheads, wouldn't know Comet from Corona. In this kind
of environment, kids weren't likely to be forced to suffer through many
teachable housekeeping moments. (Caveat: in this debate my own
hubby gets a pass. Believe you me, you do not want to be in an iron-off
with this guy. What's more, my kids' YMCA camp had a summer-long
construction program, so if you see a brand-new lean-to in Brooklyn
or Santa Monica, please give them credit.)

HAVE WOMEN MOVED INTO ANIMAL HOUSE?

"Open your fridge . . ." blogs Kirin McCrory, twenty-three, a recent Boston transplant to New York City and self-declared actor/playwright/
general badass and mild packrat. "Chinese take-out from two weeks
ago: not edible. Mustard: edible. Cheese: edible? It looks okay. You spot
a heel of bread that's wrapped up in plastic. You'll risk it. Take your
open-faced cheese and mustard sandwich back to your room as you
reassure yourself that messes, when you're living by your lonesome,
really just mean you're doing better things with your time than keeping your kitchen clean."

Is the slovenly apartment now the dusty benchmark that knows
no gender distinction, young women equal in grunge to men? Discuss.

"Of course there are individual differences in cleanliness, with
some people who are super neat and some not, but in general, men and
boys are messier," Dr. Sam Gosling observes. And no less an authority
than the American Cleaning Institute, which tried vigorously to put a
positive spin on its recent findings about the habits of young adults, also
dumped on men, deemed them "highly motivated to clean only when
their home starts to smell, are told to clean or someone comments about
their home's lack of cleanliness." My guess? That survey runner was a
mother.

There are casual observers who agree. "Men and women are both messy but different," muses a real estate agent in a college town near Toronto who has resold dozens of homes inhabited by local college students. "Women tend to leave clothes everywhere and litter the bathrooms with makeup and products," Robert J. Morrow says. "It's atrocious. But the guys have the real heads-up on absolute filth. They will leave food out on the counters and not care. I've literally seen rats going after pizza boxes seventeen in a stack. Our city is trying to close some of these student group houses because kids are getting sick."

"My twenty-two-year-old grandson Robert* has to be one of the biggest slobs on the planet," carps Teresa Brown of Las Vegas. "If he didn't have people picking up after him, you wouldn't be able to walk into a house he lived in, and when he takes off his shoes, have plenty of Glade room spray. When he eats, he leaves a mess, and the only time he's not making messes is when he's asleep. I have serious doubts if he will ever have to clean up after himself. Everyone is enabling this kid to be a slob and . . . he loves it."

"Am I a slob?" asks Robert, the grandson in the dust-speckled spotlight, a former security guard now living with his older brother while he job-hunts in Pocatello, Idaho. "That's a valid criticism." He wears it with honor. "I've taught my girlfriend laziness, but she's only half as bad as I am. We stayed together for six months in an RV without running water, and even though it was a mess, it was organized. I always knew where everything was.

"When I lived with a bunch of guys, there was junk everywhere, though. Then we got bedbugs and couldn't get rid of them. The place was rancid when we left. Currently, I don't have to worry about being a slob, though, because my sister-in-law's sister is OCD and cleans up after all of us. She thinks nobody does it to her standards."

Chapter 8

IT'S ONLY MONEY

Children are rarely in the position to lend one a truly interesting sum of money.

—Fran Lebowitz

Kids: they're the gift that keeps on taking. About 59 percect of parents provide or recently provided financial assistance to children aged eighteen to thirty-nine who weren't students, concluded a May 2011 survey of nearly 1,100 people by the National Endowment for Financial Education. We might have paid for our child's undergraduate college tuition—in whole or part—and possibly, further education. ("You call it grad school; I call it raising the debt ceiling": the caption under a Danny Shanahan cartoon I recently stumbled on illustrating a father talking to a son.) To celebrate their graduation or a milestone birthday, our congratulations arrived in the form of a check, a new couch, a car, or even a down payment on a condo.

Meanwhile, perhaps we're also bankrolling our parents, while having moonstruck moments imagining retirement. This leads a parent to wonder: When should economic stimulus for adultescents stop, as adultescents spend their twenties and thirties with the underlying assumption on both their part and their parents' that financial help will continue, putting the l-o-n-g in "long-term subsidies"?

Boomer parents realize that where the economy is concerned, we got a pretty fair shake. Even if we were functionally illiterate about finances, our lives were launched by a Wall Street headwind that created jobs and fattened stock portfolios and 401(k)s. It was enough to delude some of us into thinking we were shrewd about money, a commodity we expected would flow all our lives, a mighty Mississippi of reliability.

Frequently, the jauntiness our dumb luck wrought has filtered down to some of our children's spending habits. Do people under the age of thirty-five even realize they can brew coffee at home? That all of America doesn't spend $40 and up per person when they go out to eat several times per week? Attending faraway bachelor/bachelorette parties and destination weddings is, as a friend put it, "our kid's Woodstock," and we can't help but notice that adultescents keep JetBlue aloft visiting faraway loves every other weekend while acquiring luxury handbags *and* shiny toys. According to the Consumer Electronics Association, the twenty-five–to–thirty-four age group leads the country in acquisition of electronics, with average yearly spending at $1,099 per person, a number that spikes after college graduation.

While they're blaming themselves for—but just as often, taking secret pride in—their offspring's champagne taste, it can make a mother or father long for revisionist parenting. In the time sandwiched between the college class in the Science of Superheroes and volunteering at a Thai elephant camp, why didn't we indoctrinate our kids with a Draconian grounding in budgeting, interest rates, tax prep, all the basic drudgery, plus a tutorial in restraint?

But hey—rewind! Who are *we*, a generation of money twits, to talk? It was Grandma and Grandpa Bean Counter who own bragging rights on conserving a dollar. "Baby boomers embrace debt much more readily than people my age," harrumphs Lesley Hoinig, a bankruptcy attorney in his thirties from Mount Pleasant, Michigan. "We believe the boomers are at fault for the current financial mess. The concept of having a paid-for house is totally lost on the average boomer."

No surprise, then, given the flakiness of their role models, to learn that Americans aged twenty-five to thirty-four make up 22.7 percent of all bankruptcies, despite being only 14 percent of the population. This also helps explain why a recent American Express survey reveals that money is the overarching concern for a majority of people in their twenties, eight in ten of whom describe their current financial situation as "stressful."

When Salon.com published an essay titled "Hipsters on Food Stamps" (*They're young, they're broke, and they pay for organic salmon with government subsidies. Got a problem with that?*), the blogosphere erupted with ire. Who are these cool upstarts to be bilking the government? Poor people, that's who.

WHERE MONEY ATTITUDES GET MUDDY

The big spending that dwindles down to no spending typically starts with college loans. Two out of three students who graduate owe money for their education, according to The Project on Student Debt. The average amount that graduates need to repay is more than $27,000. Americans now owe more on their student loans than they do on their credit cards—according to FinAid.org, which estimates that America's student loan debt is growing at a rate of $2,853.88 per second. At this pace it will soon surpass $1 trillion. And there is no sign of the pace letting up, since college costs are rising a lot faster than family incomes, grants, and scholarships. The cost of a college education is increasing two to three times the overall rate of inflation, according to the U.S. Bureau of Labor Statistics, even rising faster than the cost of medical care.

"A lot of people will still be paying off their student loans when it's time for their kids to go to college," reports Mark Kantrowitz, FinAid .org's publisher. Since buying a house or starting a family or a business can become an unreachable goal if you're saddled with debt, no wonder that defaulting on student loan repayment has crept into the double digits. It's reported that Barack Obama paid off his student loans shortly before he became president at forty-seven, thanks to two best-selling memoirs.

Here's another loan repayment strategy: young women seeking sugar daddies. "Over the past few years, the number of college students using our site has exploded," Brandon Wade, the forty-one-year-old founder of SeekingArrangement.com told *Huffington Post*. Type combos such as "tuition," "debt," and "money for school" into a search engine and this site will pop up along with others where rich, older men troll for paid companions. Of Wade's site's approximately eight hundred thousand members, he estimates that 35 percent are student sugar babies, easily identified by .edu e-mail addresses.

Since few students can write a best seller or wish to avail themselves of what appears to be a digital bordello, plenty of adultescents have little choice but to seek bailouts from the Bank of Mom and Dad. A recent survey by the brokerage firm of Charles Schwab found that 51 percent of parents provide some level of financial support for children aged twenty-three to twenty-eight. According to figures from the

University of Michigan, financial support to children of that same age group averages an astonishing 10 percent of the parents' income. In the mid-twentieth century, most parents could expect their kids to be economically stable—with their own families and children—by the time they were, say, twenty-six. But fifty years later, 50 percent of people in their twenties are still supported by their parents, claims data from the Youth Development Study, which followed a group of St. Paul, Minnesota, public school students from ninth grade until they were thirty-two.

Fiscal outpatient care to adultescents is one of those sacred, opaque, and indelicate subjects that parents are likely to discuss even less openly and honestly than secret racism or the frequency of marital blow jobs. To admit that your adult child is still being subsidized can send a public message encoded with *My kid's a slacker and a moocher.* This then calls to mind *What does that make me?* even if the reason for the parent-to-child money infusion is because (a) Mom and Dad are exceedingly generous; (b) they expect their child to inherit some of their money so they feel he may as well have it now, when he needs it; (c) the child's been sacked through no fault of his own; or (d) all of the above. Complicating the picture is the reality that with the nexus of heavy student loans to repay and many adultescents either unemployed or stuck in unpaid internships, the chances for them to even have a 401(k) of their own to contribute to are negligible. Even if an adultescent's company offers the opportunity to contribute to a 401(k), the young employee might make so little that he or she can't afford the sacrifice. The median starting salary for students graduating from four-year colleges in 2009 and 2010 was $27,000, down from $30,000 for those who entered the workforce in 2006 to 2008, according to a study released by Rutgers University John J. Heldrich Center for Workforce Development.

A Forbes survey found that 59 percent of parents are offering financial support to adultescents no longer in school. Thirty-seven percent said they have struggled and don't want their children to struggle, too. Two-thirds of the adultescents surveyed said the financial pressures faced by their generation are tougher than those faced by previous generations, but only a third of parents agree. Cash infusions help offset rent, daily living expenses, transportation, insurance, and medical bills, although it's not a one-way street because, according to the study, adultescents living at home may kick in for groceries, utilities, gas for the family car, and rent or mortgage, and offer help in cooking, cleaning, or child care for younger siblings. A recent study by TD Ameritrade found that 25 percent of Gen Y reports their parents paying for cell phone bills, insurance. and car expenses.

Cynics may suggest that an inverse relationship exists between subsidizing adultescents and denying the support. Privileged parents—people with money to give and high expectations—may be likely to see their adult children as trophies who will always keep a safe lead in the escalation dominance that begins with tutors, SAT and ACT cram courses, and cross-country campus visits and continues when students get into and graduate from top colleges. It can freak out these parents to even consider the possibility that after their six-figure investments, kids' accomplishments may never yield bragging rights.

On this score—a word I pick carefully—I agree with Miriam Arond, editor in chief of *Child* magazine from 2000 to 2007, when many of today's adultescents were in middle school and high school and a mother of two daughters in their twenties. "It's very easy to be judgmental about what other parents do for their children," she asserts. "The fact is, kids who are well educated should have the world at their fingertips, but it's come crashing down on them. They also have a sense that the whole financial establishment is at risk. In their lifetime they've known only ATMs, where money comes out of nowhere, and have witnessed scandals like Enron and Madoff. They're focusing more on meaning in their lives than money, which they see you can have one day and not the next. Kids in their twenties and early thirties are more idealistic than some of us ever were. My daughter Elizabeth went to Ghana last summer to teach in a school through Cross-Cultural Solutions. When I was her age, I vacationed at Club Med. But this generation also wants instant gratification and can't make a plan without ninety-five texts.

"This puts parents of adult children in a challenging position, not that different from when they were raising toddlers," Arond says. "Kids fall as they learn to walk. They need a little pain to move on to the next stage. You want to offer some security, but not so much cushiness that a child doesn't spread her wings and fly. Parents get nervous when a child nears thirty and they're still supporting them.

"Baby boomers are friends with their kids, who don't find it as uncomfortable to be at home as people might think," Arond adds, speaking partly from personal experience: one of her daughters lived with her and her husband in their Scarsdale, New York, home for several years after college. "Parents have become conflicted, asking, 'How do you differentiate spoiling from not spoiling?' 'How do you help kids without quashing their motivation to succeed?' Your goal is not to overprovide and to remember that money represents self-esteem, which the child who doesn't support himself has less of. Money also represents nurturance, but if giving it makes parents feel they have the right to ask intrusive questions, that causes problems."

When my oldest son became a teenager, I couldn't make the rules up fast enough. During grade school my mothering had idled on cruise control, but now Jed, my husband, and I were schussing down a black-diamond trail with moguls: Curfew? Allowance? Earring or no earring? My brain hurt from all the decisions I needed to make and the belles lettres of parenting was of little help. Nowhere could I find advice on, let's say, how to handle a fourteen-year-old boy going by subway, alone and against his parents' wishes, to a dodgy part of town to get a buzz cut with the Rolling Stones logo shaved into the back of his head right before his younger brother's fourth-grade play, attended by a sea of smug, stuffy younger parents of sweet nine-year-olds who still listened to them. The shame. Rule making and boundary setting at adultescence is no different. Parents parse each new phase and schuss accordingly. Emotion as much as logic generally determines generosity.

After 9/11 many American families, for example, enrolled in a cell phone family plan. I know a doctor already in the second year of residency who's still on such a plan, paid for by his parents, who are in no rush to cut him off. As the physicians's mother told me, "It makes me feel connected to my son to pick up this tab."

Pay or not pay—how does a parent decide? "When your kid tries to be frugal and has a job that pays only $35,000 but needs a new suit to interview for other jobs, you buy that suit," says New York City mother Linda Bernstein, who has two twentysomething children who have recently graduated from law school and have yet to find jobs. "But financing your kid's apartment and living expenses while he hangs out and maybe writes poetry, that strikes me as indulgent."

Do my husband and I help our son repay his law school loan? We do, and I wish the monthly sum were four figures, not three. Were we able to offer him and his brother down payments for a home or condo, the checks would be direct-deposited today. I hope I have the opportunity to see if such largesse ruins my kids' character.

"My husband and I pay for visits to us and any other close relative," explains Betsy Teutsch of Philadelphia, whose blog *Money Changes*

Things ruminates on financial matters. Betsy has reasoned through continuing to support her twentysomething son and daughter. "We see it as an investment in family connection, since we live in three separate cities. My kids still have credit cards where we pay the bill if they use them for those travel costs. For our thirty-fifth anniversary, we took our children to Guatemala. They each added days of their own onto it at their own expense. When our son wanted to buy a condo, we lent him money for the purchase, essentially as a second mortgage at below-market rates. We have a written agreement. My in-laws did that for us and we liked the clarity."

"Four of my daughter's girlfriends have parents who pay their rent," says the Chicago mother of a daughter, twenty-five. "She almost thinks that's normal." What *has* become normal is a country ballad story line like that of Jim Snitker. A retired army officer with a second career as a business consultant in Reston, Virginia, Jim contributes more than $20,000 a year toward supporting thirty-year-old Alena, "a great mom and daughter who just had some bad breaks." Alena used to be a graphic designer for a software company in Greensboro, South Carolina. Her husband had a position with the BMW manufacturing plant in nearby Spartanburg. During the same week both jobs vanished.

"I became their only stop before foreclosure, eviction, and hunger," Jim recounts. "Alena's car died about that time and wasn't worth the money to fix, so I bought her a Ford Escape in addition to contributing several hundred dollars per month toward support for her and her family"—which included two grandsons. "Within a few months, the wheels came off the marriage and Alena filed for divorce. She met a new boyfriend and got pregnant . . . not ideal, but such is life.

"It's been impossible in western South Carolina for Alena to find a job in her field that will pay enough to offset gas to work and child care, so she hasn't worked now for years," Jim continues. "I love my daughter, although I'm not pleased with all of her choices. But I've learned that at some point you must reach past your kids to stabilize and assist the life of the next generation—in this case, my grandsons. I bought a house in a short sale, moved them into it, and pay the mortgage. I've also learned not to give cash in any large quantity."

RETIREMENT? NOT SO FAST

Situations like Jim Snitker's have handicapped baby boomers' long-term financial plans whether they have a little money or a lot, a national problem that financial experts across the country bemoan. In Knoxville, Tennessee, Trae Wieniewitz, thirty-three, is a financial adviser whose clients are largely middle-class boomers. "A lot of folks don't have priorities in the proper order," he says. "Most kids don't realize that by having Mom and Dad give them five thousand bucks every once in a while, that may mean their parents won't ever be able to retire. I have to tell parents not to neglect their own savings by giving kids too much."

Kids returning to the nest or being subsidized elsewhere can become a financial burden that can seriously derail parental retirement plans and jeopardize their financial future at a time when they need to be stashing cash at an accelerated pace, especially since many boomers are helping to support *both* their own parents and adultescents. "Nearly half of early baby boomers are considered to be at risk of not having sufficient resources to cover basic expenditures and non-insured health care costs in retirement," Stephen Blakely, a spokesperson for the Employee Benefit Research Institute, reported in a recent AARP bulletin. While the number one problem is unforeseen health problems, another is needy children. "Financial advisers and CPAs say boomers must ... stop spending excessively on their children," AARP warns.

Even parents somewhat insulated by affluence from Wall Street's random acts of lunacy feel apprehensive. Almost 31 percent of Americans are supporting older and younger family members at the same time, reports a Merrill Lynch Wealth Management survey of a thousand people with investable assets of $250,000 or more. To make this happen, 45 percent of these boomers say they have made lifestyle sacrifices. A quarter of these people sandwiched between elder care and child care responsibilities have stopped saving for retirement to take care of more immediate financial needs.

"In the last five years, I've seen an increasingly worried population," says Eric L. Abramson, a financial adviser in Paramus, New Jersey, who works with high-net-worth individuals. Clients considering estate planning and wealth transfer have started to handle their money in a different fashion. "Based on the show in front of them, the two big questions parents ask are, if they see their children moving in a problem direction, will they be able to buy the kids out of a jam without detriment to their own financial standing or retirement and will their kids, who they see as a quick-hit, drive-through generation, blow money they inherit?"

Parents raising such questions go beyond the tiny percent with mega-millions. "We're having these conversations with people worth one to three million dollars, who see their kids have a what's-in-it-for-me-today? attitude influenced by peer pressure and a false sense of complacency, not thinking about long-term stability and comfort," Abramson says. "Absolutely more parents are rethinking estate plans for reasons that have nothing to do with taxes."

Just a few years ago, when a child received a trust, it was paid out in thirds, typically at twenty-five, thirty, and thirty-five, he explains.

Now thirty-five, forty, and forty-five are the norm—or perpetuity, with parents instituting "dynasty" trusts designed to give members of the lucky sperm club access to income but never the lump sum. The high rate of divorce is a contributing factor. Statistics currently show that about half of all marriages in the United States don't last, and the younger the bride and groom, the higher the rate of divorce. "Parents don't want to give their kids money and see half of it go through the door when a marriage breaks up," Abramson says.

"COSTCO IS A MONEY PIT"

How adultescents look at their own finances is complicated. Most would be only too happy to make generous contributions to a 401(k) plan, but they don't have that luxury because they are unemployed, in an unpaid internship, or working sans benefits in today's freelance economy. Some are sufficiently spooked by their parents' financial mistakes that they have cloned Alex P. Keaton, the 1980s TV sitcom character from *Family Ties* whom boomers guffawed at while their kids were playing with Smurfs. Others are simply burned by the error of their own feckless credit card abuse. On average, Americans aged twenty-three to twenty-eight carry more than $14,000 in debt (excluding home mortgages), a Charles Schwab study found, and only one-third of those with credit cards pay off the entire balance every month. Nearly 10 percent make payments only when they can.

Meet Matthew Newton, twenty-two, of Olympia, Washington, Dutch uncle to his own father, who had to borrow $600 from twelve-year-old Matt to pay for car repairs. "My parents endured most of their married lives buried in debt with an overpriced mortgage on a humble, aging house in southern California," Matt says. He is trying to teach his dad how to manage a six-figure inheritance from Matt's grandfather.

"It's not just about keeping the money, but ensuring that my dad will be able to retire at some point. Throughout my parents' married life, they were acclimated to using a lot of credit cards. My mother encouraged me to save, though. I've had a bank account since I was ten, and every time I made a deposit she would match it. Now I realize she was trying to teach me what she wished she and my father had done."

"Most of my friends are wanderers, spending their twenties in Peru, painting or exploring advanced degrees in the humanities," says Megan,* twenty-three, of Haverford, Pennsylvania. "They're overreacting to the lives of their parents, who had a checklist for everything. By twenty-five they had the job or the degree to get the job, the marriage, and maybe the first kid. They pursued moneymaking careers and saw their marriages fall apart."

As the original jobs and marriages of boomers have imploded, they've served as how-not-to lessons for adultescents. "It took about twenty years for my own parents' marriage to fall apart," Megan says. "My mother graduated from college with a degree in dietetics, then realized she wanted to run a nonprofit. While I was in college she went to grad school and got an MBA." This is why Megan wants to take it slow. "Maybe I'll marry my boyfriend, maybe I won't. I see my twenties as a time to figure out how adult-me will fit into the world. I don't care if it takes until I'm thirty-five to buy a house and have kids, because I've unplugged my internal clock. If I need to, I'll adopt kids. Maybe I'll stay in my job as a recruiter in the technology field or maybe after a year I'll quit and pursue a Ph.D. in philosophy. My goals are long-term, so there's no push to save a ton of money." Not that Megan can afford to splurge. "If you added all my student loans together, you could buy a really nice house," she says. Her biggest recent purchase has been a TV, $400 reduced from $600. "I was really anxious about it before I pushed the button."

"I've come around from thinking credit cards were free money," says Laurel Mills, a thirty-one-year-old home owner in Birmingham, Alabama, who has paid down almost $10,000 in debt over the last year. "At twenty-seven my banker told me my seventy-five hundred dollars in debt was low—usually people my age had two to three times that." Laurel was granted a mortgage on a house. Not long afterward, she lost her position on a local magazine, leaving her with no savings. Since then, she has not had a steady job.

"It had never occurred to me that a time might come when there wouldn't *be* another job," Laurel admits. "I have a master's in English. I never thought I'd run out of money and not have a new place to get it." Through patching together freelance assignments Laurel has gotten out of hock and accumulated about $2,000 in savings. No longer is she the go-to girlfriend with the bulging closet to raid, always ready for a getaway weekend. "When my friends and I were in our twenties, we'd joke about how we lived beyond our means. Now the only people I know who are extravagant are investment bankers, not people with liberal arts degrees. I haven't started saving tinfoil yet, but I have to hold on to my money, because it *will* run out."

"I'm typical of the DIY [do it yourself] attitude you see a lot these days in Gen X and Y," says Anthony LaVia, thirty-three, a San Francisco real estate appraiser and broker who's also started a restaurant, bars, nightclubs, and a brewery. Ant is a graduate of the University of California at Berkeley. His father, Tom LaVia, is a project manager with a national construction firm; his mother, Cynthia, went from a clerk's desk at Ralph's, a California supermarket chain, to being the company's director of transportation. Neither parent has a college diploma. Both earn more than $100,000.

"These success stories aren't possible for my generation," Ant says. Nor do many adultescents cop his parents' attitude, which he interprets as, "As long as you work hard everything will be okay." "It's pretty obvious to us that even fancy graduate degrees guarantee nothing except fat student-loan payments. A corporate job means nothing." He points to his wife, Marisol Gonzalez. She worked for several years for the online shopping division of a major French fashion house. When sales dwindled, the firm folded. Marisol received no severance.

"I sensed that a slowdown in real estate was only going to get worse," Ant says, "and it looked like there was no real option except to wait out the storm, so Marisol and I decided to hop on a jet and see the world for five months. To my parents the idea of leaving was completely crazy, but we spent only about twenty-five hundred dollars a month for the trip, while staying in San Francisco would cost at least that much—eating and drinking gets pricey here. Marisol ditched her apartment." (The two hadn't yet lived together at that time.) "I rented out mine. We came out ahead, not to mention getting an around-the-world trip under our belts. Real estate picked up about a month after we came home and 2010 was a boom year," he continues. "Now it's back to bust. Marisol is tending bar while she continues to look for a better job. It's been impossible with all the unemployment around here.

"Our generation realizes the level of opportunity for financial success that our parents had is no longer available," Ant says. "Where does that leave us? To start our own businesses. We understand we can't rely on anyone but ourselves. We have a ton of friends doing craft-type businesses focusing on decor, clothing, housewares, and artisanal foods."

"Since the dawn of the Great Recession, more Americans have started businesses (565,000 of them a month in 2010) than at any period in the last decade and a half, according to the Kauffman Foundation, which tracks statistics on entrepreneurship in the United States," the *New York Times* recently reported. "The lures are obvious: freedom, fulfillment. The highs can be high. But career switchers have found that going solo comes with its own pitfalls: a steep learning curve, no security, physical exhaustion and emotional meltdowns. The dream job is a 'job' as much as it is a 'dream.'"

The way Ant and his friends earn money isn't the only difference between his generation and their parents'. What they spend on differs as well. "My parents take frequent vacations and buy the newest cars and junk. This is a typical boomer mentality that, to me, seems frivolous. When my parents visit, I think it's ludicrous that they'll spend a hundred dollars to buy us dinner at a restaurant like a California Pizza Kitchen, exactly like what they've got at home. Why not spend that money on something unique? For my wife and me and our friends, life is all about being scrappy and inventive. We buy only things that last— a memorable vacation in an exotic place instead of a routine trip to Vegas or Maui like my parents take—and shun the disposable mentality of the boomers. You'll find almost no single-use or disposable goods in our house. If my parents took up a new sport like cycling, they'd buy brand-new bikes and a full set of cycling clothes and gear. I do three-hour bike rides in a pair of 501 jeans and a T-shirt. To us Costco is mostly a money pit. What's the use of getting such a great deal on a giant box of Goldfish crackers if they go stale before you eat them all?"

After talking to Ant, I sheepishly went to my refrigerator to examine the monster hunk of cheddar that I'd been enticed by at Costco two months earlier. Moldy.

Adultescent-run blogs and Web sites like *The Baby Billionaire* ("a twenty-two-year-old who has been investing for over a decade"), *Manly Money,* and *Carrie Pink* evangelize on the folly of falling into debt and learning how to reinvent yourself as a cunning money manager.

"From my parents' perspective it looks like I'm not doing a lot, because they can almost always reach me at home," says Marc Aarons of Atlanta, twenty-five, whose Web site generated enough income after twenty-two months to cover his monthly bills. "I've opted out of the morning commute while spending as little as four hours a week managing my business. For my parents—a physician and a bioethicist from Jamaica, where my mother works in the tourism industry—time is exchanged for money. I have a severe problem with this. The second you stop showing up you stop getting paid. I got a Web site up and running while procuring a master's of science that I have yet to use in a professional setting."

For Marc, living off a Web site was Plan B. He funded both an undergraduate and a graduate degree in environmental science through scholarships to Florida A&M in Tallahassee. After graduation he couldn't find work in his field. "My dad always told me he wanted me to be better than himself. In light of not being able to get a job, I asked myself, How can I do that? The one thing no one in my family has done is master money." Hence, ManlyMoney.com, which has been featured in the *Wall Street Journal*'s MarketWatch column. Its motto is "Find Your Niche, Quit Your Job, Love Your Life" and features articles researched and written by Marc such as "Why I Turned Down $120,000 for $30,000."

Carrie Pink's* day job is with Columbia University's School of Business, where she got a master's degree. But in her spare time she's "all over the topic of financial literacy," for which she says there is a strong need in the African-American community. Carrie, thirty, presents herself as an object lesson. "When I was in college, I had a trust fund from my grandparents. I would buy an entire new outfit every week, convinced that this is what you do when you have money. I felt somehow that this money would replenish itself. But I ran out, had to switch from a private to a public school and take loans to go to graduate school...which I'm still paying off." Carrie runs pro bono money-management seminars and posts blogs on her Web site with a frou-frou look that belies its stern message:

> Our generation is much more extravagant than our parents' because instant gratification is built into our psyches. We are way more tolerant of debt because we assume this is the only way to get by. Essentially, we are all living above our means, spending more money than we make. Credit allows us to do that.
>
> Shopping is viewed as a social event attached to a sense of entitlement: you can and you should have any and everything you want because you deserve it and here, take this credit card, buy it now, take it home, enjoy it, and just pay us later! In my parents' day, credit wasn't as accessible. If you wanted something you had to either pay for it right away or put it on layaway. You had to walk by the store weekly and look at the item from the window. You valued the item because you literally had to work to get it. It took weeks and sometimes months before you finished paying something off and could take it home.
>
> We don't value the items we buy because we consider them highly disposable. "I need a twenty-five-hundred-dollar Chanel purse. My life won't be complete without it and all of my friends have one!" But in a few months, the Chanel trend is out and we now need only Gucci bags. Our generation doesn't know the difference between needs and wants because to us everything is a need!

A recent national Ohio State University survey conducted on behalf of the U.S Bureau of Labor Statistics found that instead of feeling stressed by money they owe, many adultescents feel empowered by credit card and education debts. Researchers found that the more credit card and college loan debt held by adults aged eighteen to twenty-seven, the higher their self-esteem and the more they felt like they were in control of their lives. The effect was strongest among those in the lowest economic class, though the oldest people studied—twenty-eight to thirty-four—showed higher stress. "By twenty-eight they may be realizing that they overestimated how much money they were going to earn in their jobs," reports Rachel Dwyer, lead author of the study and assistant professor of sociology at Ohio State. "When they took out the loans, they may have thought they would pay off their debts easily, and it is turning out that it is not as they had hoped."

"Do not end up like me," warns the Debt Princess, a.k.a. Jessica Streit of Middletown, Ohio, thirty-five. "There is a pit in my stomach right now that I won't be able to shake for weeks," she posts. "In the next twenty-four hours I am going to have nearly $250 deducted from my checking account and it currently holds $135. I can only sit here and watch my account dip into the negative. I have nothing more to sell. I have nothing in reserves anywhere, save for $25 in my emergency fund. I guess it's time to withdraw that and close that account. People, this is a horrible feeling. Maybe you've felt it once or twice in your lifetime. Me? I feel it every few months. Please do not end up like me. If you are spending on your credit cards more than you can pay off in a month, you need to stop. This economy is not great. People who once felt secure in their jobs are being laid off. And finding new work is not easy, this I know from personal experience. Please use me as an example of What Not to Do.

"I didn't go on trips or have electronics," Jessica adds. "I just bought a lot of stuff and paid the minimum on my cards. The worst it got was when I knew I was filing for bankruptcy and I still charged up my credit cards. I blamed the credit card companies for giving me credit when clearly I didn't need it."

Chapter 9

ONE FOR THE ROAD

Friends don't let friends drink Light Beer.

—Anonymous

I f you open my freezer, you will find a pig. This is not just any pig. It is the juicy remains of the late, lamented J.P., raised in the bucolic countryside by a well-educated young farmer and once owned by my son Jed and a group of his closest foodie friends. Last winter, when J.P. reached the tender age of ten months and became just slightly more svelte than a Smart Car, the gang gathered on a blustery morning and this little piggy went to slaughter, with the group dividing his tastiest assets. In advance of this event, Jed and his girlfriend, Anne, prepped by taking a butchering class in the Williamsburg area of Brooklyn, a date as popular as attending an Arcade Fire concert.

For a generation raised on reruns of *The French Chef*, a quintessential part of the journey for many in their twenties and thirties is focusing on food and drink: sniffing out restaurants that elevate eating, scouting for local organic resources leading to complicated cookery, and, not least, quaffing cocktails last popular when their grandparents were courting.

I knew the culinary grammar of our family had been forever modified the day my son Rory returned from applying for a summer job as a waiter to augment his covetable internship for Martin Scorsese, which paid zip. The restaurant was the kind of poisson palace that features twenty-three varieties of oysters and crows about its crabmeat hash. His interview required a written test that I would have surely failed: identify the correct temperature and timing for cooking mahi-mahi; recommend a wine to accompany haddock tart; identify the key ingredient in bouillabaisse. . . . What surprised me most was that Rory, whose gustatory pleasure I was certain had peaked at Kraft mac and cheese, passed the test and got the job. His secret weapon: The Food Network, which I noticed that he and his older brother were as likely to watch as football, so that before you can say "pea-size pieces," many male adultescents have already worked five tablespoons of butter into homemade dough. Boola boola, Iron Chef.

I regret that when my sons were in college I failed to start manufacturing trading cards with the lifetime braising averages of action heroes Mario Batali, Mark Bittman, Alton Brown, Tom Colicchio, Tyler Florence, Bobby Flay, Emeril Lagasse, and Jamie Oliver. I curse the sexist slant to this list, but these white-aproned hunks rule in a way Paula Deen and Ina Garten can only dream about. While the earth mothers prepare food that they think Americans want to eat, the hipster guys cook what *they* want to eat. Pass the fusilli with braised octopus and bone marrow, will ya? And don't get adultescents started on Rachael Ray and Sandra Lee. Any self-respecting eater in this generation would sooner gargle shampoo than consider one of their recipes, whose creations almost always contain the devil: packaged goods.

I continued to sniff out something cooking in my kids' lives when our family traveled to Copenhagen. Rory, twenty-four at the time, suggested making a dinner reservation at a spot he'd read about in the *New York Times* popular column, 36 Hours in Siberia. As we entered the restaurant Noma, we walked past an open kitchen where with the patience of poets, a battalion of chefs were slicing ingredients into morsels no larger than sugar granules. "Who picked *this* place?" my husband hissed. "It's going to cost a bloody fortune." When the bill arrived in Kroner—mange, mange Kroner—I happily pleaded math anxiety.

Even under threat of water-boarding, Rob and I wouldn't be able to recall specifics about that night's meal, except that we ate reindeer. (Tastes like chicken.) But to this day our sons tut-tut about the piquant amuse-bouche of oyster with apple ice and the delicacy of the musk ox tongue—right in line with their continued veneration of fine food. For a recent Hanukkah dinner, Jed made not just my mother's brisket and Raymond Sokolov's potato latkes, but homemade applesauce from local produce, crème fraîche with dill and salmon roe, and a salad that included treviso, which I had to use a search engine to learn is a magenta radicchio that resembles Belgian endive, and—may the God of Abraham, Isaac, and Jacob forgive my child—bacon. Dessert was pie from a sugar pumpkin fresh from the patch. No cans for my Jed, he of the CSA (Community Supported Agriculture) share and the Kitchen-Aid mixer that's been on my wish list for decades.

I can't begin to count the number of food competitions Jed and his fellow hash-slingers have entered. Who needs a varsity letter when your Apple Pie Ice Cream Cake wins the blue ribbon? And I was a proud mother indeed when Jed launched Ballfest, where all entries needed to be round and, damn the nepotism, his egg yolks poached in garlic broth won Most Creative. Rory continues to be cut of the same high-thread-count cheesecloth. After he moved to California, the first piece of kitchen equipment he acquired was a blowtorch for finishing off his crème brûlée, and he currently brews beer and limoncello in his Santa Monica kitchen. On his last visit to New York, he and Jed made a field trip not to MoMA, but to a new distillery in big brother's on-trend borough of Brooklyn.

I have a hard time reconciling that these food fascists are the grown version of little boys who were appalled at the thought of eating fish that hadn't been turned into frozen sticks and who while on their parents' watch adhered to the 3P diet: pasta, pizza, and potato chips. Rory was so fussy we referred to him as the Air Fern. Now, when these broad-shouldered gentlemen are coming for dinner, in the face of trickle-up pressure, I tremble.

I've gotten used to my kids' conversation, salted as it is with "farm-to-table," "locavore," and "slow food." It's the drinking that confounds me.

Did I mention there's a lot of drinking? That getting mildly pickled seems to be the point? Apart from AA regulars, few parents I know are teetotalers. This doesn't stop them from being deeply disturbed about how much their adultescents are drinking. We don't need the National Institutes of Health to tell us that "emerging adulthood . . . is a time of increased alcohol use and abuse," nor are we shocked to find out that this drinking "can have long-term effects on both physical and psychological well-being," or that the reasons for the problem are "developmental changes that lead to greater stress, increased freedom, less parental monitoring and greater peer pressure."

Twenty-one at twenty-one—guzzling shots to celebrate reaching the legal drinking age——has become a national ritual. According to the *Journal of Consulting and Clinical Psychology*, 80 percent of American twenty-one-year-olds drink alcohol to celebrate the birthday milestone, with the result that half of the men and more than a third of the women experience blood alcohol levels of 0.26 or higher, the rate at which a person is severely impaired and at risk for choking on vomit.

DROP THE BUD LIGHT NOW

Adultescents don't just drink a lot. They drink differently. Ten years ago, beer accounted for 59 percent of the alcohol purchases of adults twenty-one to thirty. That number has shrunk to 47 percent, and when adultescents buy beer, it's likely to be imported or "craft" beer. What they're purchasing instead of garden-variety beer is wine and premium and ultra-premium spirits. "As people care more about what they're eating, they also care more about what they drink," that noted authority, my son Rory, explains to his dim one-glass-of-red-wine-at-dinner-twice-a-week-because-it's-good-for-her-heart mom. "Cocktails and spirits have definitely picked up steam against beer and wine."

"When our son Gary came home to live after he graduated from college, he took one look at our liquor cabinet and complained about the color of our Johnnie Walker scotch," says Anita Carcich of River Edge, New Jersey. "He suddenly knew about liquor and microbreweries. I didn't even know what we owned—we inherited most of our bottles from my father when he died. It was Dad's generation that had a cocktail before dinner, not mine. My husband and I drink wine, not liquor. But we didn't upgrade for our son. He can do that on his own dime."

With the taste of beer or tequila on their lips, throughout the twenties and into the thirties Americans conduct much of their social life in bars where "the cocktail [is] no longer a fashion accessory. It [is] fashion itself," Jonathan Miles observed in his Shaken & Stirred column in the

New York Times. "The meaty center of enthusiasts is young profession-als with no big families yet, people willing to pay for quality," says Joshua Hoffman, editor of SpiritedCocktail.com.

While cooking may be testosterone-fueled, cocktail country is gender equal. For this we may thank the enduring momentum of *Sex and the City.* The series may have ended back in 2004, but the show's legacy endures, and not as you might guess—that every woman re-quires a hundred pairs of stilettos—but that a $15 cocktail is a barom-eter of success. It's become a social norm for women to drink with groups of friends.

"The cocktail is as much a fixture in the lives of twentysomethings as rent checks from enabling parents," says Doree Lewak, thirty-one, author of *The Panic Years,* which winks at the lengths some young women go to land a ring and a husband. "Among the twentysomething female set, the cocktail is king, regardless of socioeconomic or relation-ship status. It reaffirms a girl's self-worth and is her badge of honor, today's artificial measure of success." So widespread is this socializing that cirrhosis of the liver, previously found almost only in hard-drinking, red-nosed men in middle age, is starting to be diagnosed in young women.

What a woman doles out at a bar can have an inverse relationship to what she earns. "Even if she can't afford a meal that day, she most certainly will not forsake the venerated cocktail in her effort to control the illusion—the self-delusion, really," Doree points out. "We're talking about having to prove to yourself that you've made it. Hanging out in cocktail bars is a see-and-be-seen thing, going strong for the last five years, and there's no sign of slowdown, despite the economy, which is probably the most surprising part of all of this. The outside world isn't permeating their inside world. The twentysomething set is living with abandon."

Being a barfly doesn't come cheap. Alean Elston, twenty-five, of Washington, D.C., estimates that about 7 percent of her monthly net income goes toward restaurants, bars, and alcohol. "It's a staple of a young adult's social and professional life," says this freelance marketing executive. "Someone our age on a moderate income can go out and enjoy a fifteen-dollar cocktail with a really fine whiskey, but not be able to buy a fine bottle of wine," says Rory, who in seeing the cocktail glass not as half-empty but as half-full employs the same logic he used to try to convince his father and me that it made sense for us to help him rent an apartment before he had full-time work after college so he'd be "more motivated" to find a job. "People I know are willing to spend seventy-five dollars on a bottle of whiskey that will make twenty cocktails, where a seventy-five-dollar bottle of wine lasts for only one or two evenings."

It's all very two-generations-ago. "Everything of the thirties, forties, and fifties is being celebrated," says Noah Rothbaum, author of *The Business of Spirits*. "People in their twenties and thirties who have great-grandfathers' names like Max and Sam don't want to drink what their parents drank, but they'll drink what their grandparents drank. Connoisseurship of food and wine has led to a rediscovery of cocktails and spirits, so long out of favor they've became cool again."

The 1980s and 1990s were the Absolut era, all about vodka along with the growth of craft beer, wine appreciation, and single malt whiskeys, which started to appear on store shelves and in bars. Then around 2000, which happens to be the year Matthew Weiner wrote his original script for *Mad Men*, along came a generation that couldn't stop obsessing about what they ate and drank, enrolling in culinary schools and beginning careers in organic farming. Part of the appeal of the fancy cocktail is that most people can taste the difference between a bad drink and one made with fresh ingredients and artisanal spirits. It's like the difference between a Triple Whopper and a home-grilled burger made with a Neiman Marcus six-for-$72 Kobe beef patty. Customers shelling out for cocktails also notice bling-y crystal glasses and ginormous ice cubes generated by top-of-the-line Kold-Draft machines, since thanks to basic physics, the bigger the cube, the slower it melts and dilutes the drink.

Many spirits with lengthy histories were virtually extinct before adultescents brought them back from the dead. Take rye, once considered as American as George Washington, who farmed it. By the end of World War II, the whiskey had become so last-year that most of the rye fields were long gone. Today rye is very much in the wheelhouse of people in their twenties and thirties. Companies can't produce enough of it to satisfy demand.

The number of new distilleries nationwide is growing, and not just for rye, says a spokesperson for the Distilled Spirits Council of the United States, since as states have sought new forms of revenue, they've relaxed regulations and provided incentives to small, plucky producers. Colin Spoelman and David Haskell, both in their early thirties, met in a Yale a capella group; they have kept their day jobs but distill liquor at night and on weekends at their Kings County Distillery in East Williamsburg, Brooklyn. For Joe Santos, thirty-seven, a former Bacardi employee, producing and distributing his own gin "was a way to say goodbye to the lockstep march of the corporate world and hello to creativity and originality," writes Frank Bruni in the *New York Times* column The Tipsy Diaries. "He wanted to give the gin a name that communicated that." Joe's brew: Brooklyn Gin.

KNOCK TWICE AND SAY "MOE SENT ME"

Today's adultescents have left behind sticky-floored sports bars for fulsom saloons with names like PDT, an acronym for Please Don't Tell.

How cute is this? Like Clark Kent, patrons enter through a wooden phone booth in an East Village hot dog shop to indulge in Tater Tots and a signature old-fashioned bourbon infused with bacon fat. In cocktail country, New York City is the capital, known for its Manhattan Cocktail Classic, a New York Public Library gala well attended by adultescents.

The city that never sleeps also sets the pace with unmarked Prohibition-style speakeasies, but Los Angeles is not far behind, says Ben Mandelker, thirty-two, a local Dartmouth grad, screenwriter, and cocktail blogger, largely because "L.A. is the home of the quarter-life crisis. After careers in banking have already tanked, it's where a lot of people move who want to reinvent themselves at twenty-five or twenty-seven. 'At least I can do something creative,' they say. Back on Wall Street drinking might revolve around pricey clubs and vastly marked up Grey Goose. Here, learning about cocktails is the scene. My friends and I enjoy making drinks—it's our new pastime. There's a large awareness of mixology. We go to bars that serve handcrafted cocktails, nice places that are chill. It's not about getting wasted and having people scream in your ear or a drink-to-get-drunk vibe. Friends with drinking problems ruin the mood. We've been drinking beer a long time. It's about trying interesting new flavors."

"Not that long ago it wasn't glamorous to be a chef," Noah Rothbaum points out. "Now when you tell people you're a chef, you wow them. It's the same thing with bartenders." Much of the art lost in the 1970s is being revived, with bartenders learning techniques like how to infuse star anise or cinnamon bark into simple syrup. Today's bartenders don't just pour drinks. "They're madmen," *GQ* magazine raves, alchemists who make their own tinctures and bitters, scour eBay for antique glassware, peruse tattered cocktail books as if they were an autographed, calf-bound, gilt-inscribed first edition of *The Great Gatsby* and often resort to making their own ingredients.

Bartenders can command an excellent living for a calling that requires no degree. "If I worked full-time, I could make three times the salary of what I earn in my office job," says Jessica Margolis-Pineo, twenty-six, who tends bar in Boston while completing a master's degree in marketing communications and working in public relations. "It's ridiculous. I get paid mostly on tips, which are usually twenty percent. People order expensive drinks around other work people because of the image it gives—a Macallan for eighteen dollars a single instead of Jack Daniel's at eight dollars. Being a bartender is a great job if you have the right personality and can figure out whether someone wants to tell you their life story or be left alone, and know where else to send people, since a bartender triple-hits as concierge and trendspotter."

Today's cocktail culture became apparent to Jessica while earning an undergraduate degree at McGill University in Montreal, where she worked at a bar and popular drinks contained natural purees, freshly squeezed juice, or specially infused vodkas. "Since then, people mostly want to see cocktail lists over wine lists. Unusual cocktails and spirits offer something unique, which people are always trying to find. It's very civilized, in stark contrast to drinking cheap beer out of a pitcher."

In light of restaurants ditching their appletinis for more serious cocktails, *More* magazine, which addresses the demo of thirty-five-and-up—technically, the beginning of middle age—has offered its readership a guide titled *Does This Cocktail Make Me Look Old?* "What to drink, now that the Cosmo has become the official beverage of menopausal women?" ponders Pamela Redmond Satran. "Ordering the once groovy pink drink is as aging as pulling on a pair of mom jeans or hopping into your minivan." With all sincerity, the magazine asked "hip young female" mixologists to share a list of their most ordered mixed drinks, along with recipes. (You've got to love a women's magazine.) Taste-testers rejected a Skinny Bitch—"vodka, water, and a slice of lemon, the cocktail beloved by young women everywhere," along with rye-based cocktails they found harsh. The winners included a Friends with Benefits, made from white tequila, simple syrup, Chartreuse, lime, and unpeeled English cucumber for garnish, and the Parent-Subsidized Mortgage, a mix of Firefly Sweet Tea, vodka, and homemade sour mix.

I can load a bartending app like Top Shelf, Pocket Cocktails, or Nimble Strong, visit my liquor cabinet, scan the fridge and cabinets for ingredients, and tell the app what I've got on hand. It spits out directions and I can get that party startin'. I'll have my cocktail "muddled." Or was that adjective "clarified"? Maybe it was just "precious"?

"THEY TRIED TO MAKE ME GO TO REHAB . . . I SAID NO, NO, NO"

Colorful cocktails in sparkling crystal may glitz up the party, but seriously, will there be drugs? Joints? Jiggers of cough syrup? Salvia, that Mexican plant favored by shamans for its hallucinatory effects, popular with YouTube devotees who post videos of its helluva high? Not that adultescents seem as excited about them as they do their cocktails.

"In this generation alcohol continues to be more common by far, but drugs are definitely part of the culture," says Nzinga Harrison, MD, a psychiatrist, addiction medicine expert, and member of the Clinical Adjunct Faculty in the Department of Behavioral Health and Sciences at Emory University. "The attitude of young people toward recreational drugs these days is likely not different from that of their parents—something to try in order to have a good time with friends and fit in with the crowd. The terrifying thing is that the taboo around drugs seems to be decreasing, leading to using 'harder' drugs sooner than previous generations."

"These are the children, or even the grandchildren, of the sixties," says Stephen Odom, a Newport Beach, California, therapist who has been working with young adults for the past two decades in private practice as well as with Sober Living by the Sea treatment centers. He sees mostly adultescents in their twenties "who are really smart, go to great schools, and have used drugs since they were fifteen. A lot of their parents experimented and the attitude is, 'If my parents tried drugs, they can't be that frightening.' People aren't afraid of marijuana at all. It's thought of as an herbal remedy for all sorts of things. Ecstasy seems to be a teenage thing, and tapering off. There are some fad drugs, like salvia or spice, which give a marijuana high and for which there is no drug test and federal regulation. These keep rolling in waves to stay ahead of the laws." K2, for example, synthetic marijuana, is legal in some states as is another synthetic drug known as "bath salts," which has effects similar to PCP—it can make a user psychotic. Another drug on the radar: ketamine, an anesthetic often stolen from veterinary offices. There are manifold drug choices for people in their twenties and thirties, even more so than what boomers had at that age.

The biggest problem for adultescents isn't any of the above, however, nor is it street drugs like crack or crystal meth, the rural specialty. It's prescription drugs found in most medicine cabinets—Xanax, Ambien, and OxyContin. "Kids take enough milligrams so that they become loopy with a mild euphoria that makes them feel at peace," Odom explains. "Users think that because these drugs are made by reputable pharmaceutical companies they can't be bad. Kids might start with Vicodin, and then move to OxyContin, and now we're seeing a leap again toward heroin. My twenty-four-year-old daughter tells me she hears kids talk about using heroin as if they're having a drink."

Psychiatrist Arturo C. Taca Jr., clinical instructor for the St. Louis University School of Medicine, concurs. "Until recently heroin was considered an urban drug, but . . . supplies of pure, white China heroin have exploded. . . . Teens hide addiction from parents and when they try to wean themselves, withdrawal looks like a common flu, so parents just tell kids to take a few days off from school. As they become adults, addicts have to take heroin to feel better and normal. It is a horrible cycle of addiction that has exploded."

Also common: Adderall, a stimulant used to treat attention deficit/hyperactivity disorder (ADHD)—variations of inattentiveness, overactivity, and impulsivity. It's called the "smart" drug because it's known to help students concentrate on studying in college. I remember when one of my sons asked us to help him get a prescription for Adderall; so many of his college peers were using the drug, he felt academically disadvantaged. No way, my husband and I said. But lack of parental support does not discourage determined users.

"Incidents of taking prescription pills outnumber smoking pot as teens' first drug experience," Dr. Taca says. "It can start by obtaining pills from a parent's medicine cabinet. You just pop the pill . . . and the perception is because the pill is legal and widely available, it is safe."

When a parent's medicine chest supply is exhausted, prescription drugs are easy to acquire via Internet pharmacies—from Canada, for example. Word has also spread on how to describe the symptoms that will prompt a doctor to write a prescription. "How can you tell apart the kid who's telling the truth from the one who is lying?" an internist asked me. "You can't."

Odom is working with two Harvard students who've been asked to leave the university because of Adderall use. "You'll always have the alcohol crowd, though," he says. "It's the legal, traditional social lubricant. Most people are drinking alcohol, smoking some weed, and then taking pills. Back in the day you partied during college but toned it down because you graduated and got a job," Odom says. Wander years patterns make it easier than ever to extend college drug use into the twenties. "Now kids can't get jobs after college, have to return home, and keep going with drugs."

"Financial pressures seem to be greater than ever and unemployment is up, so you have less reason to go to bed at a reasonable hour instead of partying until four A.M.," points out Dr. Jeffrey Reynolds, executive director of the Long Island Council on Alcoholism and Drug Dependence in Williston Park, New York. "This generation grew up post-9/11 where things can change in the blink of an eye and the long-term consequential thinking has changed. As a culture we are riding a roller coaster of emotions, with substances doing most of the navigating."

The scuzz factor has also been rubbed off addiction, a condition with which le tout America is obsessed after watching celebrities and politicians stumble and sometimes reemerge. Adultescents know what to expect of an intervention, thanks, say, to the character Christopher Moltisanti's experience on The Sopranos. The experience at a rehab center is equally familiar, something movie and TV stars do in high-def on and off the screen—Celebrity Rehab, Vince on Entourage, or Lindsay Lohan, Robert Downey Jr., and Drew Barrymore. "A lot of kids are blasé and shrug off alcoholism and drug use," says Odom. "They don't realize they might not ever make it to rehab."

R.I.P. HEATH LEDGER AND AMY WINEHOUSE

It's not hyperbole to say we're a drinking, drugging country. Between 1999 and 2006 the number of people hospitalized for poisoning from prescription drugs including opioids (such as OxyContin and Vicodin) and tranquilizers and sedatives (depressants such as Valium, Xanax, and Ambien) increased by 65 percent, the *American Journal of Preventive Medicine* reported in 2010. As a nation, according to the Census Bureau, we're drinking 2.5 gallons per person yearly, up from 2.0 in the year 2000. Most people who experiment with drugs don't, of course, become addicted. Those most at risk, says Richard A. Friedman, MD, professor of clinical psychiatry at Weill Cornell Medical College and a frequent contributor to the *New York Times*, are likely to suffer from psychiatric, personality, or brain development disorders or are wired to have fewer dopamine receptors in their brains than nonaddicts. (Dopamine is a neurotransmitter that sends a signal to the brain and is critical to the experience of pleasure and desire.) The tendency toward addiction can also be inherited, so some people are addicts waiting to happen.

"Who can experiment uneventfully with drugs and who will be undone by them results from a complex interplay of genes, environment, and psychology," Dr. Friedman stresses. Dr. Nzinga Harrison also points out that the National Study on Drug Use and Health conducted by the Substance Abuse and Mental Health Services Administration shows that recreational drug use begins to decrease around the age of twenty-six, at which point only about 1 percent of the population exhibits drug addiction and 6 percent, alcohol addiction.

Drinking and drugging isn't, of course, limited to adultescents. If there's a massive drug crisis, it's among older adults, claims Mike Males, Ph.D., author of *Framing Youth: Ten Myths About the Next Generation* and director of YouthFacts, an organization dedicated to "providing factual information on youth issues such as crime, violence, sex, drugs, drinking, social behaviors, education, civic engagement, attitudes, media, and whatever latest teen terror *du jour* arises."

"The middle-aged drug crisis all sides ignore but stands out like the Matterhorn in Kansas," he posts on the organization's Web site, citing figures from the National Center for Health Statistics. "Drug abuse has overwhelmingly involved aging baby boomers, whose cohorts suffered the worst drug death levels at 20–24 in the early 1970s, 25–34 in the early 1980s, 35–44 in the early 1990s, and now 45–54. The fact that America's drug abuse crisis over the last three decades has centered on boomers has proven a taboo topic."

Not so taboo that I can't immediately think of at least a half-dozen people my own age who'd be happy to discuss this subject over a puff of weed perhaps grown out back next to the basil. "Boomer parents likely engaged in experimentation, if not heavy use of drugs and alcohol, and typically have a more permissive attitude about all drugs, especially pot and booze," says Dr. Reynolds. "The mind-set is 'I did it and the sky didn't fall. I didn't quit school and I have a job and a family. So it's not the end of the world if my kid does it.'"

Chapter 10

TAKE THIS CUBICLE
AND SHOVE IT

The reasonable man adapts himself to the world; the unreasonable one persists in trying to adapt the world to himself.
Therefore, all progress depends on the unreasonable man.

—George Bernard Shaw

t is a truth boomers universally acknowledge, that adultescents
in possession of a good job damn well better want to keep it. Thanks
to a mini-series of recessions, for the last few years the United States'
job market—to use the word favored by every numbers cruncher in
the land—sucks. The U.S. economy may be cautiously rebounding, but
with sleight of hand that mystifies prognosticators, it's happening
minus job growth, causing people to lose their homes, move in with
relatives, and check into homeless shelters. Here, a cheat sheet:

- Roughly two million American adultescents with at least a bachelor's degree are unemployed. The true unemployment rate for recent grads is most likely higher because numbers fail to account for people who go to graduate school in an effort to ride out the economic storm.

- Census data from 2010 show that twenty- and thirtysomethings in the United States are suffering from their demographic's highest unemployment rate since World War II.

- The growing disconnect between labor market realities and ... higher education ... is causing more and more people to graduate and take menial jobs or no jobs at all, observed Richard Vedder in a 2010 *Chronicle of Higher Education* report, "Why Did 17 Million Students Go to College?" There are 5,057 janitors in the United States with Ph.D.'s, other doctorates, or professional degrees. All told, some seventeen million Americans with college degrees are doing jobs that the Bureau of Labor Statistics says require less than the skill levels associated with a bachelor's degree: waiters, bartenders, parking lot attendants et al.

- According to the Labor Department, in May 2011, 33.6 percent of people who were unemployed had been out of work for at least two weeks, up from 9.7 percent in May 2007. The more time people spend out of work, the more difficult it is for them to land a job, in part because their skills deteriorate.

- The numbers of unemployed would be still higher if they reflected adultescents who've given up looking for full-time work and are working part-time.

- Six people are clambering for every open position.

- For recent college grads an unpaid internship is the new entry-level job.

- Even some experienced workers are interning as they come up empty in their efforts to find work, giving rise to a slippery benefit-free economy—no health care, no unemployment insurance, no security whatsoever.

In fields like film, fashion, and journalism, unpaid internships have long been the gateway for paid jobs, but the phenomenon goes beyond glitz. Three-quarters of the ten million students enrolled in America's four-year colleges and universities will work as interns at least once before graduating, claims the College Employment Research Institute. Between one-third and one-half will get no compensation for their efforts, a study by the research firm Intern Bridge found. "Unpaid interns also lack protection from laws prohibiting racial discrimination and sexual harassment," writes Ross Perlin, author of *Intern Nation: How to Earn Nothing and Learn Little in the Brave New Economy*, in the *New York Times*, which employs both paid and unpaid interns.

A common arrangement is for the unpaid intern to coordinate with her school to receive credit for work, which may mean that interns have had to pay to work for free. Internships are a windfall for colleges to provide credit; they can offer credits without paying for faculty members, classrooms, and equipment.

Enough! The dreary statistical litany has become so familiar that it no longer shocks to run across a David Sipress cartoon showing a personnel director interviewing an applicant and read this caption: "Right now it's between you and two hundred and fifty other people who came to Seattle, moved in with five roommates, joined a band, took a job in a coffee bar, got fed up, had a meeting with themselves, and decided it was time to go out and find a real job."

We hear about blogs like *Ivy League and Unemployed* and *Jobless*

Lawyer, or walk down the street, like I did, and see a flyer posted by Alice Lingo, twenty-nine, who advertised her services as a maid and asked, "Haven't you always wanted to see a lawyer clean a toilet?" No, but I was intrigued. Before her job was wiped out because of the economic downturn, Lingo says she was earning $160,000 a year as a litigator at a white-shoe law firm. "From the moment I stopped working 'til now, I haven't stopped looking for a job," Lingo told the *New York Daily News*. Besides seeking law jobs, without success, she also tried to be hired as a paralegal, a teaching fellow, a ticket taker, an usher, a waitress, and a babysitter—the last two, on numerous occasions.

Here's what does shock boomers: with faith that the universe will see them through, even during this employment pogrom, adultescents still voluntarily quit jobs, and not only Chelsea Clinton's husband, Marc Mezvinsky, thirty-three, who made headlines after he bailed on his investment banking job in Manhattan and was discovered in Jackson Hole, Wyoming, on an extended ski trip.

Together now, can we all shake our heads and shout *counterintuitive*? The millions of sidelined AARP-card-carrying worker bees legitimately carping about never having a real job again may pick a stronger word, given that unemployment among those fifty-plus has plateaued at a record high. I require no stats to know this, surrounded as I am by pharmaceutically tamed pals whose vanished jobs may never return. You recognize them by their vacant wallets and matching stares.

Never mind that adultescents saying "I'm outta here" often violate the holiest of career commandments: thou should not quit before landing your next job. The reasoning is loco—but perhaps only to a boomer like me, who more than once has forced herself to endure a stalemate of boredom, discontent, and humiliation as I faced off a boss, Mr. Let's-See-What-the-Little-Lady-Is-Made-Of, who I knew wanted me out to avoid paying my severance, unemployment benefits, and bonus. I hung on, suffering emotional gridlock primarily out of a sense of familial responsibility—two titanesque tuitions to help pay—though testing my own mettle was also a factor.

I used to be proud of my resilience. I am woman! See me stay! But lumping it is so 2001. During the wander years, when goals are fluid and improvising your life is paramount, job commitment often becomes yet another moving target. While the average American changes jobs once every three to four years, the average American under the age of thirty changes jobs *once a year*, reports Richard Florida, author of *The Rise of the Creative Class*, in *The Atlantic* magazine. Today's adultescents go through an average of seven job changes in their twenties, and according to Pew Research, six in ten have already changed careers at least once.

A recent Pew Research study also identified that people aged eighteen to twenty-nine are the only group who didn't use "work ethic" as a "principal claim to distinctiveness." In the *Washington Post*, one Jared Rogalia, twenty-five, a Hertz rental car manager-trainee in Alexandria, Virginia, analyzes his peers this way: "First, we're really spoiled and lazy. Second, we're free-spirited. Third, we'd rather be poorer and have free time than a lot of money."

To a boomer, the reasons people in their twenties and thirties quit jobs can sound cold-blooded, petulant, self-righteous, or birdbrained. Here are reasons offered by Jamie Varon, twenty-three, in a blog post called "Why It's Smart to Quit a Job After Two Weeks:"

- Your performance will be terrible if you hate your job. You'll end up quitting, so why draw it out?
- If you know going to your job will make you stressed, unhappy, and angry, continuing to go is disrespectful to your well-being. The

more you continue to disregard your own feelings, the farther away you get from happiness.

- Quitting shows you have integrity and passion. Switching jobs makes people more engaged. If you stay in a job too long, your learning curve goes down and things do not feel as new and stimulating.

- You'll do the company a favor. When you quit, the company will question what they had done to push you away—a smart company, at least. Do the company a favor and quit so they can reevaluate their training, that position and hiring strategy, so the next person doesn't want to jump ship.

- People who have self-confidence, respect, good teamwork instincts, and a sense of when it's time to cut their losses—these are the people who succeed. That's why high performers leave bad jobs.

To an employer, job defectors are a nuisance, or worse. "I've had six employees, all young, leave within the last five months, much higher than average," grumbles Obi Orgnot, CEO of OrgNot, Ltd., a London-based Internet company that hires from all over the world, although he's noticed that "this quitting phenomenon is pretty much exclusively a U.S. and U.K. young worker issue. Having people quit at a high rate increases our costs and . . . creates internal instability, because it makes other young workers look for the exits, simply from the sheep factor. A lot of our younger workers are upwardly mobile. They leave to travel, taking advantage of the depressed economy. . . . A good number of my former employees seem to be sunning themselves in Southeast Asia, where they can ride out the downturn on a shoestring."

UNIQUE SNOWFLAKES WHO CANNOT FAIL

"The biggest reason why I quit a lucrative consulting gig was that after I had my daughter, Charlotte, I was traveling four or five days a week and decided this was inconsistent with the dad I want to be," says corporate psychologist Daniel Crosby, Ph.D., thirty-one. "I also felt intellectually stifled. Our largest client was a bank and everyone on the staff took on its drab personality.

"I've always had a great ability to have faith in myself—that or narcissism," Dr. Crosby says of his decision to resign his job and start a DIY operation. "My leaving worried my parents, my in-laws, and my wife, who is a stay-at-home mother—everyone but me. It flabbergasted my employer, who had the mind-set that 'we can choose to do anything we want to these people because they're not going anywhere.' The firm had a highly autocratic leadership style."

Here we go again. "I think people older than me would be more accepting of this than I was, but when I grew up and went to school, self-esteem was the big buzzword. Adults told us, 'There are no losers,' and 'Everyone gets an A.' It bears remembering that a lot of us were raised to think we were unique snowflakes who could never fail. Although later research would prove that giving everyone a gold star isn't the best way to build confidence, this was the prevailing education and parenting philosophy of the time I was raised."

From World War I until the end of the twentieth century every generation in the United States has been more prosperous than its predecessor. Adultescents are quite likely the first generation for whom that may not be true, with dreams of satisfaction-enhanced success that may not have caught up to reality. "Part of the reason people my age wander is that it's in our collective consciousness that we need at least as much as our parents have, or even more," Dr. Crosby argues.

"Our expectation has bumped up against the negative economic realities of the last ten years. My generation gets a bad name for looking for the 'more' that's no longer there."

If you didn't snooze through Psych 101, you may recall Abraham Maslow's hierarchy of needs. In 1943 he diagrammed human motivation and personality in the shape of a triangle, where meat-and-potatoes concerns like safety form the broad base and esteem and self-actualization crowd the narrow point like a hat on top of a big, fat clown. Dr. Crosby suggests that the order of the pyramid has morphed. Adultescents who grew up in an upper-middle-class household assume that their basic human needs will be met, and they see giving fulfillment, creativity, and actualization greater importance. "A lot of my generation takes for granted that they can pay their bills—they want more."

Daniel Crosby did. "I was making one hundred thousand dollars at twenty-seven, but I was profoundly unhappy because my other needs weren't being met." So he took his degrees, experience, stamina, and hubris, moved from Atlanta to Huntsville, Georgia, and struck out on his own as a business psychologist, largely helping stockbrokers and financial analysts find their mojo. His biggest client is twenty-four years old.

But kids, you may not want to try this at home. "It's hard, hard work," Dr. Crosby stresses. "I work eighty-hour weeks, and hustling to find clients never ceases to be on my mind. I suit up every morning with my heart pounding, scared to death that it's all going to go away. But before, my heart was pounding from anxiety. Now it's pounding with opportunity. Entrepreneurship is a great option for people in the situation I was in. I've made twice as much money and have had a lot more fun."

Parents may be alarmed if their adultescent quits a job, especially if they believe a child has a sense of entitlement or illusion of uniqueness without the attendant work ethic. To this, Dr. Crosby concedes. "I think some people my age are naive about supporting themselves," he says. "We have models like Bill Gates who did it in their jeans. I don't think everyone is equally well equipped for that."

IT'S THE TECHNOLOGY, STUPID

When you look at the profiles of people in their twenties and thirties who wander off from jobs—either impulsively or after extended foreplay—you see that technology is the fairy dust so thoroughly embedded into adultescent culture that its sparkle has become the ring you wear every day on your finger and forget to notice. Adultescents started instant messaging in middle school, e-mailed their professors throughout college, and have poked potential dates. Even the oldest among them had a computer in their classroom and at home by the time they completed grade school. Younger adultescents barely know a search engine–free world, a slow-mo place where you loaded film in cameras, wrote letters, and called people's landlines after you looked up numbers in phone books.

Technology has made life move faster. According to the Pew Internet Project, 58 percent of adults aged twenty-five to thirty-four own smartphones, the invention my son Rory tells me has most changed his life. And why settle for a two-year-old smartphone—or not-so-smart job—when you can switch to a newer model? The big guns of technology haven't created many jobs compared to, say, how the automobile industry once kept Americans working. eBay employs only about seventeen thousand. It takes about fourteen thousand people to make and sell iPods, although that device has eliminated far more jobs when you consider the employees who once made and distributed CDs and records. Facebook employs about two thousand, Twitter a mere three hundred. Nonetheless, technology helps you find jobs through the incestuous connections that social media fosters and has allowed people to invent highly personalized careers.

"We grew up rewinding Boys 2 Men tapes and now we download our music," comments Jen Emge, twenty-five, in *The Next Great Generation*, an online magazine written by boomers' kids. "We went from using technology to creating it for ourselves. We went from thinking presidents could only be old rich white men; then Barack Obama appeared. So the thought of slowly degenerating in a six-by-six cubicle . . . for the next twenty years, answering to the old man who didn't get the memo about suspenders going of out style and attending company Christmas parties . . . it may be stable, but it's not fun. . . . We switch from job to job because our college applications told us we had to be well rounded. Because the restaurant manager said we needed experience just to seat people at his table. Because our parents told us they wanted better for us than what they had."

"WE WANDER BECAUSE WE CAN"

Ariel Stepp, twenty-three, of Los Angeles, sized up her employers—a public relations firm whose accounts include A-list celebrities, the cast of the Emmy-winning television series *Modern Family*, and corporations like Fox and Disney—and dismissed them as Luddites. (BTW, recent statistics suggest otherwise: Alpha Boomers, people fifty-five to sixty-four, who make up half the population, buy more techy gadgets—40 percent of the market—than any other demo, report that Facebook and YouTube are their favorite Web sites, purchase at least one product online each month, and own the most iPads and smartphones.)

"My old company's inefficiencies revolved around the lack of understanding and importance of online presence, social media, viral components, and the valuable research, resources, and marketing opportunities the Internet provides," Ariel huffs. "They couldn't grasp the business application of Twitter and Facebook. Because of the generational gap, my former employer never even offered these strategies to clients because they couldn't understand them themselves."

For Ariel, technology's opportunities were simple concepts, cost-effective and easy to accomplish, because—like virtually every adultescent—she's been on a computer forever. Her effortless wonkiness provides "access to anything and everything I want, 24/7, in a way the older generation doesn't experience. We express thoughts instantly for the whole world to view and respond to in seconds, sometimes all within one hundred forty characters or less. We blog, write statuses, make videos. Our efficiency online and with technology in general goes unmatched by the average person of an older generation. We can meet people across the world with similar taste in music we download free while sending e-mails for work as we text on our smartphone to a different friend asking for travel recommendations, upload a video to our profile, book a hotel reservation, and find the cheapest flight to visit the aforementioned friend—all at the same time—with barely any actual thought process. We use our phones and computers at the same time. We cut down on grammar, spelling, and formality for the sake of instantaneity.

"At work we put together spreadsheets, find top-level executives' contact information, book travel logistics, learn how to use new software, and answer our e-mails. Meanwhile, in that same exact period of time our older colleague has finished one spreadsheet of equal difficulty. That's all. In a meeting if a question about a recent study or new trend comes up, the twenty-three-year-old has just found the answer on her smartphone and sent a link to everyone, saving valuable meeting time, before anyone older took notes.

"We wander because we can," Ariel explains. "Having the world at our fingertips makes it immensely easy to fantasize about and plan where we want to travel or be in life—and plan it all for less money. On top of that, we witness our friends' photos of their excursions as they happen, motivating each of us to wander even more and experience things for ourselves.

"I once heard it referred to as 'World of Mouth,'" she says. "This goes for jobs, too. We wander off because we are always needed back. We wander yet we are always connected . . . through multiple sources. Doing business is all about your network and networking is all about connections, which my generation has made plenty of."

Last year Ariel survived a round of layoffs at the PR firm where she worked, yet decided not only that she could leverage technology more effectively than her bosses, but that as low woman on the totem pole she was underpaid and could make more money on her own. "My Facebook statuses revolving around my decision to leave my job and the building of my company were followed by fifty or so comments per status," she says, putting modesty aside. "Friends were supporting me, congratulating me, relating to me, referring clients to me, giving me advice, spreading the word about my company, wishing me success." Soon she'd signed on ArcLight Cinema, Equinox Fitness, and a celebrity photographer. "My friends were inspired. Thoughts arise in friends' heads: 'If my friend left her job and started her own company, why can't I?'"

Why not, indeed, if the following is true? "Every single resource you need to start your own company is online if you know your way around, which the iGeneration does," Ariel insists. "From learning about and applying for small business loans or grants to how to build your own Web page, it is all there for your consumption. And if you aren't into the concept of starting your own company . . . it's easy to find fifty jobs in five minutes and apply to them over a couple of hours per night from the comfort of bed.... Our generation will find a new job as quickly as we leave the old one, taking the place of the older person who used to hold that position and was let go. We will do the same job ... but better, more efficiently, and likely for less money with time to spare at the end of the day. We are needed by the generations that outrank us in order for their business to survive."

Tell *that* to Caleb Brown, MBA, a thirty-one-year-old headhunter in Tallahassee, Florida. "I recruit mainly in the late twenties. What I see is that these people quit jobs too easily. The grass is always greener. They'll quit because 'I wasn't feeling it.' You're not going to get that response from a baby boomer ... who won't say 'I want to take a vacation' and not even put in two weeks' notice before they quit.

"These rotten eggs create the perception that [my] generation won't pay our dues, asking, 'Why do I have to do this or that?' The approach and tone often are unprofessional or immature. They come across as arrogant, unlike a lot of baby boomers, who wouldn't think a job is beneath them and started out working Saturdays and Sunday and getting in early.... For a lot of the people my age, it's all about the title and the salary."

"THE ONLY COMPANY YOU SHOULD SLAVE FOR IS YOUR OWN"

At the Wharton School of the University of Pennsylvania, Harvard Business School, and other top institutions, a growing number of students are rejecting the traditional paths like investment banking, hedge funds, and consulting to start businesses. "The level of entrepreneurship activity here, and I presume at other schools, is up dramatically over the last two years," says HBS professor William A. Sahlman.

So it's gone for Greg Magarshak, twenty-four, whose family moved to the United States from Russia when he was an infant. Since then his life has raced on fast-forward. Greg skipped high school to start college at fourteen, and by twenty he began to work on a doctorate in mathematics at New York University. He'd planned to become a quant, the kind of Wall Street warlock who turns $50 million into $55 million by implementing derivatives and predicting market movement. But at twenty-two he got seduced by the Bloomberg media conglomerate and ended grad school with a master's, not a Ph.D.

Recognizing deficiencies in the IT system of the company he joined, Greg got busy designing and building an autosuggest system "that probably saved a few million dollars every year." The job allowed him to get a terrific apartment and a $100,000 salary. But working for the man—even if he's Mayor Mike—left him with only an item on a résumé and no ownership. After six months, Greg quit to independently design Web sites and evolved into a consultant who helps companies go viral via social media.

"Somebody once said 'the only company you should slave for is your own,'" Greg observes. "That's how I feel. I'm known in the industry and recruiters call me every week. I take a job for a few months at a time. I have a lot of freedom. My philosophy is simple: if your needs are met, you have options and can choose among opportunities in a smart way. I've gone from employee to consultant to vendor, where I can hire other people to help on projects. Finally, you can get investments in your own company"—a stage to which Greg aspires.

"I wouldn't recommend that young people with any ambition be full-time employees for long," he says. "Time is our most precious resource, and no amount of money will increase it. It would do well for parents to realize that in today's age, jobs are often only a means to get money. Much more important is . . . being able to . . . create something of value and monetize it. Young people are in a position to take these risks, because we usually don't have our own family yet.

"The culture has changed from the 1950s when company loyalty was much more important," he adds. You have only to take a look at the reaction to downsizing to understand the depth of adultescent skepticism. Greg offers as evidence a post from a blogger claiming to be a MySpace employee, when mass layoffs were announced after Facebook kicked its butt.

> At the same time execs . . . in charge of the company contin-
> ued the downward spiral . . . all were being rewarded with new
> deals, including raises and promotions, instead of working as
> hard as they . . . could to save the company and the jobs of the
> people they claimed to appreciate so much. . . . The people who
> were responsible for the continued failure will still be in charge,
> clearly intent on taking as much personal value as they can from
> the company before it dies . . . and the . . . employees that worked
> their butts off . . . to actually try to turn the company around . . .
> will be looking for jobs.

As one adultescent woman wrote to me, outraged, when she got wind of my research for this book, "Our parents stuck with the same companies and jobs since they left school. They were loyal to their companies until the day they were cut. People from my generation understand that employee-employer loyalties don't usually go both ways, and you have to put yourself first. We want to be happy with our careers, so we job-hop to better opportunities."

In my experience, it was adultescents' "greatest generation" grandparents—people like my own father—who stayed with the same company for their whole life, not boomers. Among my peers, I can think of only one person who's remained for his whole life at the same job: he's a sixty-five-year-old lawyer who now heads the stupendously successful law firm he was fortunate enough to join in his twenties. Most boomers I know have changed jobs quite a few times, though not, if they can help it, every year.

THREE YEARS = TOO LONG

In order to backpack through Africa for six months at twenty-eight, Alexis Grant quit a job that many aspiring journalists would covet, reporting for the *Houston Chronicle* on health and—boy howdy—the rodeo. "I really liked it but didn't want to stay for too long," Alexis explains, "too long" being three years. The reason for giving notice shocked her bosses as well as her father, an accountant with a stable work history. "My dad and I clashed. For his generation taking time off to travel wasn't seen as an asset, but for my generation, I think it is."

Few could quibble, given the following sequence of events. In Africa, thanks to today's technology, Alexis managed to blog and freelance for publications in the United States. After the trip, she stayed with her parents near Albany while she wrote a travel memoir and continued to live off savings until she found the right job, which she heard about through online postings from Northwestern University's Medill School of Journalism, where she earned a master's degree.

In a brandish of irony, Alexis is now an editor for *U.S. News & World Report* covering careers and job searching, though she can't predict how long she'll stay, since she's "not the kind of person who sees myself in one job for my entire career." Alexis works on the brand's Web site, which has replaced the once illustrious print magazine. Alexis says she prefers to hire "young people" for her staff rather than boomers, whose tech-wonk skills she finds plodding. Ouch.

"Job-hopping has become a natural part of the career landscape . . . for younger workers," said a report on the site with an Alexis Grant byline. "Unlike boomers, who tended to stay with one company for their entire career, Generations X (now in their 30's and 40's) and Y (20-somethings) are more apt to jump from job to job, or at least look around for more appealing opportunities. . . . One reason job-hopping has become more common is because it's increasingly easy for individuals to market themselves with free online tools. . . . If you're looking for a new opportunity, you may be able to create one rather than wait for that job to come to you."

"I loved working with physicians and nurses, but management were taking a lot of time off to play golf, and wouldn't give us peasants any time to do anything," says Jesse Waites, thirty, an air force veteran and former operating room technician in a Boston hospital. "I woke up one morning and had an epiphany that I would be happier reading books in the park and never wanted to walk back into that hospital again. Once I understood that, I wasn't afraid to quit. My mother was concerned, but there wouldn't have been any way for her to talk me out of it.

"I had planned on finding a job at another hospital, but getting the job took longer than I thought it would. In the meantime, to make rent money I started to make apps for people—I have the distinction of being the first person to develop a medical terminology and abbreviations app for the iPhone. I realized what would make me happy wasn't a big-screen TV and I was mentally prepared to be poor." But poverty wasn't in Jesse's future. "The demand for apps was much stronger than I thought. The next thing I knew I was developing software for clients full-time.

"Now I make twice as much as when I was working for the hospital," Jesse says. "I think we'll see a wave of entrepreneurs my age.

People read articles about how law school grads will never make back enough money to pay off their loans. Graduate and professional school—they're an enormous scam."

DAMN YOU, BAD VALUES

"I'm not surprised to find people quitting jobs in this economy," says author Christine Hassler. "They saw their parents sit in miserable jobs and be miserable, and a lot of them have their parents as security blankets, so why should they be miserable?" Adultescents quit for a lot of reasons—they're unhappy or bored or detest their bosses or can't quench their entrepreneurial spirit. And sometimes they switch gears because what they really want to do is *good*.

"Some people in this generation are very hard workers," Hassler stresses. "Their work ethic correlates to how passionate they feel about what they're doing, whether they respect the mission of the company and care about it, and how they are treated by the people they work for. I'd like to grow some of these people up so they can really make a contribution."

Goldman Sachs has long schtupped its executives with money. Some college grads who get hired by this richly rewarding Wall Street frat house quickly adopt a master-of-the-universe strut. Not Will Hauser. After less than a year with the investment banking group, Will quit.

Dialing back to 2008 Will was a senior at Harvard, and the autonomy and control of entrepreneurship had already won his heart. During his junior and senior years, he ran Harvard Student Agencies, the largest student-operated corporation in the world, an umbrella organization lording over companies that offer services and products that range from refrigerator rentals to the wildly popular *Let's Go* budget travel guide series. Will felt he had found his passion but no context in which to act on it beyond Harvard. As most of his classmates lined up jobs, he, too, put his name in the recruiting hat. An offer was forthcoming. "It's tough to turn down Goldman Sachs," he acknowledges, where the salary was handsome. His parents in Marin County, north of San Francisco, were, he says, thrilled.

After only one month on the job, it was clear to Will that the job wasn't, however, for him: "I didn't really believe in what I was doing. I grew up with parents who are doctors, and really respected what they do. At Goldman I didn't feel like I was contributing to the world."

Will bailed out of Goldman Sachs, sublet his Financial District apartment, slept on his brother's futon, and with savings, angel investments, and a boomer-aged partner started Two Degrees Food, a business whose mission is to fight malnutrition in the developing world by marketing nutrition bars along with a free medically formulated nutrition pack. Working with established organizations Partners in Health and Valid Nutrition, Will's company has already given out eleven thousand packs in Malawi. "Our goal is to sell millions of these bars," he says. "There's an enormous need, with two hundred million hungry kids around the world."

Does he regret that at the moment he left Goldman Sachs the company issued thirty-six million stock options at $78.78, a share price that has more than doubled as business has roared back? He says he does not. Living in the San Francisco area, Will says he can't imagine doing anything else right now.

Nor can Darcy Douglas, thirty-two, of Houston, who calls herself a "recovering attorney." When she graduated from the University of Texas, she worked for a congressman who represents Austin, then moved to Washington, D.C., to do professional fund-raising for EMILY's List and, later, Alliance for Justice.

Darcy intended to continue with nonprofits when she enrolled at South Texas College of Law in Houston. "I wanted to do politics or advocacy, but even though my original idea was to be Atticus Finch, I got involved with moot court and suddenly decided I was going to be the best litigator in the world," she says. "After law school I worked for three horrible years at plaintiff firms and quickly realized that it's rare to find an attorney who is trying to fight for a good cause. It's all about money, working with not-very-nice people with no interest in work-life balance.

"There were times when I'd have to call my mother in the morning for a pep talk because I was so unhappy I didn't want to go to the office. My boss would send me e-mails at three in the morning and get angry if I didn't respond. One Sunday at church while my BlackBerry was set on vibrate, the guy sent five e-mails, the last one in all caps.

"Finally I called my dad and said, 'I can't even work. I'm paralyzed.' I felt I needed my parents' approval to leave. He said, 'You need to quit.' Up until then they'd been very impressed with how much money I was making," the magic number of six figures.

"I had no job lined up, but I couldn't look for a new job while I was at the firm because I was working eighty hours a week." (Here, the second magic number.) "My family refers to the time after I quit as my Post-Traumatic Stress Disorder period."

Now Darcy is the development director for Breakthrough Houston, an education program that helps put academically talented, low-income teenagers on the path to college. Her salary is half the amount of her last job. "I always had the suspicion I wasn't going to love law, so unlike a lot of my friends, I never bought a new car or a new house," she says, "but still, I'll be paying back student loans forever. I don't even want to know the number."

"We work much differently than our parents," says Krista Chapman, thirty, of Nashville. "My generation tends to go upstream when we should be going down, though . . . we do feel a sense of selfishness when we quit a job, because we know there are people who'd kill to have what we're walking away from."

This is what Krista has done, several times. "Job-jumping has been my pattern since college. This year, two months shy of my twenty-ninth birthday, I left a great job as an event and wedding planner at a club in Nashville after working my way to nearly the top after two years. I was making seventy grand—more than my parents. I could have bought a three-thousand-square-foot house in Nashville for thirty thousand dollars. But while my job had prestige, my relationships were damaged, and I couldn't conform to the company's culture. My boss valued numbers, not humans." After downsizing, another colleague's tasks were dumped on top of Krista's load. "At the holiday rush I started to lose my mind . . . with no outside life and every single problem falling on my shoulders," she says. "I was afraid that in four years I'd wake up alone. 'This is not me,' I thought, and gave notice. My boss said it was a stupid decision, but I answered, 'Not a point of discussion.'

"I'd gotten sucked into the idea that success is money, that we need the best car, the best handbag, the hundred-thousand-dollar wedding—and that we shouldn't quit," Krista says. "A lot of people get caught in the wheel. I forced myself to do some soul-searching."

During a three-week solo road trip, Krista revisited her past in her college town in Mankato, Minnesota, her home in Green Bay, Wisconsin, and her grandparents' farm on a lake in northern Wisconsin, a Huckleberry Finn–ish Brigadoon. "It's weird how quickly you can detoxify, and very Midwestern, I think, to go after what really matters. I figured out I like to write and guide people and made the decision that I was going to own my own time." She returned to Tennessee to work as a blogger for a wedding marketing company based in Knoxville and augments her wages—considerably less than her former salary—with freelance event management

"I've chosen to be more thoughtful about my spending, which aligns with my values. I've canceled my gym membership, don't buy expensive wine, and shop a lot less. I used to buy clothes twice a week, almost a self-medication thing. But as soon as I left the toxic environment, this need went away. I purged all of my professional wear to make a clean break. Now I can work in my bathrobe. Luckily, I had emergency money in the bank. For the first couple of months, I worked off savings and paid off my debts. Now I can pay my bills, though I have to be careful with extra stuff."

RESET: EACH GENERATION QUESTIONS THE LAST

Doing work right is a puzzle each rising group of adults is convinced that it's solved. Krista Chapman describes herself as a planner by trade, "a financially responsible type-A," the antithesis of her father. "He was born in 1952. It took him seven years to go to college. He's low-key, and my mother is the same type. Hippie stuff is still very much there for them. They're liberal and socially conscious but financially not very smart. They've lost a lot of money. I am the hyper-reaction to them, more focused and sensible."

Before she had four children, my grandmother, Ida Hertz, emigrated from Lithuania at age two, taught English to immigrants in St. Paul, Minnesota, and according to family legend, regretted that she'd been unable to go to college. My mom got the degree my grandmother always craved. But after she worked as a social worker, my mother married, moved to Fargo, and became a stay-at-home wife, then a stay-at-home mother, in the style of the day. During my childhood I slowly came to believe that she'd have been far happier had she been able to plug in her brains nine-to-five beyond our sedate North Dakota household and constant volunteer work. I was never prouder than when she chaired a regional convention for Hadassah. (Really.) I also read a subliminal warning in the depression she faced when she hit middle age.

These observations dovetailed with the 1970s electricity that encouraged women to take their jobs seriously and to keep them after they had children, which I did. I started at the bottom rung on magazines and I found that I liked virtually everything about what evolved into my life's work, not least that I was an equal to my husband in taking care of our sons, providing for their excellent educations.

I have no daughters, but if I did, I suspect I might feel more than a tinge of disappointment—and to be gut honest, rejection—if they didn't find me a role model worth mirroring. I would have wanted my mythical daughters to chase a passion that put them to work. I'm hoping my future daughters-in-law will find a continuing way to be financial partners with my sons: it troubles me to think of Jed and Rory carrying 100 percent of a family's fiscal burden. If these wives mutter, hey, I'm not signing on for *that*, I'll try very hard to butt out, understand, and not come off as the world's most judge-y mother-in-law.

Everywhere, I meet women confounded by the comparatively blithe work attitude they notice in some adultescent women. "Do not leave before you leave," Sheryl Sandberg, chief operating officer at Facebook, told the 2011 graduating class at Barnard College as she reflected on how many women dial back aspirations, picking the less challenging road in hopes of finding "balance for responsibilities they don't even have yet. Do not lean back," she lectured. "Lean in. Put your foot on that gas pedal and keep it there until the day you have to make a decision."

"Young adults seem to drift along, trying this and that, with the underlying assumption on both their and their parents' parts that parents will help them financially," fumes a friend who is the mother of two current college students. "What you see is long-term subsidized lifestyles that I think have crippled a lot of kids. Many of them want careers in the arts but not on their own dime. Nobody has forced these kids to reckon with the realities of the grown world, where you really are responsible for yourself.

"I'm a boomer who went off to college at sixteen. I started working full-time at nineteen while I was still finishing college. I never accepted a penny from my parents—I wouldn't have thought of it. Not every job I had was great. Most of us realized that at a certain point we were going to have some shit jobs. We put up with them, and worked hard until we found something better. These kids expect to have jobs with meaning and purpose from the get-go.

"Career choices are hobbies if you don't think you have to earn enough to live on," she says, barely catching her breath. "You have to lay the blame at parents who have permitted their kids to be spoiled brats who never grow up. I find it hard to avoid the conclusion that the best approach is tough love."

This spring her daughter, an outstanding student and an English major, will graduate from an Ivy League university. So far, she hasn't been able to find a job. "There's no justice!" the mother says.

No, there isn't.

"My daughter has done everything right," my friend continues. "She's very distraught about her possibilities. Obviously, I'm not going to cast her out before she has a job, but I don't want to start on that slippery slope of subsidizing her lifestyle."

Oh to be a fly on the wall at their household in a year or two. Will my friend's Dickensian stridency and certainty prevail? It's ugly when principles go bad, but I can't help but wonder if there won't be some revision.

Sometimes we're forced into evolving. Sarah Lee Marks, fifty-three, of Henderson, Nevada, is a fourth-generation working mother. Her great-grandmother was a clerk in a millinery shop. She supported her husband during the Depression and worked until she passed away at eighty. Sarah Lee's grandmother graduated from college and worked as a secretary. Her mother was a teacher and her aunts had jobs, too.

"My own perspective of work is based on the idea that we were the generation that was going to break the glass ceiling and enjoy the newfound freedom of the feminine mystique," Sarah Lee, my sister-wife in rhetoric, says. "Being a mom was okay, but having a career was a big deal. We valued the job as a prize to which, in many cases, our self-esteem was tied. Women my age were pressed to go to college to have a great 'career'"—of which she's had three: in arts and crafts supply sales, telecommunications, and, currently, the automotive in-dustry.

For her daughter Rebecca's generation, the need to feel passionate and appreciated is, Sarah Lee observes, not tied to a paycheck. "Our kids watched us grow up as women putting in all these hours to prove ourselves against the men. Maybe they learned from us that they wanted to enjoy that 'mom and dad' feeling more. They also saw a lot of divorces and came away with huge lessons from female working baby boomers. The money and trappings come at a price and, hey, look what just happened to our economy. They're saying, 'Whoa, all that cool stuff doesn't guarantee you a job, because my parents were loyal and it didn't mean anything.'"

Sarah Lee has arrived at the attitude that this awareness is not such a bad thing. "If you think, 'This is just a job,' it's okay to quit if you don't see a future that registers as promising." This has made it easier for her to accept that her daughter Rebecca, twenty-four, walked away from a job without having another position in hand—at the same time that Nevada's unemployment rate had the ignominious distinction of being number one in the nation.

Rebecca had debated before accepting the job in question. It was for a regional theater company, required constant travel, and she'd just met a guy she liked. "The job is a stepping-stone to your career and you don't know if this guy will be around or not," Sarah Lee had advised. But after a few months Rebecca told her mother she hated being away from her boyfriend and wanted to quit.

"It's a lot easier to find a job when you have one," Mom countered.

"Except that when I'm traveling, I can't interview where I want," her daughter shot back, and added, "Will you disapprove of me if I quit?"

"Hold on," Sarah Lee told her. "I'm not taking the blame for telling you to expand your career or your associated miserableness, because it's not up to me to make you happy. But if you want to do something about it I won't disapprove." Once Rebecca absorbed this, she agreed that it was her decision, which Sarah Lee believes she came to with considerable angst. "I felt terrible," Sarah Lee says. "What did I do to my kid that my opinions and disapproval mean so much?

"I would have held out and taken my beatings until I found another job," she adds. "But I realized Rebecca's perspective on what makes a person whole, fulfilled, or driven is totally different from mine. When she gave notice, I sensed that she felt like she'd lost a hundred-pound gorilla.

"For all the rhetoric about my daughter's generation feeling entitled or not being committed, I don't think this was the case for Rebecca." Sarah Lee has continued to tweak her attitude. "My daughter put in over two hundred and fifty résumés and ultimately got a job teaching drama in a charter school. She was willing to take entry-level money, not something I would have done, but that helped her get another job fast. She's happier than a pig in slop right now."

Chapter 11

OOPS, I FORGOT TO GET MARRIED

A guy's idea of a perfect night is to hang around the PlayStation with his bandmates or a trip to Vegas with his college friends. . . . They are more like the kids we babysat than the dads who drove us home.

—I Don't Care About Your Band: What I Learned from Indie Rockers, Trust Funders, Pornographers, Felons, Faux-Sensitive Hipsters, and Other Guys I've Dated by Julie Klausner

Some couples in their twenties, even their early thirties, are merry old souls. They've won wars, supported families, become parents, and faced disasters. Not me. Not my husband. At that age the two of us were not quite smart enough to get out of our own way. Our vision of married life was foggy and we were oddly matched: East Coast /Midwest, extrovert/introvert, fan of golf tournaments/

period drama, jock/not. We bickered. We bitched. We were *young*. Yet at twenty-three, against all reason but like many couples of our age at the time, we married.

Soon after I arrived in New York City a dust devil blew into town from my mother, shouting *Get married or move on!* And here's where it gets quaint: I listened—to my mom—never questioning whether at that time, or ever, marriage made sense for the two mere spores that were my beloved and me. Every morning I'd turn to Rob and ask, "Is this the day we're getting engaged?" Forget *The Rules*. This is the strategy to beat a man into submission, and one day my boyfriend produced a ring, which led to the end and the beginning: marriage.

We were living together. Back in the day that put us ahead of the curve. Now it's the norm for more than twelve million unmarried couples aged twenty-two to thirty-five, although others opt for "stayover" relationships, a trend reported on in the *Journal of Social and Personal Relationships*. Couples maintain separate residences but regularly spend three or more nights together.

At twenty-four our son Rory told us he was considering moving into the Santa Monica apartment of his girlfriend, Kim, whom he'd dated for a year. Rob and I were wary; it had been our experience that once you've commingled your wineglasses, the next thing you know you're marching down an aisle, and Rory, our baby, struck us as young for such a step. But how could we protest, when at an even more tender age we'd done the same?

Jed, the older brother, had a more vocal position. He told Rory that living together was emotional dynamite; he'd seen too many such couples who'd split in breakups as harsh as divorces. Nonetheless, Rory moved in with Kim. A year later, Jed reconsidered his position when he lost his heart to a blue-eyed beauty from Berlin whom he met when she needed her H1B work visa notarized and he wielded a no-tary stamp. To hell with principles. A year later he asked Anne to move into his apartment and she has never left.

As a parent of cohabitating sons, it's been tricky. It didn't take long for Rob and me to feel increasingly attached to Kim and Anne, delightful women who could be deleted from our life in the time it takes for them to call Moishe's Movers. The only thing clear for parents whose kids cohabitate is the lack of clarity. While some parents maintain a certain distance, scheduling family vacations sans girlfriends or boyfriends, for example, Rob and I chose to treat both couples as if they were a little bit married. When Anne's father visited from Germany, I invited Herr H. to dinner. Intrusive or gracious? In truth, I was curious to meet the man who'd fathered the woman who'd turned my boy to butter.

If adultescents find what seems to be a committed plus-one, moms and dads often start asking, early and often, Is this arrangement going to lead to marriage? The answer? Dunno, because what's different from the bad old days is that partners living together are now less in-clined to wind up married. The percentage of people who marry in their twenties in the United States has plummeted, according to Cen-sus Bureau stats, with 45.3 percent of those aged twenty-five to thirty-four still single, while ten years ago the number was close to 40 percent, and in my day, barely 16 percent escaped a wedding ring. The propor-tion of Americans aged twenty-five to thirty-four who are married is less than those who have never married—46 percent versus nearly 45 percent, according to an analysis by a demographer at the Population Reference Bureau. You can throw a dart at a map of Europe and the United Kingdom and see the same trend. In France, for instance, straight couples are shunning traditional religious marriage ceremonies and opting for civil unions.

When people do marry in the United States, it's at an older age. The median age of first marriage has increased to the highest age recorded: 28.2 for men and 26.1 for women. That's up from 26.8 and 25.1 ten years prior. The women's sports pages—the *New York Times*' Style section—is loaded with brides and grooms well past thirty. Personally, I've been invited to only four weddings of men or women younger than thirty, and one of those unions never made it to the first anniversary.

There are still cultural pockets where young marriage is the custom. The president of the Mormon Church recently admonished men to marry young and in Orthodox Jewish circles, brides and grooms are encouraged to marry at tender ages as well, although rampant anorexia and bulimia in this enclave have been reported, and some cultural observers link these eating disorders to young women hoping to postpone marriage. Beyond celebrities, who seem to marry and divorce more frequently than lesser mortals clean their closets, the demo with the greatest enthusiasm for marriage seems to be same-sex couples living in states whose laws prevent their unions.

"HARD IF NO ONE TEACHES YOU"

You can't look at the decline in marriage today without considering its dark side: divorce. In 1980 the United States had about eleven million divorced people; recently, the tally was twenty-six million, a sum most definitely including many parents of adultescents, who are—understandably—spooked about the institution. Forty-four percent of marriages end in divorce, 19 percent of them within the first decade. Who wants to catch that social disease? Not college-educated Americans. Curiously, only 11 percent of this demo divorces within the first decade today, compared with almost 37 percent for the rest of the population, claims a 2010 study by the National Marriage Project at the University of Virginia. Divorce has taken on an ick factor.

"I've never been able to work out if marriage is good or bad!" Georgia Aarons, thirty-two, told me. "I didn't grow up in a household where marriage was valued. My parents each married at least twice, and my mother has lived with a man for thirty years who has still been married to another woman. Hollister's parents were each married three times—he's from Holland, where I think people are much more liberal about relationships, so it was never a huge priority for him, either. It's hard to know how to do something important if no one teaches you.

"Hollister and I met when I was a senior in college and have been living like a married couple since I was twenty-one. We bought an apartment together, but aside from that, we've remained financially independent. I did well working on Wall Street, so I never felt the need to find financial security in someone else, which might partly explain why we never got married. We first talked about it when I was twenty-two, but I told Holly I was way too young and I'd let him know when I was ready. Somehow, years went by.

"My generation is very noncommittal and expects everything to just sort of fall into place, without realizing you have to earn it. I've learned that it's work to keep a relationship thriving. If I didn't know that, it would be easier to get married. When you've already lived with someone for many years and seen how challenging it can be, it's harder to commit.

"Last year Hollister sat me down when my father was diagnosed with terminal cancer and said that if we didn't get married soon, my father would never know. He thought it would be nice for Dad to know I was taken care of in the old-fashioned sense. I was also feeling pressure from my friends, half of whom are married, and was sick of the constant probing I got from them and strangers. It's crazy how people have such strong opinions about marriage! So, I agreed.

"When I turned thirty, I realized I'd fallen into my career track rather than having planned it. I quit my job to spend time with my father and see what else might be out there for me professionally. After Dad passed away, it seemed like the perfect time to make a change. Hollister and I moved to London. We definitely will get married, but I'm not sure when."

"The unmarried people *least* likely to say that they want to get married are the ones who have already tried it and divorced or whose siblings and especially their parents have failed marriages," says Bella DePaulo, Ph.D., social psychologist and visiting professor at the University of California in Santa Cruz, in *Psychology Today*. "Divorces hover in the background like a bad fairy sorority."

As divorced boomer parents try to parse why their kids remain single, they may charge themselves with guilt by association. "I've been mystified as to why my daughter and the guy she lives with haven't gotten around to marriage," admits Bruce Solomon,* the father of a thirty-three-year-old woman who graduated from Washington University in St. Louis, went on to law school, and now has a job in local Chicago government. "She and her boyfriend appear to be building a strong relationship. His parents have told us how they think Sophie* is perfect for him. Why isn't anything happening?

"She won't discuss the topic, so I've come up with several theories—that her boyfriend had a heartbreak that's made him gun-shy, or might be upset that she outearns him, or that neither Sophie nor he sees any compelling reason to marry. But what I've decided is that Sophie has been scared off because of me leaving her mother." She was eleven when the couple separated. Bruce stayed single for many years. "How could I be judgmental about the way she's behaving toward marriage when I myself have questioned the institution? After my divorce, getting remarried didn't seem to be relevant"—although it seemed relevant to his girlfriend. Eventually, they wed. "I'm coming around to the position that my daughter should be paying attention to her biological clock and take care of that, rather than forcing a formal marriage. I plan to tell her just this."

What would you pay to eavesdrop on *that* dinner? Bids? Anyone?

UNSOCIAL NETWORKING

The bogeyman of divorce is a curse, just as stagnant or nonexistent paychecks among adultescents also muck up the marriage machine; it's hard to sustain a social life without money. But the decline in marriage rates may also connect to a trend noticed by the Centers for Disease Control: Americans are starting to have sex later. Even as hookups are part of college life, 28 percent of people aged fifteen to twenty-four say they've not had oral, vaginal, or anal sex in the past decade, a number that has shot up from 22 percent. We may live in an erotically charged society and there is plenty of casual sex on college campuses, but female college students also outnumber men, which means they wind up competing with one another for guys, reports Mark Regnerus, coauthor of *Premarital Sex in America: How Young Americans Meet, Mate, and Think About Marrying*, a book based on four national studies representing twenty-five thousand young people aged eighteen to twenty-three.

Pushing that line of thought, could the poky crawl toward the altar be because, given the dearth of men, college is a hot spot of sexual experimentation between women, giving rise more than ten years ago to the term "LUG": lesbian until graduation. After years spent in Sapphic embrace, does it take a while to reorient to men? Nah. Turns out, the CDC also found that college-educated women are *less* likely to have a same-sex experience than women who don't pursue higher education. Maybe the LUG phenomenon was merely titillation for men.

The CDC finding may flip the wigs of parents convinced that lascivious unions are happening on every school bus and whose emotions curdle when they hear their thirteen-year-olds in crotch-revealing pants blow off blow jobs as "not really" sex. We're confronted with a riddle wrapped in a mystery inside an enigma that's not inside a vagina. Experts point out that the younger generation may be cautious because of an awareness of sexually spread diseases and the effectiveness of abstinence campaigns, but I'm wondering, given all the sexting and trying to build a brand in order to get admitted to college, if these kids are simply too busy being extracurricular sluts to bother with sex. Virginity is R&R.

Another thought: the biggest relationship buster of all might be technology, which disconnects people, especially young ones, as much as it brings them together. While cell phones have become ubiquitous in American households, most cell phone owners use only two of the main non-voice functions on their phones: taking pictures and text messaging. Among Millennials, however, a majority also use their phones for going online, sending e-mail, playing games, listening to music, and recording videos. Are adultescents simply too busy doing the thumb dance on their toys to develop the sort of meaningful relationships that come from actual talking and touching?

Facebook has become one of many giddy intruders we invite into our life, a trend with benefits that allows us to see whose life is so small she posts a picture of her pedicure and which friend is simply a relentless self-promoter. It's ugly when social networking goes bad. If your mother and your friends are friends, that's troubling enough, but it gets worse. There's also the humiliation of being defriended. It's enough to get rejected in real life—does it have to happen in the online world, too? A new study suggests a link between social networking and depression in children, with Facebook the mall where you read graffiti from bullies and a friend tally that either anoints you as popular or confirms your loser-ness. Friends' hyperbolic status reports, photo updates from countries you can't afford to visit, and hundreds of thousands of connections may present a skewed view of reality that can make you feel you don't measure up. And where you used to be able to simply roast marshmallows over the bonfire you made from your former lover's pictures, digital images never incinerate.

Worse still: a change in romantic status can be reported by a vengeful partner before someone knows she's been dumped. "My husband moved out last year because he was 'depressed,'" Michele, thirty-one, told *Glamour* magazine. "I bent over backwards trying to save our marriage, then got a Facebook message from a girl saying they'd had a long relationship and she might be pregnant." Have a nice day.

Between couples, social networking sites are like an extra person in bed. Couples sharing passwords to e-mail accounts and photo-posting sites have become intimacy's new currency. When you merge in cyberspace, you commit to the other's friends' networks. Social networking gives couples no space at all. "There's so much fear and jealousy, with people checking their partner's cell phone or Facebook page constantly to see who has friended them or who they've texted," says Sherry Amatenstein, a New York City couples counselor whose practice focuses on people in their twenties and thirties.

The insta-reporting of Twitter and Facebook have also crimped adultescent meeting-and-greeting, since new relationships no longer stay discreet. "Twentysomethings aren't having one-night stands anymore," Jennifer Wright, twenty-four, posts on Gloss.com. "There was a period of socially acceptable one-night stands . . . let's say it lasted from 1963 until 2003. What happened in 2003? Facebook . . .

"Jackie Susann's novels chronicled beautiful women bed hopping their way through Manhattan. . . . These days the pictures would be up on Facebook the next morning, and the stud would want to confirm you as a friend on LinkedIn. Your friends won't morally judge you for sleeping with someone, but you can be certain you'll have ten odd comments either making fun of you or asking you for specifics. . . . And we *want* this. No one is forcing twentysomethings to buy into the myriad of social networking sites we log on to with frightening regularity. We've created a community where near strangers can fill the role that used to be taken by nosy 1950s-style neighbors."

"Technology is a double-edged sword," says Ben White of Aspen, Colorado. "I like that you can access information easily and in an instant look up all the art gallery openings that night. It makes making plans easier. But while technology operates in the guise of connecting us, my suspicion is that on some level it's the opposite. I just ended a relationship with a girlfriend who had a circle of about thirty people she contacted on her iPhone in a loop all day long. It was hard for her to be present, a major issue between us.

"I also hate that my generation relates so much with texting," Ben complains. "You don't have to bring yourself to the relationship. This technology connects us in a distant, hands-off way and that's something I've tried to fight. When I get a text, I've irked more than a few people by calling instead of texting back. I'm looking for deeper connection. I'm the person who walks away from the table to have a conversation."

"When I meet someone and he actually calls instead of just texting, I get really excited," Kate Longyear, twenty-three, of San Francisco told *Time Out New York* magazine.

Technology also enters into dating through Internet meeting sites, which have ceased to be considered creep magnets since almost anyone you ask knows of a romantic success story produced by meeting online. Yet the sites are also cyber watering holes where people post carefully crafted profiles that often reveal more about their writing talent than the truth. "The fact that you can't get away with lying in your profile for long doesn't prevent a lot of people from doing it," notes Nick Paumgarten in *The New Yorker*. "They post old photographs of themselves...or click on 'athletic' rather than 'could lose a few pounds,' or identify themselves as single when they're anything but. Sometimes the man says he's straight but the profile reads gay. Sometimes he neglects to mention that he is a convicted felon."

"From what I've seen of this generation, the older they get, the more particular they become," says Barbara Weisberg, a Louisville, Kentucky, mother of Brad, thirty, and Danielle, twenty-seven, who both work in Chicago. When her children visited Louisville last year, Barbara noticed her son trolling JDate.com, a Jewish singles site. After Brad left one evening, Mom surfed through listings and, by the time he returned, had compiled a list of hot prospects for her son.

From this motherly intervention, Danielle hatched the concept for TheJMom—"matchmaking Mom's way"—a Web site where Jewish mothers post their single kids' profiles and pictures for other moms to consider and recommend to *their* son or daughter. Perhaps you'd like your daughter to meet Scott of Las Vegas, the Brown University–educated professional poker player "often mistaken for Seth Rogen" or your son to meet Daphna, the fashion stylist from Texas in the goofy pink hat. Who is Daphna looking for? "[I]t wouldn't hurt if he were good-looking and reasonably tall," Selma, her mother from Houston, confides in cyberspace.

Did Barbara worry that the site plays into the most cringe-worthy stereotypes of the meddling mother, I asked, knowing that if I'd ever posted a profile of either of my sons on such a site they'd consider it grounds for a momectomy. Barbara answered my impertinent question. "I'm speechless!" But she didn't stay that way long. "We're more *vocal*, not more interfering. When a mom searches the site, she makes a suggestion for a date, that's all. TheJMom offers another way to meet people similar to you—similar background, education, and goals in life—qualities I feel are most important when you marry, since you're marrying the whole family. My kids are expanding the site to include other ethnic groups. The concept isn't that different from a blind date.

"The next generation isn't going to live the way we have in terms of affluence," Barbara added. "I just want my kids to be happy. I've lowered my expectations. When my kids were born, I hoped they'd grow up to be CEOs and marry movie stars," she said. "Didn't you?"

Ah, no. When my kids were born, I didn't even know them yet—why would I imagine one of them as a CEO? But Barbara and I found a point on which to agree. "You're only as happy as your least happy child," she said, quoting the dead-on balls-accurate cliché. Every stressed-out parent of a wandering adultescent—whether you think your child is a fugitive from hard work, good judgment, or quotidian good fortune—suffers when they think their child is miserable. And when it comes to *affaires de coeur*, a lot of adultescents are suffering.

SINGLE WOMEN—STAND UP AND TAKE A BOW

Another reason why marriage seems to be on the way out is that there are fewer reasons than ever for people to wed, especially female people. Young women rock. To start, they outstrip men in graduating from college. Among Americans aged twenty-five to thirty-four, 34 percent of women but just 27 percent of men have earned a bachelor's degree. Women's grade-point averages are also higher and classroom glory carries them along more often than men to graduate school, which gives them brighter employment prospects. Adultescent women then work hard for the money and, while single and childless, frequently outearn men. Single, childless women under thirty earn 8 percent more than their male peers, whom—in their dreams—they'd like to date, if only the guys showed interest. The radioactive tut-tut among women in their twenties and early thirties: adultescent men are genetically marked for staying single, at least for the immediate future, with way too many of them living in a Judd Apatow stoners' screenplay, playing Total War IV, eating Froot Loops for dinner, trading fart jokes, hooting at Cartoon Network and Daniel Tosh on Comedy Central, and sleeping until noon, possibly in their boyhood bedroom.

This leaves adultescent women on a parallel line, spending their evenings and weekends in herds. "Among pre-adults, women are the first sex," gloats Kay S. Hymowitz in *Manning Up: How the Rise of Women Has Turned Men into Boys*. "The single young man can live in pig heaven—and often does. Women put up with him for a while, but then in fear and disgust either give up on any idea of a husband and kids or just go to the sperm bank."

Be that way, snort plenty of adultescent men. "Marriage and parenting and mortgages can wait," Nathan Rabin, an editor at *The Onion*, writes in the *Wall Street Journal*. "We're all about living in the sacred present tense and chronicling its key moments 14 characters at a time. Scoff all you like at the shaggy, hang-dog 27-year-old next door dressed in a baggy college sweatshirt and cargo shorts, taking empty pizza boxes and beer bottles to the dumpster. He . . . might just be getting ready to change the world with what he creates in his unkempt guy lair."

Or be another boychick wait-listing adulthood.

The parents of Natasha Bashri,* twenty-seven, with whom she lives in Los Angeles, can't understand why she doesn't have a boyfriend.

"Men in their twenties are just looking to have fun," she tries to explain to them. "They want a career first and a relationship second, while women can learn to integrate the two. We manage our time better. Among my friends, there are an overabundance of accomplished, interesting beautiful women and not as many similar men to choose from," Natasha says, its echo the gripe heard 'round the land.

There are more single adultescent women than men in most eastern seaboard cities, but New York City, in particular, resembles an overcrowded women's penitentiary, where the female/male ratio is almost two to one, and there isn't as much sex in the city as you'd guess, with, according to the most recent census, some zip codes showing two girls for every boy. "Guys in New York are perpetual bachelors who want the cream of the crop," grumbles Sharon,* a twenty-six-year-old Bay Area transplant to the Big Lonely Apple. "It's difficult to connect with someone of substance who's not just a hookup. I always have the fantasy that I'll meet a guy walking in Central Park, in a coffee shop, or on the subway, where he'll hold the door for me. But for a city with so many people, it's isolated. Nobody talks to strangers. I can't even imagine being in a relationship here.

"The older you get the more you think that if you ever want to get married and have kids, when will that happen?" Sharon asks. "My parents are liberal, but I know they want me to eventually get married and have children. I hope I can be married in my early thirties so I can have kids when I'm thirty-five. I expect to be an older mom."

"Parents of adult children cannot fathom why their offspring are still living alone or moving from one transitory relationship to the next," Jack Werthheimer wrote in Commentary magazine. Changed dating and marriage patterns cut across the races, religions, and socioeconomic subgroups, from coast to coast. Everywhere, you find women putting their best flirt forward and men looking over their shoulder for someone better.

"I have watched normal, rational moms turn into Mrs. Bennet overnight, sharing their frustrations with the lack of suitable men for their daughters who are longing for marriage and children," blogs Midwestern mother and grandmother Karen Campbell, a self-professed church lady, in ThatMom.com, which addresses the homeschooling demo. "Why are so many young Christian men delaying marriage?" she asks. "This seems to be the burning question all around Christian websites these days. . . .

"Most relationship pundits conclude that the reality of more and more young men delaying marriage is because of a latent adolescence, an inability or lack of desire to be responsible, resulting in 30-something men who are content to play video games and hang out at bars with their friends rather than to grow up and invest their time and money in family pursuits," Karen Campbell writes. "There are plenty of things that could cause a young man . . . to delay marriage. One is that our society has a skewed view of what a woman should look like and many young men are looking for airbrushed perfection. Why would we think Christian men are any different?"

"COUPLES TRY TO TALK THEMSELVES INTO THINGS"

"I see people stuck in childish thinking, very self-absorbed, saying, 'Give me what I need!'" Sherry Amatenstein observes. Attach this attitude to the thought that "life is long and maybe I'll have five careers" and you've overengineered today's marriage picture into a Rube Goldberg design. How can an adultescent commit when there are couches left to surf and five more career paths to explore?

Looking at ladies first, so it's gone for Katy,* who has wandered her resolutely single way to thirty-four. The maze of her life in the last decade is representative of the adultescent genus. She started at Boston College, missed her home state of California, transferred to the University of San Francisco, and then switched to the University of California in Los Angeles. After graduation an Italian captured her heart and Katy moved to Tuscany and worked as a tour guide. The romance fizzled. Law school in California became her default.

"I found myself falling into the entire line of what you're supposed to do to be successful after law school and got a little lost," Katy now realizes. "I interviewed with big firms, didn't pass the bar, became disenchanted and decided I wanted to escape to where people would appreciate me just as a nice person." For Katy that meant declining a $125,000 offer from an international law firm based in Los Angeles and moving to Alaska to clerk for the state appellate court. The clerkship didn't last—"I had a low level of self-confidence with respect to my legal abilities"—so she joined the Peace Corps. After a stint in Tanzania, she returned to San Francisco and for one year was a case manager for Tenderloin Housing Clinic, which provides legal aid to tenants in an area rank with poverty, drugs, and crime. On a second try, Katy passed the bar. Soon she returned to Alaska to clerk for a criminal court judge. "I intended to stay in Alaska, but within months I knew it wasn't for me—too homogenous and insulated, with no diversity of opinion." Katy moved back east and earned a master's degree in social work from Columbia University, one of the best but costliest schools in the country. At thirty-two she graduated.

"With only a six-month grace period left before my loans were due, I felt anxious about returning to California without a job, so largely on a gut feeling, I became a school social worker in the Williamsburg area of Brooklyn." This is where Katy is now. Throughout her ramble,

Katy has had boyfriends but has never lived with anyone: "I'm not interested in making that commitment.

"Around twenty-seven I had a lightbulb thought, that I might not have my own biological children. Adoption on my own is something that could work well for me. I'm very comfortable with this idea." Less so, her mother, who married at twenty-one and lost her husband in a plane crash at forty-six. "When my mother was my age, she had five kids. I know she's proud of me, but there's a lot of concern, because my wandering path is unfamiliar to her. Around my age it becomes very clear that if children are something you want, you take steps in that direction. I don't feel this tremendous biological clock *yet*," she says and pauses. "Check back when I'm thirty-seven."

"For many emerging adults, especially women, age thirty is the deadline age set for marriage because it fits in with their plan for the rest of their life," writes Clark University psychology professor Jeffrey Arnett. "Thirty gives women two or three years to establish intimacy with their spouse and still have time to have a child or two before they pass their prime childbearing years. . . . Thirty is also the age at which they feel other people expect them to get married."

This can make skeptical women scream, wondering if all their friends have redeemed a *Brides* coupon the magazine neglected to send to them. "I feel as if everybody around me is growing up and getting married like wildfire while I keep staying the same age," grouses Cincinnati native Kara Guilfoyle, twenty-seven, a registered pediatric nurse working at night toward a master's degree to become a nurse practitioner. "It seems all pretend. How can these people be so sure? I think sometimes couples try to talk themselves into things. I look at some of my friends holding on to relationships because they're comfortable. They'll settle, not try for something better. I've dated a lot of guys, usually doctors or men I've met when I bartended or coached soccer, but I can't even imagine picking one or planning a wedding."

Nor can Sarah Foster* of Baltimore, thirty-five, who was recently invited to four weddings within five weeks. "One of my least maternal friends suddenly got married and immediately had a baby, which especially threw me for a loop. I felt like all these people were in on some big secret. How did so many of them find 'the one' so quickly? And why couldn't I? I surely don't have that many more issues than everyone else—or do I?"

Sarah has the kind of regrets you hear twanged in a country ballad: "I feel like I'm running out of time, wasting years with the wrong kind. When I was twenty-six, my live-in boyfriend told me he wanted to propose, but I felt we were too young, although I'd gotten my master's in Virginia, where people get married early. When I was thirty-one, I met this guy I thought I wanted to marry, but he was a player and wasn't interested. Then I went back to an old musician boyfriend who offered the security of guaranteed attention, but he was always literally walking a step ahead of me. Now I've exhausted my friends' friends and it's hard to figure out how to meet people. I wish I'd seen a long time ago that marriage was something I wanted. I'd always had this idea that if you found someone you loved enough, then you would get married, but marriage was not an end-all-be-all goal, and it was weird to specifically search for a marriage partner. Now I'm grasping at straws, trying to find someone."

As decades fly, men get to lose their hair, grow love handles, and eventually shuffle to the drugstore to refill their Viagra prescriptions, all with love lives intact. A recently widowed friend in his late sixties has been besieged by the brisket brigade of single women dropping off dinner as a way to meet. ("My mother tells me that if the food arrives in a nice dish, it means the woman hopes to strike up a relationship because you need to return the dish.") Recently I wanted to introduce an attractive single friend in her fifties to a man I know who is fourteen years older. "Women I go out with are no older than fifty," Mr. Not-a-Dreamboat sniffed.

"Men don't seem to have trouble meeting women at any age," confirms Kathy Berkman, MD, a psychiatrist practicing in New York City. "It's committing that's the issue. They ask, 'What if somebody better shows up?' They feel cornered, afraid to give up this 'fabulous' freedom that they don't actually have."

With no biological imperative to reproduce at an early age, men have the luxury of snickering at age deadlines for marriage. But as every journalist knows, deadlines can be merely pesky suggestions. As women get older, their ideas toward living together and marriage begin to mutate, too. While hurrying to achieve other goals, thirty looks more like a blur on the side of the road as hunting for Mr. 85 Percent Right gets back-burnered or falls off the list.

IS MARRIAGE OBSOLETE? DISCUSS.

"Financial pragmatism has become a reality for a lot of people in my generation," says Bonnie Johnson, thirty-one and not rushing to change her single status. Bonnie's professional life started out smooth as pudding. After grad school, she lived for five years in Las Vegas, employed by a major corporation, and invested in a condo. Then, kapow, layoff, right in the old kisser. "There's no idea of professional fidelity anymore," she says, thrumming with indignation. "I was forced to walk away from my underwater condo—you could have bought a car for what it was worth. This promise of the American dream is practically a punch line." Bonnie headed home to live with her mother in Park Ridge, the leafy suburb near Chicago's O'Hare Airport where Hillary Clinton grew up.

"When I was out of work, one of my older, married sisters began to actively search for someone for me to date. I told her, 'I need a job, not a man'" (which is in line with how 63 percent of users answered a question on a prominent dating site, admitting they'd rather "have the most amazing career" than "meet the love of my life"). It took Bonnie six months to find that job, becoming the executive director of Sister-House in Chicago, a small nonprofit women's recovery facility. Now she's searching for a "bohemian" apartment in a city neighborhood "within walking distance to at least one cool coffee shop. This is my vision of me happy. Why should I settle for less because social norms say I'm supposed to have kids and a white picket fence in the suburbs?"

For a lot of people her age, marriage, Bonnie has decided, is obsolete. "How many marriages actually last?" she ponders. "One of my sisters has been married for ten years and that's extraordinary, though it shouldn't be. Another sister had a baby five years ago, and right afterward, her husband lost his job. They've been struggling for their son's whole life.

"But one thing I know is that I don't know," Bonnie adds. "If I fell madly in love, I could see getting married, though I don't think I could see kids. Being the spoiled brat I was, with a parental scholarship for both undergrad and master's degrees, I'd feel remiss to not give a child whatever I was offered, and I don't see myself in that position anytime soon. I volunteer, work out, collect rare books, travel, and visit friends in other cities. Most of these things would be set aside if I had children. I see this firsthand. My sisters, who are mothers, no longer own their lives. They never get a break and have to consider their families and their children in all decisions. My dog—ten pounds of pure toughness—can be left alone and loves me unconditionally, which is twenty times better than the alternative, which seems depressing.

"What makes me okay with the idea of not having children is that I've been instilled with a vision of service, having a social justice impact in the world, doing something good. Every day I know I contribute without having a little baby staring me in the face, depending on me. It might be the most selfish and egotistical decision of my life to say I don't want to take on the responsibility of another life, but then I think of the Philip Larkin poem 'This Be the Verse,' and I think it makes sense. '*They fuck you up, your mum and dad,*'" Bonnie begins, ending with "'*don't have any kids yourself.*'"

The older females get, the less likely they are to want to marry, claims a recent Match.com study conducted by biological anthropologist Dr. Helen Fisher and evolutionary biologist Stephanie Coontz, Ph.D., of Evergreen State College. In the twenty-one to thirty-four age group, 62 percent of single women say they hope to wed, but by thirty-five to forty-four, the number sinks to 40 percent. The study also found that women want greater independence in their relationships than do men—more personal space, nights out, and vacations with their girlfriends—oh, and their own bank accounts. "This survey busts entrenched myths about women, men, sex and love," Dr. Fisher says.

Yet when I spoke to Alexa* of San Antonio, it was the fifteenth of February and she was cranky. "I despise Valentine's Day," she says. "When people find out I'm not married, they ask, 'Why not?' I know they're thinking, 'What's wrong with you?'"

This is not a question Alexa asks herself. At thirty-seven she is a part-time college professor and full-time executive at a company that sells power equipment. She has been engaged three times, twice to the same man. Alexa was twenty-three when she dumped her first fiancé because he cheated. The second time, the air force serviceman she expected to marry abruptly decided he didn't want her to live with him abroad. She returned his ring. A year later, he proposed again but broke it off by e-mail, complaining that Alexa had too much debt—$50,000 in car payments and school loans for a master's program from which, incidentally, she graduated with a 4.0, summa cum laude. "I dare a man to find a woman in her thirties with no debt!" she says. "This time I didn't return the ring—I hocked it to pay down the debt.

"I asked my parents if they were worried that I would be alone after they passed away. They said yes. My mother married at nineteen and had me nine months later. She has this idea that I need the same stability. My parents haven't seen that many independent women. I'm the first college graduate on both sides of the family. All my cousins are married with at least one child except the older gay ones. Many of them have moved back home with their parents with their kids because they're divorced and can't make it on their own. I've found that my life is complete despite not having a boyfriend or husband. I did the online dating thing, but once men realized I had a brain it was over—or else they didn't have their baggage under control. I have five friends who've divorced in the last five years, so at the moment I'm letting them do the dating. I live vicariously when the drama hits."

There's something to be said for taking care of yourself, says Mara,* twenty-eight. "I've had three relationships that have turned my life upside down. I ended all of them."

Bachelor number one was her college sweetheart in Indiana, a pilot she followed to Bakersfield, California. "After a year I felt bored. I thought, 'There's got to be something more.'" On the rebound, Mara connected with Bachelor number two, a classmate from junior high school whom she moved in with four hours away in San Diego, where she's continued to live. "That blew up in my face. It always seems to be the same issue: the men I give time to aren't emotionally mature."

Bachelor number three was a navy man with a grown son. This time, Mara got pregnant. "I wanted my boyfriend to be my knight in shining armor. 'We're going to do this together!' But in my core I didn't feel support and I had an abortion. My mother had offered to raise the child and was very disappointed with me. I couldn't explain to her—or to myself, completely—why I had an abortion. I felt torn between motherhood and moving forward in my career. I hold a degree in communications and have always wanted to be a news anchor. Having a child would set me back. I had images of me alone with a broken relationship, a screaming baby I could barely afford, and all my family back in Indiana.

"Every time I've broken up I'm starting over, but I'm learning lessons. I will never again give up my independence and space and compromise, and unless I have a ring on my finger, I won't cohabitate. All my friends from Indiana and every other woman in my family are married with kids. I want to fill my life with something, but I'm not sure it's kids. I'm too selfish for that now. I watch my sister and see how much motherhood and balancing the relationship with her husband takes out of her. It's tough, overwhelming! I try to picture myself in that same position and I'm not there yet. I'm relieved to not be married. Maybe ten years from now I may feel differently, but maybe not. Is there ever really going to be the right time, with the stars aligned? I feel it's never going to be that perfect."

Cathy* will be thirty-five next month. She canceled an elaborate wedding in 2006 after relocating to New Orleans to move in with her fiancé, a petroleum engineer. "We bought a house," she says. "Hurricane Katrina smacked it. The house made it through, banged and bruised. We did not. After seeing who I was stuck with in crisis mode, I decided I would be making a mistake. My dad told me, 'Better a minute before than a minute after,' and to charge a one-way ticket back to New York, stay with friends, dust myself off, and start over. Now I'm writing a book about how to investigate your date. I want someone with me who really wants to be with me, not a man who is worried about how his actions will affect his wallet. I'd love to meet somebody and be in it for the long run, but I'm not sure about marriage."

PICKY, PICKY, PICKY

"By thirty-five women may seek professional help because they can't find the guy at all," Dr. Kathy Berkman has noticed. "I hear a lot of 'good men are hard to find.' It's difficult for some women to acknowledge that they may be acting impatient or remote or believe the man should have a different personality strictly on their account. They aren't willing to compromise, finding things wrong with every man they meet without any awareness of what they might be doing to sabotage the relationship. They often think the problem lies with the other person." As a commenter said on Karen Campbell's blog post about why Christian men are delaying marriage, "Jesus himself would not be good enough for some of these girls."

But right back at you, *Homo doofus*. The same could be said of men, and often is, by the women who'd like to love them. "A matchmaker told me I'm the pickiest guy she ever met," says Mark Herschberg, thirty-seven, of New York City. "I've been looking for years for a wife and I'm not a hunchback in a terrible job. I'm six foot one, in shape, with three degrees from MIT. I build and fix start-up companies, do volunteer work, teach, and was a top ballroom dancer. I've gone on literally hundreds of dates yet struggle to find someone.

"I'm looking for a woman with positive values and an upbeat persona who has drive and intense passion about . . . something. It could be quilting. One ex is a top Sudoku champ, another was a whiz at jigsaw puzzles. But the problem with all the girls"—a word a lot of men use, although you rarely hear a woman say "boy"—"is that they're smart, pretty, nice, and went to good schools but they seem like they're bobbing along, waiting around to get married.

"Women in their twenties ruin it for everyone. The typical girl moves to New York in her early to mid-twenties because she always wanted to work in fashion or media. She earns about thirty-five thousand dollars a year, which in the city is dirt poor, but this is her dream even if it means sharing an apartment with three girls. She wants to date guys in their thirties because older men open doors and take her to nice places. It's not that these girls are all gold diggers, but it's hard for guys in their twenties—even if they earn seventy thousand dollars—to afford to take a girl to dinner.

"In their twenties girls just want to have fun. Right around thirty they flip. They become aware of their biological clock, want to settle down, and look for a guy who's thirty-four or thirty-six—and find that all these men date the twenty-five-year-olds. For a man, there's a tiny sweet spot in the thirty to thirty-two range before women start getting unhappy and feel the pressure of thinking, 'How soon can I marry this guy?'"

"At thirty women suddenly feel that if they're not married, they're a loser," says Rob Braddock, thirty, a political fund-raiser in San Francisco. "Some are jaded. They've been in relationship after relationship with a guy who has treated them poorly, so they think all guys will behave that way." At that age women's panic or clarity may show as clearly as a visible panty line. "I've been on a second date where women say, 'I want to get married and have kids.' Women don't have a good poker face about wanting marriage. They should be way more subtle or I feel as if I'm being suckered. In a few years I might be at the exact same mental place, but I hope I won't blatantly advertise it." A corollary

Rob finds is that many women are looking for a guy "to complete them—a recipe for disaster, because one complete person has to meet another complete person."

Here's where it starts to seem as if the dating scene is as unjust as the fact that we call a male dog "a dog" and a female, "a bitch." "At risk of sounding totally misogynistic, a lot of women put too much value on their looks," Rob suggests. "In fairness, I suppose we can blame our culture, which says a woman's worth is based on physical appearance. But thinking this way, every day your value depreciates is a biological fact. You're not going to be as cute at thirty-two as twenty-two, while for me, a man, every day my perceived value increases, because I'm becoming more established in my career."

Arrogant much? Yet the man who spoke the words above, disturbing on several levels, was eminently pleasant. "I'm not looking to date a supermodel with a doctorate," he stresses. "I'm looking for a decently good-looking girl, decently smart, someone who should be able to have a happy life without me. I will be completely disinterested in a woman who is smoking hot but stupid, or totally ugly but smart."

MEN FEELING THE PAIN

In the social sweepstakes, it's hard to avoid concluding that adultescent men come out the winners, yet many seem deeply confused, frustrated, and unhappy. In the last five years, Nicholas,* thirty-three, of Brooklyn, has had two serious girlfriends who left him, "probably because I've had a wandering path." Currently Nicholas is waiting for approval from the New York Department of Education to become a substitute teacher. He's done freelance writing and has worked with kids in various capacities, including being a male nanny. "The people I think of as impressive aren't the lawyers and businessmen—they seem miserable," he says. "I'm impressed with entrepreneurs and authors, but I've shied away from that when I saw all the work it takes. After a while, girls start to think about the future, where I'm living very much in the present, doing things that are fun and interesting, though it's been hard for me to make anything profitable. I seem to have problems with ambition and, as a result, come off as insecure, which isn't attractive, although my personal security isn't in jeopardy, because my parents will continue to support me if necessary. They've always been supportive of whatever I've done." This generous family also sets a high bar. If anyone would Google them, they would find writers, thinkers, cancer curers, and a winner of the Nobel Prize.

"My roommate is thirty-eight and has been searching for a woman to settle down with for over a decade now," says Paige Hays,* of Philadelphia. "Sean still hasn't found his Ms. Right. It's a cryin' shame because this is a really good guy—smart, educated, domesticated, well groomed, with a master's in divinity, wants kids, white picket fence, the whole nine yards, and he can't find a woman who isn't crazy, married, kid-phobic, or plain narcissistic."

Logistics make it hard to date, Sean Slack says in his defense. The forty-hour workweek—he is a community organizer—is obsolete; finding time for a relationship is the first hurdle. "The second challenge is emotional," he says. "Being single this long, I've been turned down enough to get gun-shy. Third, I grew up as the proverbial nice guy in the 'just say no' era. The comment I heard over and over was, 'Don't ever change.' Women will say they want a guy like me, but if you watch who they get involved with, they want another type. It took me a long time to realize the important trait for a man who wants to find a wife is confidence, which tends to get bundled with good looks and athleticism.

"I realize that I've never developed the willingness to be rejected."

Teaching children to handle rejection has never been high on the boomer curriculum. "I grew up in Bucks County, Pennsylvania, a high-achieving community where everybody was on a college track with many AP courses. I was overscheduled, with no time to date or develop social skills. All the emphasis was on getting into a good school, which I did—Notre Dame. But when I got there, there was no casual dating. Couples either were boyfriend and girlfriend or single, nothing in-between. Now I'm trying to reconcile how to be confident in a sexy way with the compassionate, nice person I want to be."

When siblings and best friends find someone, those are game changers, says University of Michigan graduate Dan Adelman,* thirty-three, who works for a television network based in New York. "We shout 'man down' at each wedding. You don't want to be the guy left behind and feel especially left out at Christmas when you're visiting your parents and they ask if you want to spend New Year's Eve with them.

"Now with so many people losing their jobs it's okay not to be married at thirty-five, but if you're still single at thirty-seven, that seems dreadful. I feel I'm at the peak age to get married. I've got a short window here, so I'm really looking. I meet women in bars, sports events, through setups, college events, and charity stuff where you're already vetted. Online is also a great option. You write a hundred e-mails and maybe get five responses. I've got a nice apartment," Dan says. "But after two weeks of dates I see women ogling my closet space, looking as if they want to move in. Once they get to five dates they are saying, 'Are you sleeping with anyone else?' which is code for hoping to becoming exclusive. I find this off-putting."

Enough men are flummoxed about how to meet women and fall in love that Jordan Harbinger has been able to quit his job as a Wall Street attorney to establish himself as a dating coach. His mission began with podcasts he created while at the University of Michigan law school. After taking the bar exam, Jordan traveled in Southeast Asia and Europe. By the time he returned, the podcasts had such a following he began broadcasting *Game On*, a Sirius radio show dedicated to helping men improve their success with the opposite sex. This led to The Art of Charm—"either you have it or you learn it from us"—which instructs guys via Skype and in New York and Los Angeles, where Jordan has moved. The company has seven employees. ("We started with sixteen but fired a bunch of lazy bums.")

Only recently has Jordan, thirty-one, decided to "wife it up in the near future," lest he become "sixty with a ten-year-old kid." It's difficult to find the right girl, he acknowledges, even when you're a (self-trained) professional. Jordan's theory: to constantly date. "The passive person says, 'I'm so busy.' They wait to win the lottery but don't buy a ticket." Jordan admits he used to be passive himself, never going beyond texting women he'd met or drinking with them in a group. "Now as long as I'm physically attracted, I make an effort to get to know someone." This is, of course, advice that every mother has offered since Eve, garnered from noticing that people start to look more physically attractive to one another the better we know them.

Jordan's second commandment is for people to relax their requirements. "No one wants to be seen as dating *downward*. For guys, this means seeing someone less attractive than their ex, and for women it's social status. It becomes a really big problem. Women don't find happiness. They find rich guys."

Ironically, a parent's contentment can be a factor that puts a child's lack of social life in bold relief. "I think both of my daughters have impossibly high standards for finding a man and I have unwittingly had some hand in it," says Joan Minkoff,* of Milwaukee. "Jessica, my younger daughter, has said more than once, 'You and Daddy are so lucky—you're attractive, intelligent, and ambitious. I don't want anything less than that. I don't want to compromise.'

"My daughters grew up in a household where they watched a mother and father devote themselves to one another. My husband is a very accomplished physician yet has always encouraged me. Where someone else may have said, 'You've turned left and you've turned right—enough already!' he's cheered me on as I've gone from teacher to school psychologist to physician."

Joan and her husband, Scott,* both came from "pedestrian" households. They went to the local branch of the state university and lived at home during college because neither set of parents could afford for them to live in dorms and no high school guidance counselor walked them through applying for a scholarship. "Scott and I met as freshmen on the commuter bus. We married at twenty-one—the only way we knew to leave home—and took nothing from our families just as we knew from nothing. Two babies acting like grown-ups.

"We've gone far beyond what our parents could have imagined and we've raised our two girls as if the world is their oyster. We've wanted them to have every opportunity we never had—fancy private schools, summer camps, and travel programs all over the world. When my daughters still lived at home, I saw life through the illusion that I was doing all the right things," Joan says. "The girls always performed well in school, had friends and outside interests, and never did what they weren't supposed to do. They lived a copacetic existence, with not a lot of drama or need for it." Ellen,* now thirty-eight, marched off to Harvard, earned a Ph.D., and is a professor at a prestigious university. Jessica, thirty-six, majored in Middle Eastern languages and culture at Yale and moved to Israel, where she practices law.

"Everything turned out the way it was supposed to." Until, in Joan's opinion, now: neither Ellen nor Jessica has had a serious boyfriend since graduate school, although both, according to Mom, are near perfect.

"They know that I'd like for them to be married, so they each have someone in their life who loves them as much as I do," Joan says. "I don't want to be The One because there isn't someone else. I'm restless in the middle of the night, ruminating about my daughters staying single. I don't want them to be alone. Who will worry about them? 'I don't want to get married so badly that I'll just take anyone,' one daughter said. On an intellectual level I agree, but I think, 'What if you can't find that special love?' The older a woman gets, how many good guys are going to be left who haven't been snatched up? I gently suggested to her that she might consider having a child on her own. 'I'm trying to get tenure,' she said. 'I'd like to think I will still meet someone. I haven't given up hope and hope you haven't, either, but if I reach forty, I'll know what to do. You need to trust me.'"

Chapter 12

A WOMAN WALKS INTO A SPERM BANK

I believed I wanted to have a child, I was not surprised to find myself at thirty-five, and then forty, without one. . . . [M]y body was no longer what it had been, but I found it difficult to believe that the possibility of having my own child could expire without my explicit agreement.

—*Great House* by Nicole Krauss

When a friend asked me shortly after I had become engaged, "Do you think you'll have kids?" I felt bonked on the head. Finding a wedding dress that didn't look as if it had escaped from a Cinderella comic book had been challenge enough. I was assuredly pro-choice, but *that* choice? Off my radar screen. Only when nailed to the wall did I realize I'd assumed my marriage would one lucky distant day be at least a three-legged stool: daddy, mommy, and a bun in my own Easy-Bake Oven. The chutzpah!

After we married, my boy-husband and I dodged conversations about parenthood. It took four years to get to what the hell, why not try for a baby? Apparently, the moment we made that decision the cosmos got the message: nine months later we counted ourselves among the fortunate when we delivered a healthy baby boy. Among my high school friends from North Dakota, I was an old mom at twenty-eight; for my friends in New York City, I was strangely young, out of sync with all things cool.

Having a second child was not the same slam-dunk. Again, we were in no rush; one child had seemed like plenty of novelty, responsibility, and intimidation for two parents as gaga and inept as ourselves. When we ultimately decided to go for baby number two, there were, in ob-gyn speak, secondary infertility issues. It took almost six years to give our first son a brother. I was thirty-three. My doctor had invoked the age of thirty-five as the Berlin Wall of childbearing, mentioning any number of grotesque possibilities that might befall the hoary, fossilized, thirty-five-plus mom known as an *elderly primapara*. If I wanted more than two children, he urged me to make haste.

Decades later, the decision to remain childless by choice or childless but hubby-free is not uncommon and far more openly discussed than years ago. According to a study by the Center for Work-Life Policy, 43 percent of college-educated women between the ages of thirty-three and forty-six are childless. Recent census figures confirm that there are far more women in their forties without children now than there were in past decades. In 1976, just 10 percent of all women aged forty to forty-four had no children. That percentage had jumped to 19 percent by 2010.

A 2010 Pew Research survey found that 52 percent of Millennials say being a good parent is "one of the most important things" in life, but just 30 percent say the same about having a successful marriage—meaning adultescents value parenthood over marriage. Pew Research surveys also find that Millennials are less likely than older adults to say that a child needs a home with both a father and mother to grow up happily and that single parenthood and unmarried couple parenthood are bad for society. The delay in marriage among today's young adults has been accompanied by a corresponding increase in the rate of out-of-wedlock birth. It is more likely for a woman who has never married to have a child now than it was in the 1970s, census figures show. Just 3 percent of women who had never been married had a child in 1976. Now the number is about 21 percent, up sharply even from 2008, when it was 15 percent.

If women do embrace the idea of a baby-maybe, they are wired for waiting. Adultescence is a young enough stretch to allow for women to stay on the fence and postpone making a decision about whether or not they want to become mothers one day, whether by reproduction or adoption, or to opt for the freedom that remaining child-free allows. Longing to have a baby may be on the docket—but only after marching through school, invading the workforce, auditioning numerous partners, and making the usual detours to standard wander years' destinations. "I absolutely think I was raised with the idea that there wasn't a time limit, that I could do it all," says Shannon Davidson of Toronto, who spent the last half of her thirties grappling with how to answer the baby question.

A FERTILITY CRIB SHEET

Women's groupthink may have changed, but the human body hasn't gotten the memo. The twenties remain prime time for pregnancy. By then, wacky menstrual cycles common to teenagers have stabilized and ovulation tends to become predictable. A woman's eggs are also freshest and healthiest in the twenties, making them choice contestants for fertilization. Add on the yoga payoff, which puts women this age in peak physical shape, untouched by the veritable *Grey's Anatomy* of insults that even the thirties brings: decreased fertility! miscarriage risk! pre-eclampsia! thyroids in a tizz! and cancer. A 2009 study of Swedish women of childbearing age found that the incidence of breast cancer associated with pregnancy more than doubled between 1963 and 2002, partly—the scientist-authors suggest—because of births to older mothers. There are also chromosomal abnormalities to ponder, which from age twenty to twenty-nine are found in only one in every 375 births, but by age thirty-five affect one in 178.

"From a biological standpoint, peak fertility is in the twenties, which once, culturally, was when people usually conceived," says Owen K. Davis, MD, associate director of the Center for Reproductive Medicine and Infertility at the Weill Cornell Medical College and a board certified obstetrician-gynecologist and reproductive endocrinologist. "Now people who are in their twenties think they're immortal."

High school health and sex ed classes emphasize contraception and avoiding sexually transmitted diseases. There's scant information on the time horizon for conception. "You'd be surprised at what intelligent men and women who walk in my door at thirty-eight don't know," Dr. Davis frets. "Since educated adults are taught to religiously use a barrier method of contraception for protection against pregnancy and disease, there's an essential assumption that the minute you stop you'll conceive." Yet when you look at the numbers, you wonder how the human race has managed to stick around:

- Fertility starts to decline in a meaningful way around thirty-three, with a steep downward plunge at thirty-seven. Natural fecundity in the mid-thirties is about 30 percent per month but by the forties drops to a mere 5 percent per month.

- In leading IVF (in vitro fertilization) programs, by the age of forty-three, the live birth rate per try is only 12 to 15 percent, "although this is ten times more successful than trying on their own," Dr. Davis says. By forty-five the number sinks to fewer than 10 percent.

- It's not only women who need to heed the booming biological clock. Men over thirty-five are twice as likely to be infertile as those under twenty-five, reports Harry Fisch, MD, director of the Male Reproductive Center at New York-Presbyterian Hospital/Columbia University Medical Center and author of *The Male Biological Clock*. Studies also show that, as with older women, older men are more likely to have babies with birth defects due to the decreased genetic quality of their sperm. "Every cell in the body ages," Dr. Fisch says. "Why would you think the sperm or testicles don't age?"

"I married at thirty-four and we decided to try to start a family right away," says one of Dr. Davis's former patients, a Harvard Business School grad. "My son was born on his due date thirteen months after we married. With my MBA hubris intact, I had the false confidence that the next pregnancy could be as easily managed. At thirty-eight my husband and I began to try again. I had three miscarriages. We went through a battery of tests, but no obvious problems were revealed. Fortunately, after one round of fertility drugs, I got pregnant, stayed pregnant, and had my daughter a month after my fortieth birthday. Now when I see other childless women moving toward the fertility abyss that forty can be, I want to tell them not to delay motherhood if their circumstances permit. We've changed. Biology hasn't."

"I'LL HAVE WHAT SHE'S HAVING"

"If they're thirty, single, and hope to have a child, women should put looking for a mate on their shopping list, just like getting an education," advises Dr. Michael Feinman, a reproductive endocrinologist and infertility specialist who is medical director of HRC Fertility, with offices through the Los Angeles area. Ph.D. in neuroscience? Check. Leopard-sighting in Sri Lanka? Baby-daddy? Check.

That the media is engorged with tales of glowing, bold-faced mommies cradling infants they gave birth to at ages we associate with bifocals only adds to the delusion of conception being a medical act you can delay indefinitely. Stand-up comedienne Kathy Griffin presented a special titled *50 & Not Pregnant*. She didn't need to look far for material. Former supermodel Cheryl Tiegs had twins at fifty-two. Actress Holly Hunter did the same at forty-seven. Why not you, too, when Celine Dion, Madonna, Nicole Kidman, Halle Berry, Salma Hayek, Geena Davis, Courteney Cox, and Julianne Moore all had a child at forty-one or a decade later?

"The bump of women expecting miracles started in the 1990s and has been noticeable for many years," Dr. Feinman says. "Whenever a celebrity story breaks, our phones light up with questions about how so-and-so had a baby with 'her own eggs.' The truth is that most of those celebrities have had donor eggs and are lying about it. I've seen actresses who've said 'my eggs' when I *know* they weren't. And it's often twins. Isn't that interesting? How does a woman miraculously conceive twins with her own eggs in her late forties or fifties? Doesn't that tell you something? Many births to older celebrities create unfair expectations for other women, who feel as if the rich and famous can avail themselves of special technology. I feel bad when people call us and say, 'I'll have what she's having.'"

"You hear about the one woman having a baby at forty-three with her own eggs, not the nine hundred ninety-nine failures," protests Dr. Mark Perloe, reproductive endocrinologist and medical director of the Georgia Reproductive Specialists in Atlanta. "The media suggests that everyone will have success. There are limits to having a child with your own eggs."

Young women make many assumptions their older selves later question. Dating that unemployed drummer with the video game addiction? Quitting law school? *Going* to law school? Who thought these were swell ideas? Early attitudes toward having or postponing kids are often not irreversible decisions, but their psychic fallout can mount.

Wandering takes adultescents far and wide, and given the high rates at which women go to college and grad school and succeed in the workplace, for some the journey is often a vertical trajectory as they clamber up a corporate ladder. "I never thought I'd have children—I was too in love with my career," says Cassi Christiansen of Fairview, Oregon, a suburb of Portland. "By the time I was thirty, I'd become the first female vice president and member of a senior management team at a coffee company. There was no way I was going to give that up."

Cassi met her husband, Jeff, when she was in her early thirties. He wanted kids. She did not but softened after they married and went off the pill at thirty-five. "We thought we'd wait a few months and bang, I'd be pregnant." So convinced were Cassi and Jeff about being able to engineer conception, it became part of an overall design in which little was left to chance, including the blessed location. They planned a trip to Italy because they considered it the most romantic place on earth to make a baby.

Italy wasn't the charm. In fact, Cassi spent the next five years sweating out fertility tests and treatments, popping herbs and supplements, seeing a physical therapist that specialized in female reproductive issues, practicing prenatal yoga, and experimenting with acupuncturists, psychics, shamans, and a Mayan abdominal masseuse. "And this," she allows, "was only the short list." The more months that went by, the more focused and determined she got, which led her to quit her sacred job because she thought its stress was contributing to her inability to conceive. Not working failed to help and jacked up her frustration. "I was used to setting a goal, doing whatever it took to make it happen, and reaping the rewards," she reflects. "Our generation was taught we could have it all—on our time line—but the things that helped me excel in the business world weren't the same qualities it takes to conceive.

"I finally told myself if I wasn't pregnant by forty, I'd let go of the dream." A few days before that bingo birthday Cassi became pregnant. "We were overjoyed. Then I miscarried. It was heartbreaking, but I truly believe that little soul came into my life to tell me not to give up, that it was possible for me to conceive." At forty-one Cassi had a child. "In the meantime, I was able to build an independent coaching business. More than half of my clients have struggled with infertility due to waiting."

"Fertility is not endless," Dr. Perloe stresses. Nonetheless, there is considerable reason for infertile women to be encouraged; medical research has found countless ways to lend a hand. In the last decade, 1 percent of all infants born in the United States have been conceived using assisted reproductive technology (ART). The most common and oldest procedure is in vitro fertilization (IVF), where egg cells are fertilized by sperm outside the body. IVF has been practiced for more than thirty years, with some of today's adultescents its insouciant result. But assuming that IVF will work is like banking on poker for your retirement plan. While a woman under thirty-five has a 35 percent chance of having a baby after a single IVF attempt with her own eggs, by the time she hits forty-one her chance is below 10 percent. IVF is not always covered even in part by insurance plans and the United States is one of the most expensive countries in which to have the procedure. You find ads for potential donors in mass-market magazines geared to young readers like *Time Out New York* and on Facebook, Craigslist, Twitter, and billboards. Recently, a chipper advertisement of this sort popped on the screen at my local movie theater between a pitch for a realtor and a pizza parlor. Ads in newspapers at Harvard, Princeton, and Yale promised $35,000 for donors; one ad placed on behalf of an anonymous couple in the Brown *Daily Herald* offered $50,000 for "an extraordinary egg donor," tempting women to repay their college loans by donating eggs. The Web site EliteDonors.com has cited up to $80,000 for a blue-ribbon donor.

"There are as many egg donor agencies as Starbucks," Dr. Feinman says. "Donor eggs can return a woman to IVF success rates that she'd experience with her own eggs under the age of thirty-five," but the process, he says, "is pricing itself out of the realm of regular people." In 1987, Dr. Feinman helped found one of the first anonymous egg donor programs, working with leading ethicists to develop guidelines for egg donation; women were paid $500. A study in a leading bioethics journal found that the compensation currently being touted in ads aimed at students at prestigious colleges often vastly exceeds industry guidelines. The study examined more than one hundred egg donation ads from sixty-three college newspapers and found that 25 percent offered compensation exceeding the $10,000 maximum suggested by the American Society for Reproductive Medicine's voluntary guidelines.

CHOICE MOTHERS VISITING THE SPERM BANK

There's a shimmer on a child's hair in the sunlight. There are rainbow colors in it, tiny, soft beams of just the same colors you can see in the dew sometimes. They're in the petals of flowers, and they're on a child's skin.

—*Gilead* by Marilynne Robinson

Men can wait to have kids; women can't. If becoming an adult is defined by self-sufficiency, perhaps the most independent, take-charge, and harrowing act of all is for a woman to stop waiting to find a perfect partner and to adopt or intentionally get pregnant on her own.

"The older you get the sooner you realize in a relationship whether it works or doesn't," says Samantha Mendelsohn,* a Chicago attorney, who decided to have a baby on her own when she turned thirty-six and was relationship-less. "I found that a lot of guys my age either didn't want children or weren't in as much of a rush. They can marry someone in the twenties later when they decide they want children."

Raise your hand if you think being a parent is easy. No one? I found bringing up children to be the most daunting responsibility I've ever had or expect to have—and I did it with a hands-on, equal partner, a feminist's dream of a guy who rarely took a business trip and who happily shared in every task except those I co-opted: birthday party planning, clothes shopping, and haircuts. Which is why when I meet women who've gone rogue to have kids on their own, most often by making one or more costly withdrawals from the sperm bank, I can barely find the words to express my awe for and curiosity about every one of these gutsy broads.

If you can make one generalization about women who have a baby on their own, it's that they're independent thinkers. Shannon Davidson of Toronto didn't start college until the age of twenty-three and "five months after graduation had the most desirable sports PR job in Canada." She dated and lived with two men, but says she never wanted to settle for less than what she felt she deserved.

"At age thirty, I said if at thirty-five I wasn't married, I'd think about having a child on my own," Shannon says. "I woke up on my thirty-fifth birthday and spent the following year furious. All these high-maintenance women around me had solved this problem! Why not me? Then I decided I could fix this and for the next year I mulled options for having a child on my own, knowing full well I was privileged enough to consider them.

"The adoption process could be endless, I learned, since as a single woman I'd be at the bottom of the food chain, so I had my doctor explain how it worked to have a baby on my own. Within three months I chose my sperm donor from an international bank. There were pictures available of him, but I didn't want to know what he looks like. I didn't care. Friends helped me check into everything I did think was important, from health history to spirituality. I particularly focused on the essays attached to an application where a man explains why he elects to donate sperm. I ultimately chose a photographer who'd donated at nineteen. Back then his language was arrogant and self-absorbed, but when he donated again at thirty-five he'd grown up. I liked that."

Her first four insemination attempts failed. "Looking back, I'm not surprised. In anticipation of being pregnant I'd amped up my career 280 percent. My doctor said, 'Let's chill and start again.'" Shannon took off a few months and on her next attempt conceived. She was thirty-nine and sailed through pregnancy.

"I was texting in the delivery room, where my sister and a good friend met me. Delivery was easy-peasy—no drugs. I used midwives and was home an hour and fifteen minutes later with my son, Jack

Winston, and made dinner. I stayed home for three months. Now I work full-time for an ad agency and JW goes to his caregiver five doors away, his 'big family at the end of the street.' I never thought, 'I need a child.' I always asked myself, do I have what a child needs? Before I got pregnant, I made sure I had a network and backup system, which includes my family, who has been insanely supportive."

Throughout her twenties and thirties Wendy Dembo of Santa Monica sampled job after job, none in a cubicle or nine-to-five—working for *Spy*, the iconic humor magazine, and Jive Records, a hip-hop label, presenting public art. "Years ago I interviewed with Faith Popcorn, the trend spotter, who looked at my résumé and said, 'You've worked at so many places!' I thought, 'You're Faith Popcorn. Don't you know this is what people's lives are like now?'" Eventually, when Wendy discovered there was money in tapping into her natural ability to tell people what to see, where to go, or whom to hire, she became a professional trend spotter, like Popcorn. It was not a life that synchronized with a sustained relationship. "Once I made a New Year's resolution to spend one night a week at home—I worked long hours and was always at art openings, parties, events, and clubs.

"In New York City, being single is what's normal," Wendy explains. "The city practically enables it. It's almost strange to have a partner." She had no serious relationships and did nothing to try to have a child. Still, she always thought she'd be a mom, possibly with donated sperm. "When I was thirty-nine I read a *New York Times* cover story, 'Looking for Mr. Good Sperm,' and thought, wow, other women are doing this. I didn't realize it was organized and happening."

It was. The population of single women who are "choice mothers" has vastly expanded, though by precisely how much is hard to guesstimate, because the National Center for Health Statistics doesn't break out numbers for women who use donor sperm, nor does Single

Mothers by Choice, an extensive networking organization with thousands of members throughout the country. What we do know is that by the Centers for Disease Control's best estimates, the number of babies born to unmarried women between the ages of thirty and forty-four in America has risen, while the number born to unmarried women between fifteen and twenty-four has dropped.

"Not long after I read the *Times* article I visited my parents in L.A. and met one of their new friends. He owned the California Cryobank, the largest sperm bank in the country. If that wasn't a sign, I don't know what is. When I got back to Manhattan, I discussed insemination with my gynecologist. He wasn't enthusiastic. When I pressed him months later, I learned he was concerned about my being able to support a child. This was *my* problem, not his, so I went ahead. I picked a filmmaker, because he seemed like somebody I might know rather than, say, the Peruvian doctor or the Swedish skier. I made sure to use an 'open donor' who'd be willing to be contacted by any offspring after they reached the age of eighteen."

Using a sperm donor is as easy as ordering from Zappos, but again, it's expensive—$5,000 a pop for each insemination—and not covered by insurance. Wendy conceived on her third cycle of insemination. She was forty.

"When I went into labor it was 11 P.M. I called my Mom in L.A., who hopped on the next flight. When I got to the hospital I was dilated to 9.75 centimeters. My mom arrived at 9:10 A.M. and I had my daughter, Ruby, fifteen minutes later."

"I FELT THE UNIVERSE WAS TELLING ME NO"

When her husband didn't want kids, Teresa* divorced at twenty-three. At thirty she gave up waiting for another man, nested in a house near a Minneapolis lake, and shifted from advertising into feature films, which meant long hours and little opportunity for romance beyond her film crew. Her life allowed for time off to travel, which she did extensively, including "the grown-up version of backpacking" in Europe.

After several years, Teresa says she realized if she wanted a family something had to change. "When the call came for the next movie, I turned it down and started producing a show on HGTV. My doctor said thirty-five was the worry line and I had already crossed it. At thirty-seven I panicked. I didn't want to have a child by myself. I was strong but had my limits. Really, no thank you. I put out the call to family and friends that I was serious about dating, signed up with dating agencies, and spent money on a matchmaker."

Ultimately Teresa realized she would have a child on her own or not at all. "I didn't want my baby to not know his father, so I arranged with various friends, including a former partner, to be a donor. Each time their life kept taking them in another direction."

Teresa reluctantly decided to take a number with adoption. The list of countries at the time that would accept a single woman—China, Mongolia, and Russia—was short, with waiting lists long. "The universe was telling me 'no.' I focused on work, building a cabin on a Wisconsin river, and crossed the Gulf in a chartered sailboat. But my dreams of having a child wouldn't let go. I'd changed careers for a more stable schedule. If I gave up now, what did the last eight years of my life mean?"

The answer came in a passing comment from a friend who said, "I hate to see you give up—you'd make a great mom." Teresa's soul screamed, "Yes! I don't want to look back with regret." She reactivated the adoption process, this time in Guatemala. Tragically, her first child died of SIDS (sudden infant death syndrome) right before she was due to pick him up. "After that I almost gave up for good, but at forty-two, I became a mother to my beautiful baby boy, Cole."

THE FREEZER SECTION

"Women used to grow up with their mothers instilling in them that they had to get married and start a family," remarks Roberta Victor, MD,* a Boston dermatologist. "My mom got married at twenty-one, but she sent me a different cultural message and it represents a significant social shift: to think I could do anything and everything!

"I was never the girl who dreamt about the wedding dress, the husband, the baby. I was my high school valedictorian, graduated from an Ivy League college with a chemistry degree, got a master's in molecular biology, and went on to get a joint MD-Ph.D., all by twenty-nine. I was consumed with becoming the professional person I wanted to be. Every single guy I dated wanted to get married. I had zero interest.

"At a certain point my mother tried to reason with me, saying one day I'd wake up and have regrets." She was right. Roberta's regret detonated like a time bomb. "At thirty-two I was walloped with baby lust. Babies, babies, babies! They were all I saw or thought about—that and pregnant women. Ever since then I've needed babies in my tummy. When I talk to my family, I deny wanting to be a mother, but I do and it's frustrating. My last three relationships with men have been short-lived. I felt so much pressure to have this part of my life resolved, I couldn't be myself.

"I don't want to feel this desperation to find a mate," she moans. "I used to date only one guy at a time, but I can't afford monogamy anymore. From now on, it's the pair and a spare. There is a level of shame or guilt associated with this, but I don't want to worry about it. I'm turning thirty-seven and have promised myself if I don't find a suitable mate in the next year or two I will freeze my eggs and it's sperm bank time, baby!"

If only I could develop an app for freezing women's eggs.

"There's quite bit of interest in this option, but the paradox is that the women who generally have the resources to freeze eggs generally don't have the eggs," says Dr. Perloe. "The majority of women start too late, when their fertility is in rapid decline. Woman who ought to be freezing their eggs are about twenty-nine. They wouldn't need to put away many to be successful in having a baby later, and at that age, the average egg retrieval is twelve to eighteen per try. But for a woman this age, time and money are a real issue." At Dr. Perloe's clinic patients who wish to freeze eggs select from packages costing $20,000 per cycle, plus drugs at about $3,500 per cycle. "At, say, thirty-eight a woman would have a reasonable chance of retrieving maybe only three or four eggs per try," he says, "and the chance of an egg resulting in a live-born birth is only two to three percent."

There is also a difference between freezing eggs and preserving fertility. Given how recent the technology is, doctors don't know much about how viable eggs are for conception after freezing, Dr. Perloe concedes. "Not many women have come back yet to utilize their eggs." But even with the iffiness of the process, women in their late thirties and up are plunging ahead with fingers crossed.

Brigette Mueller started her work life as a concert promoter, which she continued throughout her twenties. Next up, she was a filmmaker in Los Angeles, where her movie credits include *Waitress, The Open Road*, and *Bride and Prejudice*. At thirty-three she and her boyfriend ended a seven-year relationship. "I would have had a child by thirty-five had that relationship continued," she says. "At a certain age you ask, 'What is the rest of my life about?' For me it meant children." At the same time a married sister used IVF to conceive twins at age forty. Another sister, who was single, became a mother at forty-one via a sperm donor. "She said it was easier to pick a donor than doing online dating." Brigette's sister had sperm shipped from California to her doctor in Philadelphia. On her second attempt, an egg was fertilized that became Brigette's niece.

This sister took on the wingman role, urging Brigette to "do something." Though Brigette's Beverly Hills ob-gyn insisted that she had ample time to conceive on her own, Brigette did independent research and decided that freezing her own fertilized embryos would be her best option. Now Brigette is forty-two with forty eggs in a Santa Monica freezer. "I hope this will give me four tries to get pregnant, since you need about ten per try. I still want the chance to have a genetic link to my child and with frozen eggs I could theoretically give birth ten years from now, even when I'm in menopause."

Egg freezing is no St. Patrick's Day parade. Brigette had to pump herself up with hormones, which caused the equivalent of rabid PMS (premenstrual syndrome), and it cost approximately $60,000 out of pocket. After this investment of time, money, and stress, she has no immediate plans to use the frozen eggs. "I will only try to become pregnant with my frozen eggs if I'm in a relationship, because I don't want to go through pregnancy by myself," she says. "If I'm forty-five and still not in love with someone I'm planning to have a child with, I'll use an egg and sperm donor or even adopt. Knowing I have the eggs frozen makes me feel more empowered and relaxed." Educating women about fertility and conception has become her mission through a documentary she's completing called *My Future Baby*.

Where does this leave adultescents' parents? Confused when they observe the lives of accomplished mid-thirties daughters. "My daughter has kissed a lot of frogs," says Karen Bates* of Washington. "Jill* is beautiful, a successful labor lawyer, sings with a band on the weekends, and was getting to that age where she didn't know what she was going to do because she really wanted kids. We talked about it all the time. I'd do the motherly thing: commiserate. When my daughter came up with the idea of egg freezing, it gave me pause, from the ethical viewpoint, and it's very expensive." While Karen was coming around, Jill decided to go ahead with the procedure, her mother at her side. Doctors harvested a dozen eggs.

Not long after, online dating finally yielded one non-amphibian suitor. Now Jill is engaged and Karen looks forward to joining the ranks of boomer grandparents, a group so eager for this experience they would have the grandchildren themselves if they could, and once in a while do. As a former editor of women's magazines, I had story pitches cross my desk at least once a year like the tale of the fifty-nine-year-old Del Ray, Florida, mom who gave birth to her own twin grandchildren. In this case, her daughter had undergone a hysterectomy at age twenty-five after being diagnosed with cervical cancer. Doctors had harvested the daughter's eggs prior to her treatments and hysterectomy and they were implanted in Nana's uterus. If moms will do this because their daughters are ill, why not because twenty- and thirtysomethings are building a sewage system in a Third World village or a criminal law practice? The boundaries of helicopter grandmotherhood are simply an envelope ready to be pushed.

More important, where does this leave adultescent women? Inevitably, Mother Nature raises the question, and in wander years fashion, adultescents answer by improvising.

"When I discovered I was pregnant at twenty-three my initial reaction was numbness," says Erica Zidel, now twenty-eight. "My boyfriend Ted and I had been together at Harvard for several years, but we'd broken up. I had moved to Manhattan for a job. It was a complicated decision, but I chose to have the baby and co-parent with Ted." The couple did not discuss marriage. "The decisions to be together and to raise our child were separate," Erica says. "Ted and I aren't great romantically, but we're good co-parents."

When their son, Gavin, was three months old, Erica followed Ted to Seattle, where he'd gotten a job offer with McKinsey and Company, the consulting firm. For a time, Ted's mother, who lives in Idaho, moved nearby and helped the couple. All along, Erica, the formal custodial parent, has worked as a management consultant. Erica and Ted divide their expenses proportionally, according to each of their incomes, which fluctuate. "I know we should have a legal arrangement," she says, but they don't, and Erica relies on trusting that they will continue to "be on the same page with finances and child rearing."

Now Ted and Erica are business partners as well—seeing a need, they've started an online babysitting co-op service, SittingAround .com. Dating? "Not a priority," Erica says. "Between work, Gavin, and the new company, it feels like a lot of effort."

Chapter 13

A GPS FOR THE FUTURE

> If you don't hurry up and let life know what you want, life will
> damned soon show you what you'll get.
>
> —Robertson Davies

F or the past twelve months, I've been immersed in examining
and thinking about the forms the wander years take—from
adventure seeking in countries whose names I can't spell to
adultescents moving back home to their childhood bunk bed. I've met
women with freezers full of their own eggs and men who scrap six-
figure jobs to brew beer, people who toast to not being married as well
as those who've started a business to help guys put a ring on it. After
ruminating on what the wandering trend and its tentacles mean to
parents and adultescents, I've ended not with a Cliff Notes manifesto,
but with a few festering thoughts.

The younger generation strikes me as exuberant, clever, and often idealistic. They may be slimed as a bunch of slackers, but I've met mostly hard workers. Many merit sympathy, in fact, because—no argument—compared to previous generations they've been burned and humbled in their ability to earn a living. It's excruciating to think of how many college graduates are un- or underemployed, especially given the sacrifices parents have made to educate children and the ongoing student loan debt that both generations will be shouldering for possibly the rest of their lives.

What is the secret of life? a wise man asked. Making good choices. What's the secret to making good choices? Experience. How do you get experience? Through making bad choices. The upside to random acts of wandering is—in the best of all possible worlds—that by experimenting with living in different cities and countries and sampling assorted work scenarios, an adultescent will hit on a combination to the padlock that allows lasting contentment to spring free.

I also deeply hope that by intellectually and creatively cross-training, many in the younger generation will, instead of settling for mind-numbing careers, invent wildly successful businesses that create jobs for others. I have faith that many will.

Nonetheless, so ends my hagiography. At risk of sounding like the Angel of Death—or just an infuriating biddy—I've completed my journalistic *wanderjahr* still wishing more adultescents would stop pretending that procrastination represents moral superiority and just try to get on with it. Even after developing a considerable affection and empathy for almost every adultescent I've met, I wonder whether many aren't simply taking longer to make the same mistakes their parents did. Career advice blogger Penelope Trunk, who occasionally doles out wisdom on CNN, may say, "It used to be that graduating from college was a sign that you had entered adulthood. But really, let's get serious. It also used to be thought that a bar mitzvah ushered in adulthood, and we all now know the bar mitzvah thing is really just a sign that you are starting regular wet dreams.... If life were *Alice in Wonderland* ... then your twenties is falling through the rabbit hole."

Perhaps, but at the end of the bottom of some rabbit holes, I picture regret that might have been avoided. Adultescents are as defensive as any other group, convinced that they aren't drifting, taking the time to do things right while they foster bliss their parents never knew or dared to imagine beyond quickie vacations.

"We're embracing our youth to learn from the previous generation's mistakes," one inflamed young woman snarled when she got wind of my research. "I hope you realize that your generation was not the model for all others to follow."

Point taken. Certainly I find it hard to be proud of how many politicians, mostly baby boomers, clobber one another with invective instead of owning up to our country's myriad problems, taking strategic steps to solve them in calm, grammatical dialogue. We can enumerate the public and personal boners boomers have made and make, just as we can be collectively mortified by the level of self-absorption boomers have displayed. That we continue to represent the demographic bulge is no excuse.

This doesn't mean, however, that today's adultescents couldn't benefit from a gentle attitude adjustment. Perhaps young wanderers are experiencing more immediate joy in the moment—couch surfing into their thirties, ditching business-boring jobs to ruminate on developing apps while they listen to the drumbeat of their heart—but any moment is fleeting and I'm not persuaded that the joy will last. When I think about adultescents caught in this gridlock, I can't help but wonder if years from now many of them, along with their tottering parents, won't look in their rearview mirrors and wish they'd done a few things differently. "I can't go back to yesterday, because I was a different

243

person then," Lewis Carroll wrote. How many adultescents are going to evolve into different and certainly more cynical people who wish that someone had kicked them in the butts when they were younger so they'd gotten their acts together sooner? Many, is my guess.

The wander years are about celebrating the feast of the epiphany! Then the adultescent gets Mister'd or Ma'am'd, plucks the first gray hair—assuming, if he's a guy, he still has some—or realizes that after a weekend of binge eating and drinking, those five pounds no longer evaporate despite how rigorously he or she adheres to the Belly Fat Cure. Three weeks later, the belly's there along with the to-do list that, although a ten-year college reunion has come and gone, contains an alarming number of unchecked items.

I worry for a lot of adultescents. There is never enough time in life to do everything you want. You think that each light in front of you will always turn green, but it won't, and not making a plan becomes a plan, usually one that falls short.

The passage of time is terrifying, as a dark inevitability always is. I can attest to this. Lately I've been shocked to see that certain body parts about which I used to be ridiculously vain no longer merit braggadocio, secret or otherwise. At a few movie theaters I'm already considered a senior, a person I associate with my late mother in her sensible shoes, not, for God's sake, me. What's more stupefying is that there are so many countries yet to visit, languages to learn, jobs I've yet to have, courses left to take, homes to own, ballets to see, recipes to try, books to read—let alone write. You get it. But I don't. How did this happen? Ten minutes ago I was thirty-five, when everything seemed possible.

What makes me feel cretaceous are my own children. When I look at them, a gooey Alan Jackson "Remember When?" sound track merges with "Sunrise, Sunset." Remember when thirty seemed so old? Now lookin' back, it's just a stepping-stone to where we're at, where we've been. Is this the little boy at play? No, this is the big guy getting married, making business deals, raising money for charity, manning up to serious and poignant challenges with grit and grace.

A ONE-TWO PUNCH

When I consider adultescents, one top-of-mind thought is about the bruising realities of the workplace. I'm not referring to the bias against young hires thought to lack experience and gravitas. Nor am I referencing the truly rotten luck of grads from the toughest years of the economic downturn—2008 through 2010—who've had a more hellish time than others finding jobs. If they've been enterprising, they've moved on to Plan B, C, or D, embodying the words of Teddy Roosevelt: "Do what you can, with what you have, where you are." This usually involves following a need they noticed that requires filling rather than chasing a fuzzy dream they were urged to find and follow by a commencement speaker who had no better advice than, as David Brooks called it in a June 2011 column, "the whole baby-boomer theology."

I worry about adultescents aging out of opportunities while they're logging years in graduate school or zonked out on a mushroom cloud of illusion. I've met many people who don't launch a career path until well into their thirties and then feel too ancient to start at the ground floor, where they may have bosses younger than they are whom they resent along with the killer hours or nonstop travel required. What's worse is that at a time when people want or need to work until they're older than ever, today's early-onset age discrimination can run you over decades sooner than you might imagine. In England, the director-general of the BBC recently caused a flap when he described a forty-year-old female newscaster as an "older" woman—and being a newscaster used to be one of those occupations, like shrink or cleric, where age earned you dividends.

Consider Elizabeth Weidland of Boulder, Colorado, ostensibly one of the country's self-anointed capitals of progressive attitudes. Deeply experienced in the green gizmo business, Elizabeth applied for a job with a high-tech energy company led by a dynamic twentysomething founder. "I was perfect for the position," she claims. "I'm an innovative leader in this area and they were looking for someone to start up a new product line in which I have just the right background."

A company insider recommended her to the hiring manager, yet weeks passed with no interview scheduled. "I was surprised and asked around. What I heard was, 'Oh, their HR director throws out the résumé of anyone with over fifteen years' experience—she says that person's too old for the job.' I thought this was crazy so I followed the woman on Twitter and, sure enough, she tweeted, 'Never put more than fifteen years of experience on your résumé—it dates you.' I was floored. Last week I taught a group of twentysomethings *how* to tweet."

In Silicon Valley, Jason Wong* has been struggling for the past year to land a job. Previously he followed the distinctly non-wander-years-esque path of working at Hewlett-Packard while getting a bachelor's in engineering, then earned a master's in engineering at night, and in 2004 topped off his education with an MBA. By thirty-two Jason had started a consulting company and the next year cofounded an Internet company. At thirty-five he was an executive at a midsize software company and at thirty-seven became a director at a larger company of the same type.

Last year his employer eliminated his job due to cost-cutting and outsourcing to India. Recently, he was interviewed at a similar company by a man who said he was forty-three, the oldest person at the company. The interviewer asked, "Would you have a problem working with people much younger than me?" Jason answered, "No, of course not." Next, a manager whom Jason estimates to be no older than his early thirties met with him and stressed that the company employs mostly "very young" individuals. A week later, when Jason followed up, he was told the budget had been cut and that he was too expensive.

"I do not look old and had yet to reveal my age, but apparently the second guy saw me as someone who might not fit into their youthful environment," Jason says. He is forty-four.

If you're an African lady elephant, your job tenure is ensured, since the herd recognizes that older matriarchs have the best chops for fending off those pesky male lions. And an employer would sooner confess that he masturbates behind his desk than admit to age discrimination, which is "hard to prove, subjective, and full of legal loopholes," points out Anthony Quinones, a New York City career consultant who helps those thirty-five and over make successful transitions in their later years. ("Later years" and "thirty-five" in the same breath? Get over it.)

Age discrimination starts at about forty-two, Quinones argues, but some experts feel it begins at an even younger age. "If your goal is to work in certain industries, your options start to foreclose at about thirty-eight," observes Leonard Emma, an employment attorney practicing in the Bay Area. "People in their early thirties have reported that when they interviewed at some of the emerging companies, particularly those in social and new media, almost everyone was in their twenties.

"The perception exists that older people have ideas that are more embedded, certain traits that are less desirable, and are less willing to use new skills or change existing habits," Emma says. "You hear code phrases like 'not a good cultural fit.'" Translation: too old. Yet for wandering adultescents, the years thirty-eight to forty-two are when some barely hatch careers. They may also be still paying off student loans and, because they are having a baby, starting to save for their child's college education and hoping for flexibility in the workplace.

That is, if there are children. For me, the other deeply troubling dynamic is the delay of childbirth among adultescent women who wish to have kids. Relationships are a crapshoot at any age and I'll steer clear of the argument for marriage over cohabitation. I also say vive la différence to women who choose to opt out of motherhood altogether, although adultescence is too young an age for most women to make a definitive decision in that regard. But given how much I adore my sons and how empty I imagine my life would feel without them, I ended my research wishing that those in the younger generation who are hell-bent on wanting kids were more willing to take a chance on earlier baby-making. A character, a mother, in *Three Stages of Amazement*, a recent novel by Carol Edgarian, says it best: "Twenty-six, my friends, becomes thirty-eight just like that." And thirty-eight is a risky year to first start thinking about trying to conceive.

When fertility specialist Dr. Owen Davis told me, "No one should have a child before she's ready," I couldn't disagree, but I found equally memorable a remark from Roberta Victor, who at thirty-two has become distressed by being single and childless. "The smart thing would have been to have . . . had children when I was in my twenties, like my mother," she says in neon hindsight. "If I ever have a daughter, I will pressure her to have children young. There's no way I'd like her to go through what I have."

Many young mothers now look at my generation of working moms with our frantic do-it-all philosophies—what I always called "good stress"—and have decided that people like me have screwed up. For themselves they want an old-school version of parenting, with more balance, less working. Good luck with that, given the economy. I can't help but wonder if the generation that follows today's adultescents, stunned by stories of infertility and lonesome, unwanted childless-ness, will dial back to their grandmother's era and have kids at a much earlier age.

Hey, you heard it here first.

LADIES AND GENTLEMEN, YOUR ATTENTION, PLEASE

Younger generation, you can stop reading now, because even though as parents we've done everything we can to give you the impression that it's all about you, it isn't. What I want to say next—or bray, if I might—is directed toward my baby boomer parent peers, although it applies as much to myself.

It's time to say "enough." *People, step away from the adultescents.* All together now, let's push back. The best way for a lot of us to show our love would be to learn to un-mother and un-father. "By trying so hard to provide the perfectly happy childhood, we're just making it harder for our kids to actually grow up," therapist and mom Lori Gottlieb—the same woman who raised hell with her book *Marry Him: The Case for Settling for Mr. Good Enough*—wrote in an *Atlantic* maga-zine article titled "How to Land Your Kid in Therapy: Why the Obses-sion with Our Kids' Happiness May Be Dooming Them to Unhappy Adulthoods." Amen.

"What we talk about when we talk about tomorrow is the great fear that our kids will never find their way, now that opportunity is just another word for no," blogs Timothy Egan in the *New York Times*. Egan was part of the Pulitzer Prize–winning *Times* team that wrote the series "How Race Is Lived in America." "By we, I mean parents of a certain age. . . . Baby Boomers who rejected 'Mad Men' conformity groomed their offspring to expect only the best, to climb a ladder that would end in startups cranking out stock-option millionaires. . . .

Maybe if I knew that our children would be coming of age in an economy that would crush even the best and brightest among them, I would have cared a little less about their score on an advanced placement history test, and a little more about helping them find happiness in moments at the margin. I hope many of them are doing just that—without our help."

But it's not just that. Put aside, for a moment, the grandest of understatements, that the economy hasn't done our adultescent children any favors. They've gotten the national short straw, as have many of us, with our hollowed-out pension plans and stock portfolios. I also sense, however, that for hard-core adultescents, we baby boomers, with our quest for agelessness, have contributed to making our children drift by making them feel ever-young, not just happy-happy-happy geysers of self-esteem.

If we're not old—and who among us doesn't feel thirty-five?—then for adultescents the years must be standing still.

If we're not old—with our covetable lives, joint replacements, face-lifts (which are no longer only for the ladies; this surgery increased 14 percent for men in 2010), high-fiber granola with antioxidant-rich blueberries, Spanx, Pilates and Bikram yoga, white-water rafting trips, and treks through Patagonia—how can we expect our kids to grow up?

If we're not old, our children must be babies, big babies we adore and whose attention we crave as much as they crave our support in its myriad forms.

The boomer generation, with its idiomatic immaturity and fury at the very idea that we have to age, is in no small part to blame for adultescents feeling as if there will always be time to break up with one more partner or employer, to search for someone or something better, to get another degree or to surf another couch, to wait around to reproduce. Thanks to our own parents listening to Dr. Benjamin Spock and to us sucking up TV ads that pandered to our kiddy greed, we established the 2.0 model for unprecedented self-involvement, enhanced by our ceaseless boasting. "The upwardly moral children of the bourgeoisie are obsequiously, uncompromisingly virtuous," Joe Queenan grouses in the *Wall Street Journal*. "They ride bikes everywhere. They never eat red meat. They refuse to watch television. They eat with wooden chopsticks. They only read books by authors named Jonathan who live in Brooklyn. They themselves are named Jonathan and live in Brooklyn. That is because everyone who is good and just and whip-smart and special in this society lives in Brooklyn." Like one of my sons.

Our offspring have simply leveraged our braggadocio, good intentions, and overinvestment. Adultescents have taken egoism and not infrequent narcissism to the next level, a broad savannah of entitlement that we've watered, landscaped, and hired gardeners to maintain if we're not there hoeing and mowing ourselves. Our young adult children now exist in a perfect storm of overconfidence, a sense of never-ending time, and a grim reaper of a job market.

Nothing in my life has been as challenging as raising kids. Being a mom or dad is astonishing, gratifying, and enduring. It also requires constant renegotiation, and this is where we boomers tend to bomb. Just as we want our fannies and faces to show no signs of aging, in parenting we cling to the familiar, remaining overinvolved in adultescents' lives. This is yet another twist on not wanting to get old. It's hard for us to realize that, like graceful actors, we need to evolve in our roles and adopt less-is-more, fade-to-gray parenting.

It's one thing to provide our children shelter in a storm and another to function as their entire weather system. Once kids graduate from college, it's time to collectively peel off the bumper stickers and remind ourselves that the ultimate goal of being a parent is to become if not completely obsolete, lovingly marginalized.

The biological imperative is for children to be able to manage without us. It may be difficult to stop trying to vaccinate our kids against every conceivable catastrophe, but the ultimate and most lasting major gift we can offer our children is the chance to grow up and develop independence, to learn to ably handle their lives on their own so that one day they can teach their own children—our grandchildren—to do the same.

This is very hard to do because we lust for their attention. We really, really like them, these remarkable people we've nurtured, whose complete childhoods are archived in our hearts with four-color illustrations and footnotes.

On the spectrum of motherhood as I know it, I'd always felt I'd been pretty laid-back. No smother-mothering for me, especially as my children became older teenagers. Both sons did most of their college visits on their own, for example, and during the four years they were away at school, I didn't self-destruct if I hadn't heard from one of them for a week, nor did I expect them to spend every vacation with Dad and Mom. After they got their diplomas, each son immediately moved to the opposite coast. Roots and wings, I thought. Yeah, that's the ticket.

But if I was such a cool cucumber, as I was finishing this book and one of my sons began to plan a wedding, why did I feel an unfamiliar emotion hovering between elegant melancholy and uncommon panic?

I knew my dismay had nothing to do with my son's choice of mate. He could not have chosen better. My anxiety was because nothing says "you're fired, lady" like knowing your boy will take a wife, with whom he will establish a household that surely will *not* be a franchise of your marriage, right down to the last Happy Meal. In addition, knowing that your reward for decades of parenting will be to become a mother-in-law—in Borscht Belt humor, more reviled than a debt collector—does not make this transition easier. According to an old German saying, a mother-in-law's role is *schenken, slacken, und schweigen*: give presents, swallow (or hold her tongue), and shut up. How's that for a nice clambake?

In the middle-of-the-night self-examinations, what I realized was that I was gripped with a particular worry. Now that time was winding down, I was wondering if I'd done enough as a mom to prep my child for flying solo. Did he have every tool necessary to evolve into the world's most wonderful, caring, sensitive, compassionate, fulfilled man? Could he iron a shirt, clean a wood floor, write a thank-you note? When he was a tot, I used to say, "God made you smart and handsome, but only you can make yourself a nice person." Had I done my job to see that he was?

Tough nuts if he wasn't, because the statute of limitations on my aiding and abetting that process was running out. Was I ready to let go? That was the real question. The answer: I'm not but I'm trying, because I know this has become the most essential part of my revised job description.

I'm remembering that when my younger son was in grade school he continued to grasp my hand at city intersections as we waited for the light to change, as I'd instructed him to do at age two. Other boys shook off their mother's hand at seven or eight, but his behavior kept going until about ten. I didn't want to be the one to let go. Clearly, he needed to know I was there.

One day he wrenched away his hand abruptly. Message received. The light had changed in my parent-child relationship, only not from red to green. And now it's changed forever from green to red. Nothing could be a clearer signal of that than a child marrying, but the incremental steps that led to this stage—going away to college, moving to the opposite coast, assuming one responsible job after the next—were all there, a road to full independence, even if it's full of potholes. I have it easier than some, because marriage is a 3-D announcement of launching yourself. It's a lot harder for parents to let go if adultescents continue to lead lives that outwardly appear much the same as five, ten, or fifteen years ago.

"Alas, after a certain age every man is responsible for his face," Albert Camus wrote. It's up to parents to let our adult children determine their faces and their fates. This means being the generation that acts more like tough but tenderhearted athletic coaches than fairy godparents with limitless credit cards and an indefatigable ability to solve problems.

We can start early, or at least earlier, to push our kids to develop practical plans as we also give them a crash course in the DIY drudgery—from tax prep to turkey-trussing—that doesn't make it onto school applications and résumés but is all in a day's work. "I brought up my kids to thrive without me, but I think a lot of parents don't allow that, and their expectations handicap the children," says Reina Weiner, a wise mother turned motivational speaker from Leesburg, Virginia. When Reina's local library asked her to speak to a parents' group, she told them, "If you want to raise children to be problem solvers and decision makers, you allow them to make reasonable choices and expect them to be responsible for their outcome. You're there for them, but you know they can do it themselves. If you step back, they'll be able to step forward." Boomer parents of adultescents, let's sing out that last sentence as our mantra.

With the time we gain by not shadowing our adult children's lives, we can put more effort into not only our own work, friends, other family, and projects but solving societal problems. Panic isn't a strategy, but it strikes me that as a country, job creation is. On a micro-level, if a boomer is an employer, it would be a public service if he or she offered an adultescent or two a job, and it's no less valuable if the hire is someone the boomer knows. As a whole, we need to come together and address the brain drain and social tragedy resulting from so many of our bright, well-educated kids lingering jobless, especially those who graduated in the dog years of 2007 and 2008. These kids aren't damaged goods. They just look that way to many employers, who when they do have a job to fill prefer a more freshly graduated model.

We can also try to figure out how technology can improve our relationships with our kids. I'm wondering, for example, how I will forge a bond with my future daughter-in-law. No more do most of us usually call the family landline, if there is one, and have an amiable chat with whoever answers. Virtually all my conversations with my son—soon her husband—usually take place when he's on his cell phone suffering a long commute. Communication has become other-specific, and thus it's easy for connections to never be made. I'll be figuring out new patterns, just as other parents are deciding that when their families spend time together, the mobile devices need to be put away. During the moratorium, generations will actually talk to one another.

We can also—even if we're not there yet—ponder the next-stage role of grandparenthood, especially as we take in the helicopter grandparenting filling the airspace around us. Surely, boomer grandparents have the ability to enrich their grandchildren's lives and offer help that eases the stress their own kids may be experiencing—all this while they savor the elation of getting to know and love a new generation of their family. But I'm wondering about slippery boundaries as I hear of grandparents who move a thousand miles away to settle next door to grandchildren, of nanas and papas who visit grandkids' schools almost daily, of boomer couples who no longer see their own friends on weekends because they are the regular babysitters, and of grannies who take the shuttle from New York to Washington every week to read a story to their little pumpkin. I've been told about a couple in suburban Chicago who built a full-size basketball court in their basement for their grandsons and legions of grandparents who Skype multiple times a day with faraway grandkids. It makes me convinced that the over-bearing behavior that's prompted the wander years is already taking root with grandchildren, growing as fast as bamboo, crowding out more restrained forms of plant life.

"Make somebody happy one day," said Ann Landers, that wise woman of baby boomers' childhoods. "Mind your own business."

Retrenchment may smack of tough love. But forcing ourselves to back off is no harder than what we expect of our adultescents, whose wandering, I hope, leads them on a path to deep and lasting fulfill-ment, happiness, and calling home, often, so that both generations can say "I love you."

Namaste.

Acknowledgments

I wish to thank my sons, Jed and Rory, and husband, Robert, who have redefined the meaning of generosity by allowing me to use their names and experiences in *Slouching Toward Adulthood: Observations from the Not-So-Empty Nest*. With these men, who bring so much love and laughter into my life, I have won the Triple Crown.

I could not ask for a sharper team than those at Viking, led by Clare Ferraro, an incomparable, far-sighted publisher. I am honored by your support. A standing ovation to Carolyn Carlson, the editor every writer wants, whose incisive critiques and continuous encouragement helped build a better book. Amanda Brower, the interest and digging you offered were enormously helpful. Jim Tierney, your cover made me smile. Nancy Sheppard, your marketing efforts made all the difference, as did those of publicity director Carolyn Coleburn in collaboration with Sonya Cheuse. Sharon Gonzalez , you and your copy editors did an ace job, and sales force, woo-hoo! You are simply the best in the business.

Special gratitude to Carin Rubenstein, Ph.D., for your astute slicing and dicing of all those pesky numbers, and to Mary Dell Harrington, who could find a monkey on Mars. The crackerjack research both of you provided vastly improved every chapter.

Christy Fletcher, there should be a new name for the role you play in an author's work. Thank you for planting the seed for this book after hearing my family sagas. Melissa Chinchilla, Mink Choi, and Alyssa Wolff, I am truly grateful for your cheerful professionalism and work, past and present, on my behalf.

To my sister Betsy, much appreciation for your intellectual curiosity and unflagging enthusiasm on the topic of wandering adultescents. You missed your calling as a cheerleader and sociologist.

A big shout-out to the smarty-pants Monday night workshop circa 2010 led by Charles Salzberg. Gang, your collective feedback on my embryonic proposal gave me the confidence to plow ahead.

Most of all, I am deeply indebted to a hundred-something people in their twenties and thirties—along with parents—whose candid observations make up the DNA of *Slouching Toward Adulthood*. To my fellow baby boomers: repeat after me, we're not just getting older, we're getting wiser. To adultescents everywhere: Godspeed in your journeys.